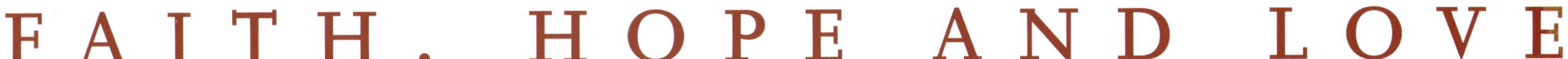

FAITH, HOPE AND LOVE

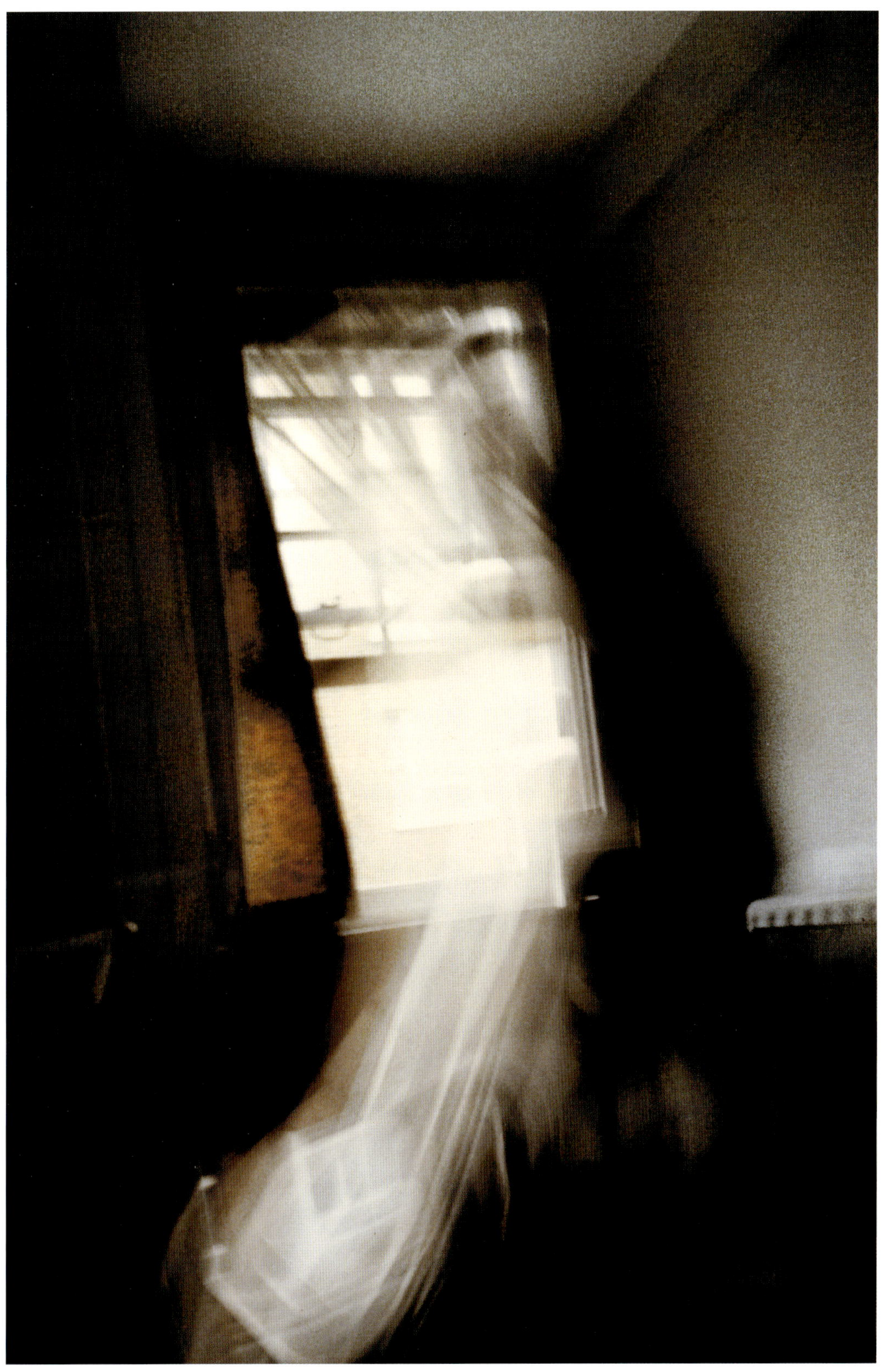

Curtain I, c. 1990, color photograph, 10 x 8 inches.

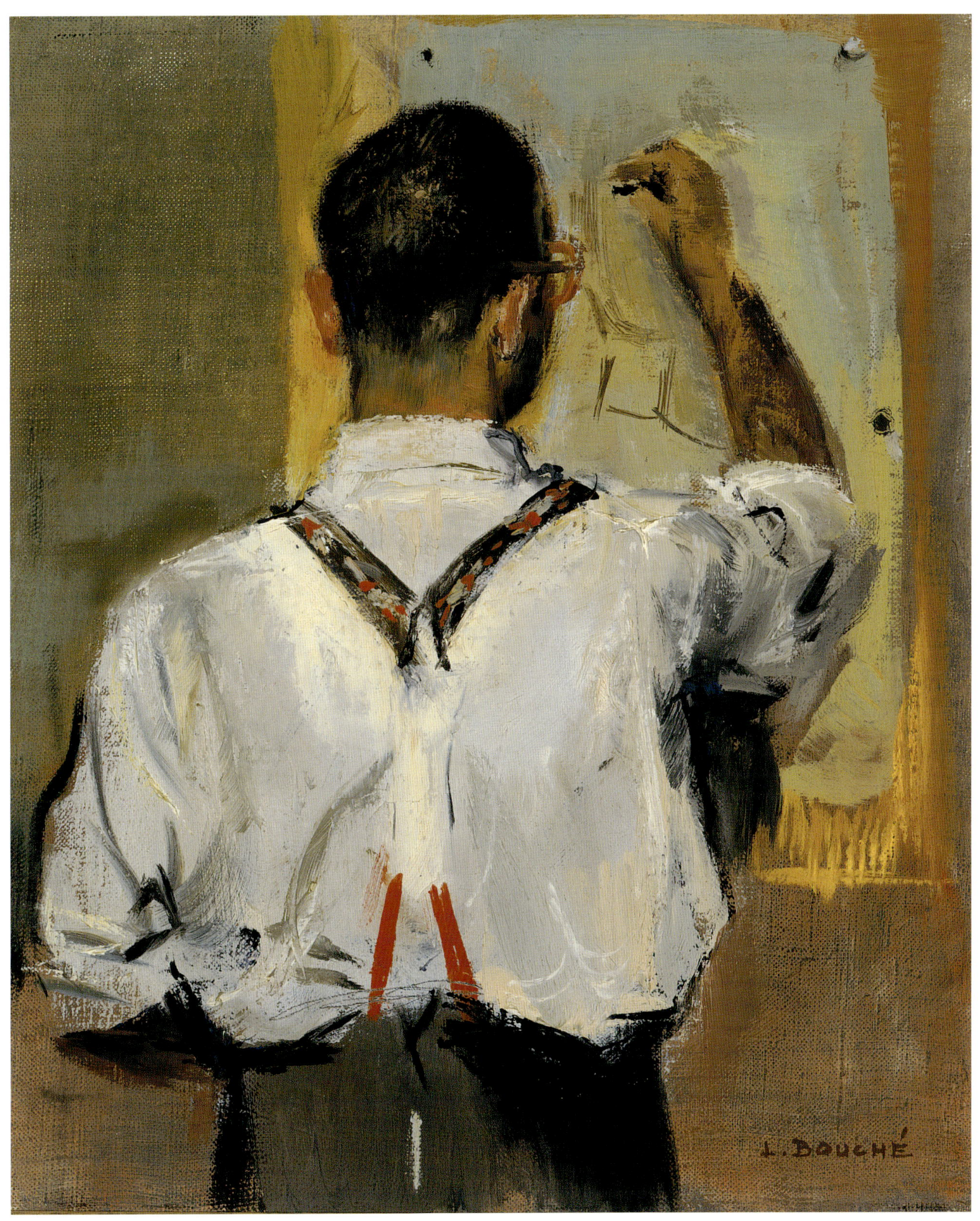

Louis Bouché, *E.P.J. from the Back*, 1945, oil on canvas, 15 x 12 1/4 inches.

EDWARD POWIS JONES

FAITH, HOPE AND LOVE

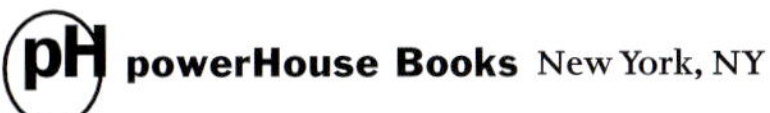

powerHouse Books New York, NY

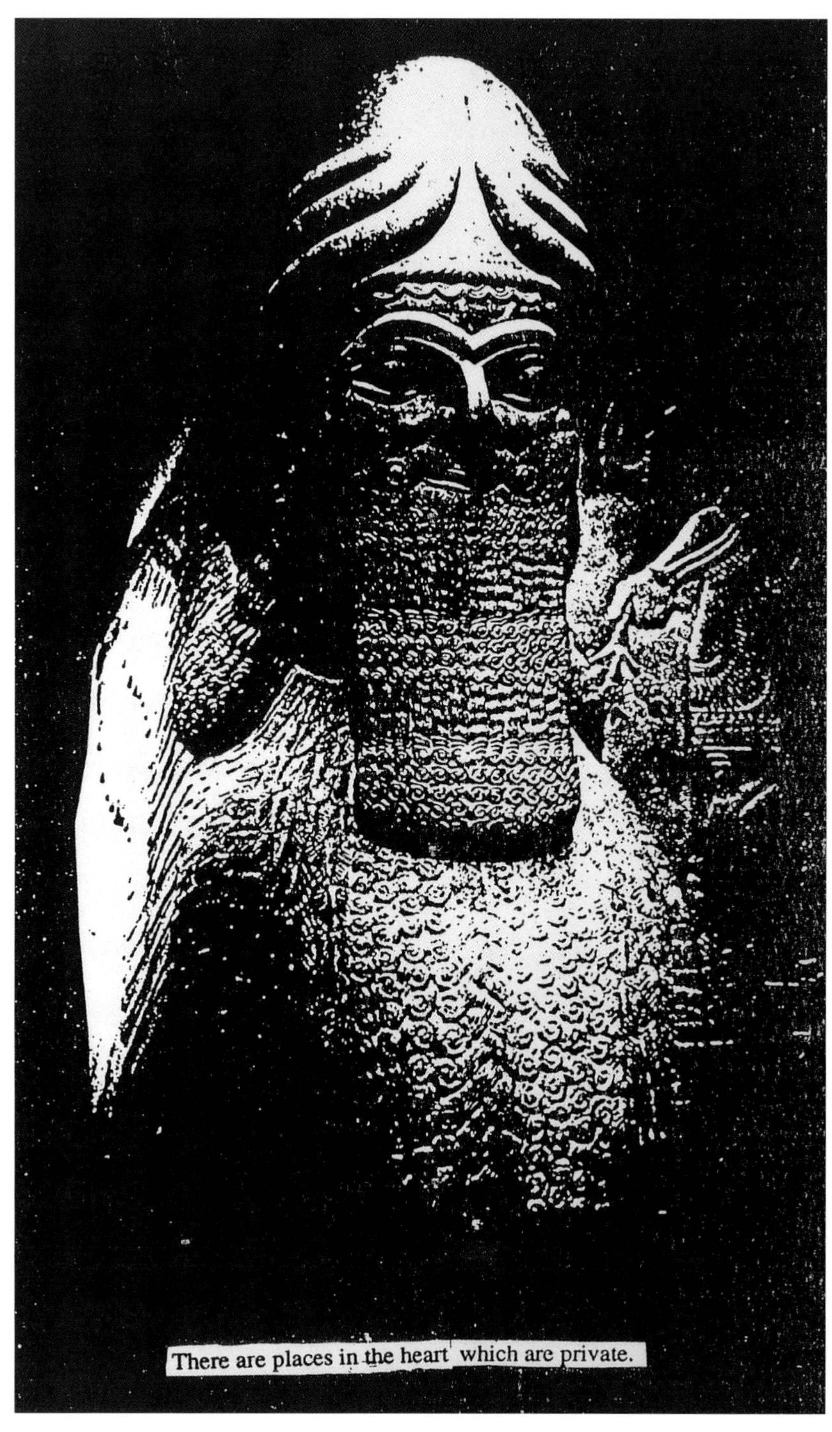

Places in the Heart, c. 1985, copier print, 13$1/4$ x 7$1/2$ inches.

PLACES IN THE HEART WHICH ARE PRIVATE
MARK HOLBORN

Dislodge a pebble and the whole mountain can come crashing down. Early one morning in a grand hotel in Rome sometime in 1928 an American rose to face the day. A scene followed. You can only imagine the interior. He started shaving and there was the slightest slip of the razor, drawing blood. He washed the cut. The water was in some way contaminated. The poisons entered the bloodstream and within days he was dead. The tragedy gathered pace. The family came to bring the American's widow and her three children back to America, where the widow, having never recovered from the devastation of her loss, died three years later. One of the children, a boy aged nine that morning in Rome, was Edward Powis Jones. Such a loss would drive any child back into the most secret places in the imagination, unreachable to others, forever marked and isolated by the tragedy. Just one slip of the hand and the whole mountain had indeed come crashing down.

In 1988, when he was nearly seventy, Ed Jones published a poem that opened:

'No pockets in a shroud'
They say, 'No pockets in a shroud'.
There are pockets in the mind
Though that makes us cry aloud.

Ed Jones had joined the National Guard before America entered the Second World War. A part of him was prepared for war, but what he saw on Omaha Beach in Normandy in 1944 as a lieutenant in the Corps of Engineers took him beyond what was bearable. The pockets in his mind were too deep – tragedy too compounded. His life and work can be seen as a measured response to these events as if through his work he was laying stepping-stones on a path to reconciliation with his past. In Christian language that reconciliation might be termed redemption.

Ed Jones was an artist born in 1919. He lived and worked most of his life in New York, a city he adored, and where he died in 1998. His final New York exhibition was held at PS1 in 1980. He began as a painter immediately after the war, at the same time as he entered marriage and became the loving father of three children. He became enthralled with printmaking and established a collection of prints and works on paper by the old masters, produced sculptures, became fascinated with the potential of the photocopier and finally he became a photographer. This body of work should be viewed not as a series of disparate sorties into diverse media, but as a whole. What emerges is a view that ranges from the peace of domesticity to a profound meditation on mortality, especially the artist's own mortality.

Under the title *Faith, Hope and Love* the most mundane details acquire a particular resonance. In several cases it matters less what details Jones's paintings describe than what atmosphere they exude. They become psychological probes rather than descriptions of objective facts and, in so doing, establish the tone of his art. The simplest of his subjects sometimes bristle with uneasy qualities – an elevator shaft or stairwell, a knife sharpener and even an empty chair by an open window (a repeated subject) are unsettling. A subject as simple as a railway track or train, which he painted several times, marks the route to and from the great city he left in order to establish a quiet family home, and the route of return when he brought his family back to the heart of the city. A simple passage in a traumatized mind can become a route to Calvary. *Faith, Hope and Love*, qualities like the art itself, were the means with which to rebuild and by which to live.

First, *Hope*. There is a snow scene he painted in 1947 from the red porch of his house in Barrytown, New York, where he had moved with his new wife and was starting a family. The house looks across a bare orchard below, to water and a line of hills. Space unfurls. From around the same time there is a painting of Rhinebeck station, close to the Hudson, with two figures waiting for a train on an empty platform. From this station you can go as far as Canada or even find a connection to the Pacific. These paintings offer promise.

Uncluttered highways, gas stations, the lines of telegraph posts, street lamps, simple houses by the track, a water pump, cranes and chimneys, smoke from the engine, flags and washing on the line – the whole catalogue of vernacular America unravels through these early paintings. The high-priest of the American vernacular, Walker Evans, and others had established their working vocabulary amongst the domestic and industrial vistas of the nation. A dark, empty lot with abandoned chairs or a dump of waste factory piping and plumbing are the subjects of two of Jones's grittiest but better paintings. Out of the mundane and discarded he could find his excitement. The tackle shop in Red Hook, like his painting of the banners for Congo Mae, would have charmed the photographic eye of Evans. At the bottom of the Red Hook tackle shop window he painted a box labelled LUCKY. Maybe Ed Jones felt he was.

His interiors are enigmatic, mysterious and in some cases heavily laden with memory and association. In one painting the clothes slung over the chair and the suitcases by a mirror suggest a hotel room. In fact the painting is of the room at The Pierre in New York, where he and his wife, Anne, spent their wedding night. It is in every sense a beginning. A hanging rose-patterned bedspread in meticulous detail suggests a loving pleasure in the act of painting, not a labor. He liked painting chairs and they become portraits of a sort. In his pictures the waiters are waiting, the tables are empty and the chairs stand in attendance. When he painted himself with his son Peter drinking a bottle of ginger ale, the real meal begins. He painted the food onto his plate, the drink into the glass at Goodies, the Coney Island bar, and the match that lights the cigarette of the bare-breasted lady in Maine. He could paint pleasure at will and choose his nourishment with a brushstroke.

Shortly after his marriage Ed Jones wanted to buy a Seurat drawing with his wife. He said with conviction that they had to buy it – there was no question in the case of such a work – and buy it they did, paying for it over months. Anne never regretted the purchase and it became the start of a special collection of works on paper that she continues to nourish to this day. Ed Jones had a friend at Knoedler's in New York through whom he acquired two Rembrandt prints – the *Descent from the Cross* and an *Artist and Model*. There followed a Tiepolo drawing of Punchinello by Giambattista's son Giandomenico. In the 1730s both Tiepolos, father and son, had greatly admired Rembrandt and particularly his painting of *The Lamentation*, which was owned by the British consul in Venice. Though separated by geography and a century, the Tiepolos and Rembrandt sat side by side in the Jones collection, where Punchinello and the Passion coexisted. The collection also accommodated several versions of *The Flight into Egypt*. In the early Sixties, when Ed Jones was ill, Anne wanted to buy him a present and went to find a print at Lucien Goldschmidt's on Madison Avenue, where they had bought a number of prints and illustrated books. The lady who attended her said, 'When I think of Mr Jones, I always think of Rembrandt.' By the late Fifties Ed Jones had begun his own attempts at printmaking and by the Sixties he was in full flow.

Secondly, *Faith*. Ed Jones's formal conversion to Catholicism took place in 1950. By his bedside he kept the Bible and Butler's *Lives of the Saints*. He regularly read the Old Testament, in which he must have discovered the story of Sisera, the captain of a host of 900 chariots of iron to whom the children of Israel were delivered and, according to the Book of Judges, under whom they suffered for twenty years. Sisera, with all his chariots, was defeated by Barak and an army of 10,000, then fled on foot from the carnage. Jael, the wife of an ally, took him into her tent, wrapped him and gave him a drink.

Then Jael Heber's wife took a nail of the tent, and took
an hammer in her hand, and went softly unto him, and
smote the nail into his temples, and fastened it into the
ground: for he was fast asleep and weary. So he died. *

And the hand of the children of Israel prospered…The tyrant was defeated in battle, then slain in his sleep by the woman who offered comfort. Liberation followed. In 1958 Ed Jones produced an ink-and-wash drawing as well as an etching and aquatint of the great battle leading to Sisera's defeat below Mount Tabor. Four years later he made a set of etchings and aquatints of Sisera's

* The Book of Judges, Chapter 4, verse 21.

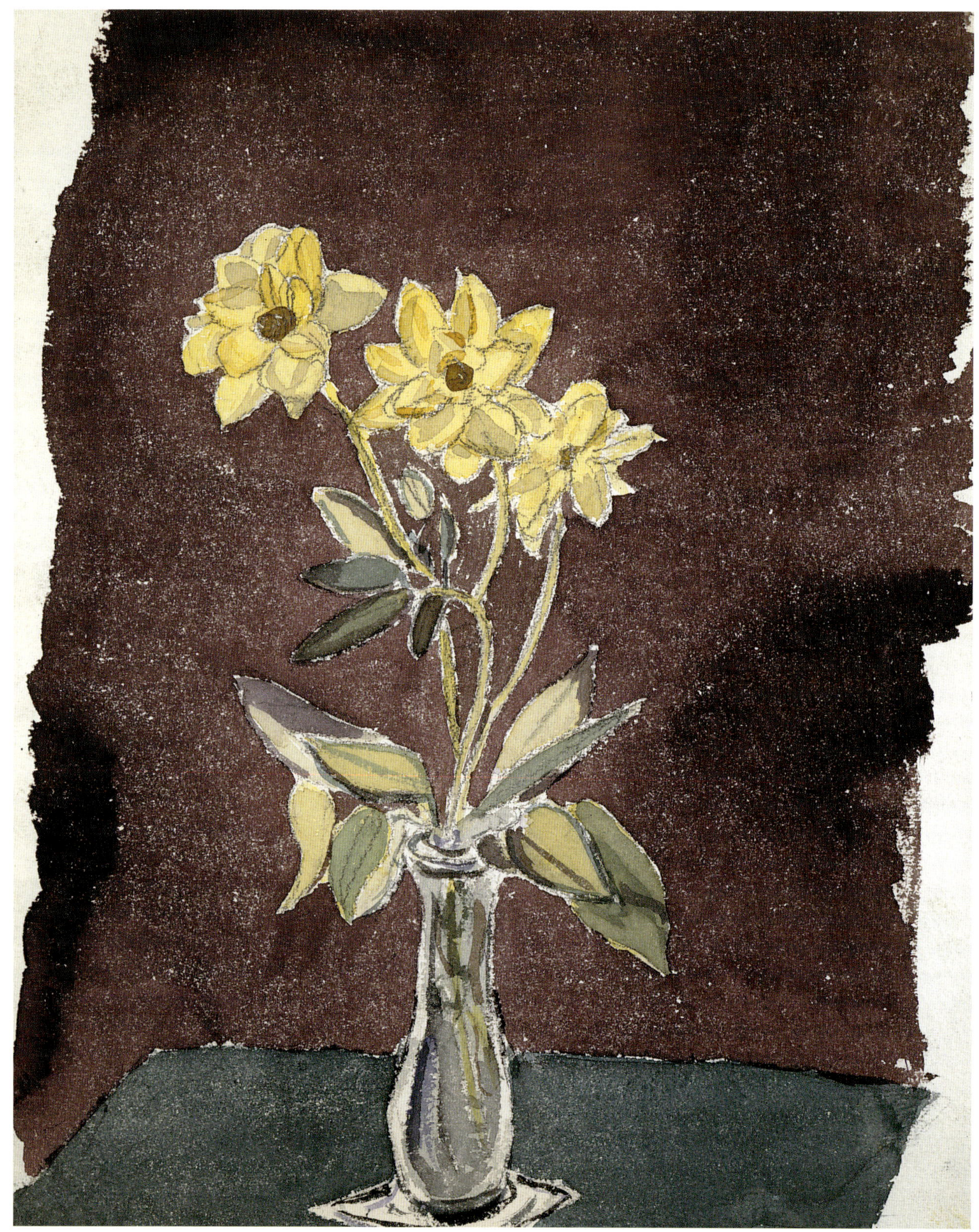

Flower, c. 1960, watercolor, 14 x 11 1/2 inches.

death within the tent. What drew him to this passage of the Old Testament, and why? Was it the flight from the horrors of the battlefield or the justice in the murder of the tyrant? Perhaps it was the aptness of the tyrant's death not by the sword in battle, but at the hand of the woman when he was unsuspecting. A single nail from a tent was the weapon that achieved what an army in battle could not complete.

That the story was predominant in Ed Jones's mind is confirmed by an extraordinary painted plaster skull he produced in 1978. It remained untitled and enigmatic, especially as from the top of the head protruded a nail. It is of course the head of Sisera.

When memories become too hard or the imagination too vivid, the human response is the predictable desire for oblivion. One numbs the mind. There are painkillers of choice, acts of self-destruction, or metaphorically one drives a nail through the brain, so piercing the seat of the memory. There is also the analogy with the nails of the Cross. In 1960 Ed Jones made a series of etchings and aquatints of the Stations of the Cross, and in 1963 he produced a large oil painting of the Crucifixion itself. The nail in Sisera's head may have been the pivot of Ed Jones's imagination around which his memories, both poisonous and sublime, circulated.

Injustice still preyed on his mind. Shocked by the murders of Medgar Evers, Emmett Till and Martin Luther King in Mississippi and Memphis, in the mid-Sixties he made bronze heads of the three, which have been given to the Mississippi Museum of Art in Jackson. One summer in London and lacking a studio, he created a large papier mâché head of the Ugandan monster Idi Amin. On a private note, when he felt he was cheated of a Degas print at auction – he had signed the bid and the auctioneer reopened the bidding – he turned the subject into an etching, with the auctioneer depicted as a skeleton in a room full of skeletons. Fury too could be harnessed through art.

His later discovery of the changing technology of reproduction, notably the arrival of the photocopier, thrilled him. Again in London, without a studio, in 1980, he turned to radically distorting the *Self-Portrait* by Gwen John, which he saw at the Tate. The chance nature of the results excited him, resulting in a portfolio of copier prints of Gwen John in 1984, about which he has written explicitly. One of his first copier prints, based on the photograph of Ruby's shooting of Oswald, with the head of Hitler and other modern tyrants, was titled *Dictators*. The ghost of Sisera remained.

He photographed on the street and varied his results by sometimes hand-coloring either the photographs or the copier prints he produced from the photographs. He was drawn to the surfaces of walls, posters, graffiti and shop windows, especially those with mannequins, clothed and unclothed. He tore fragments of posters from the walls and constructed a huge collage of the material in his studio. London and New York were his stalking grounds. There he would pass the frozen models and hear the voices scratched on the concrete, 'Stefney, you sexy bitch.' These explorations revealed he had also become a photographer.

Towards the end of his life his trips to hospital provided yet another subject to photograph. 'I never go to hospital without my camera,' he said. The drip stands, hospital curtains and machinery of medicine that surrounded him proved irresistible subjects. The photographs constitute the trail of a man who experiences the world by framing it, even as the curtains were drawing. The results are not so much photographs that are constructed as photographs that are lived. The street outside, the dead insect by the curtain, his reflection in a bathroom mirror, and even his face suddenly caught in a rear-view mirror are fragments that in fact complete the life. The work of fifty years, in all its different forms, amounts to a single self-portrait.

Finally, *Love*. His wife, his children, his sister, the city where he worked and the art that moved him were all subjects of his love. He was gregarious and sustained his friendships, many from childhood or from the war years. He loved good company and good stories. His collecting too was less an act of mere acquisition, and more a love for what mattered or for what made sense. His greatest feat of collecting was assembling a set of Manet's six lithograph illustrations for Edgar Allan Poe's 'The Raven'. In May 1875 Manet completed the set based on a translation by Mallarmé. The prints were made by transferring his brushstrokes onto zinc plates. They have a looseness about them that makes them look as if they were effortlessly drawn. The raven appears across the rooftops through the open shutter of the window. The raven, or its spirit, enters like a breeze through the open window. The final image is almost abstract — an empty chair beside the shadow of the raven 'that lies floating on the floor'. Ed Jones, it seems, frequently returned to the open window and caught the breeze. The raven that entered was the demon that haunted him, or the spirit that released him.

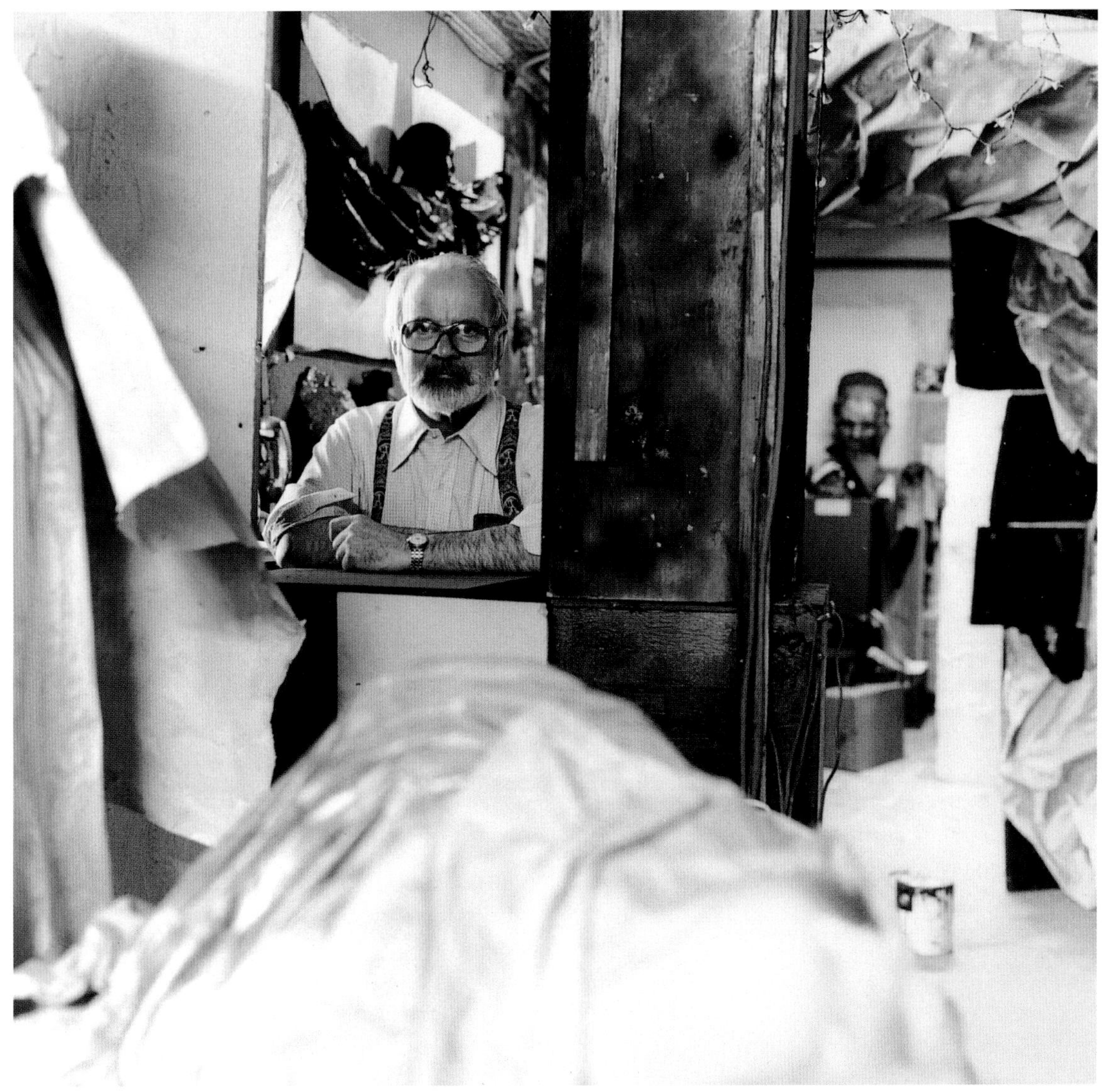

Edward Powis Jones in his 87th Street Studio preparing for his final exhibition in New York at PS1 in 1980 (photograph by Peter C. Jones).

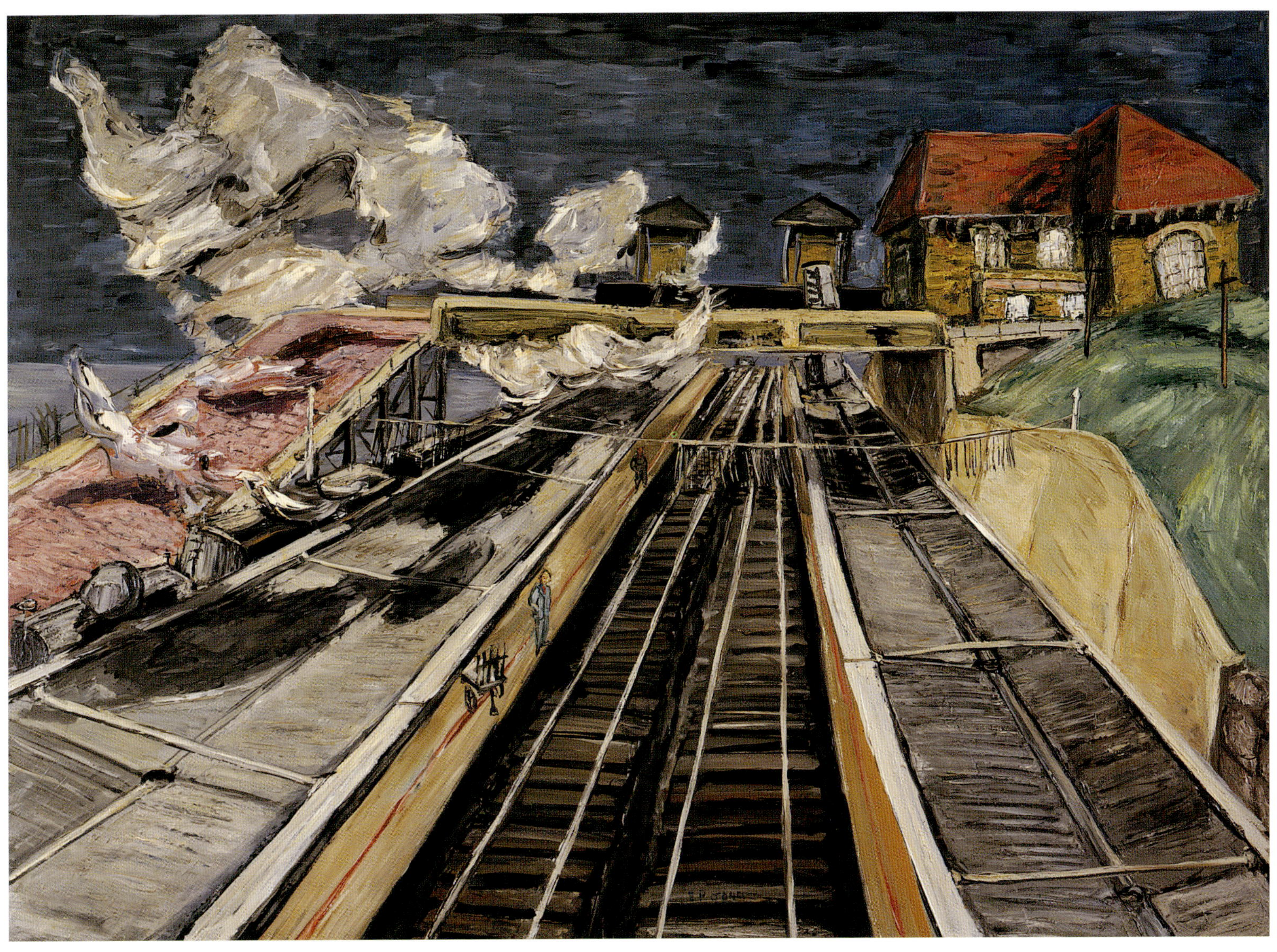

Rhinebeck Station, c. 1946, oil on canvas, 30 x 40 inches.

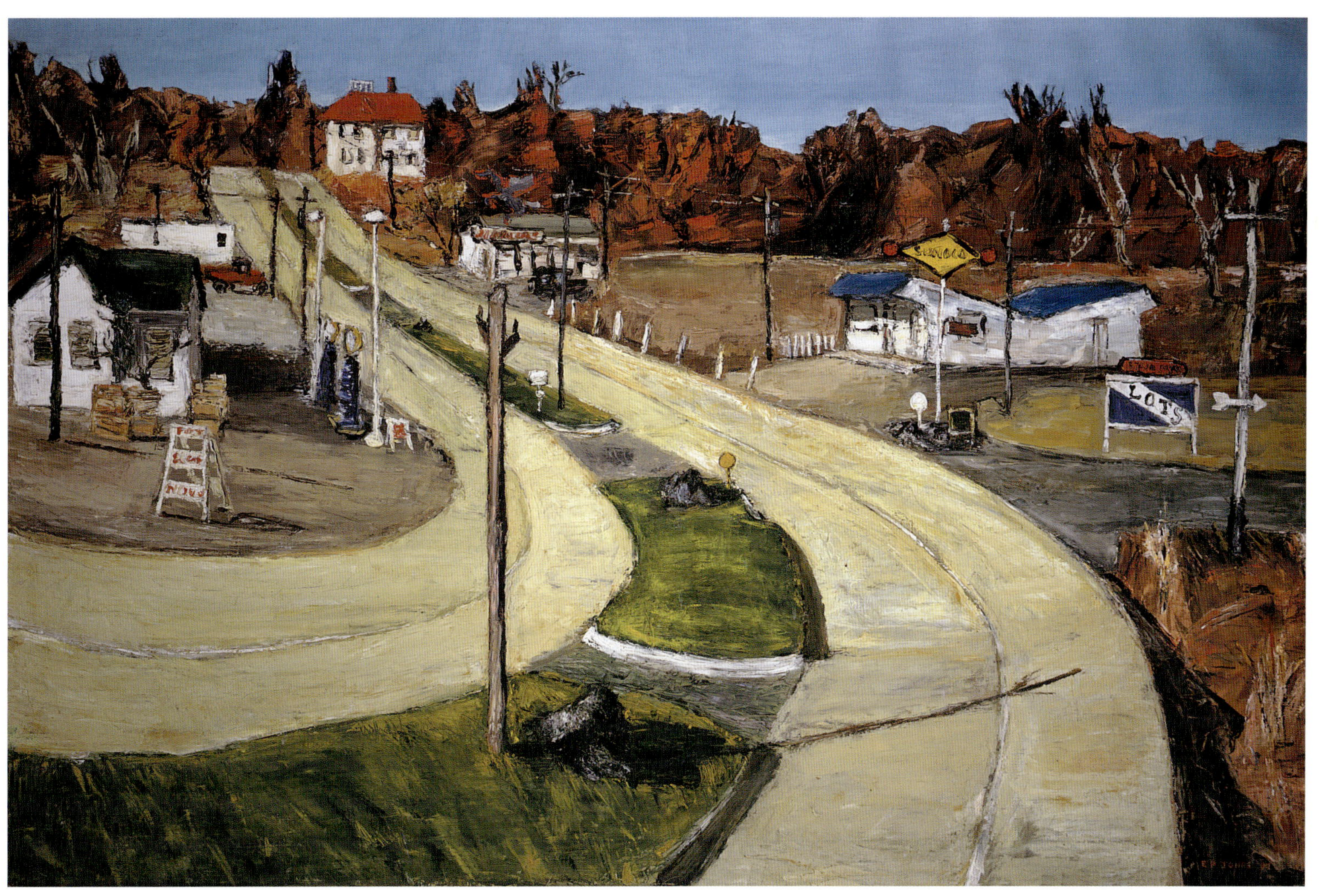

The Road, 1948, oil on canvas, 40 x 60 inches.

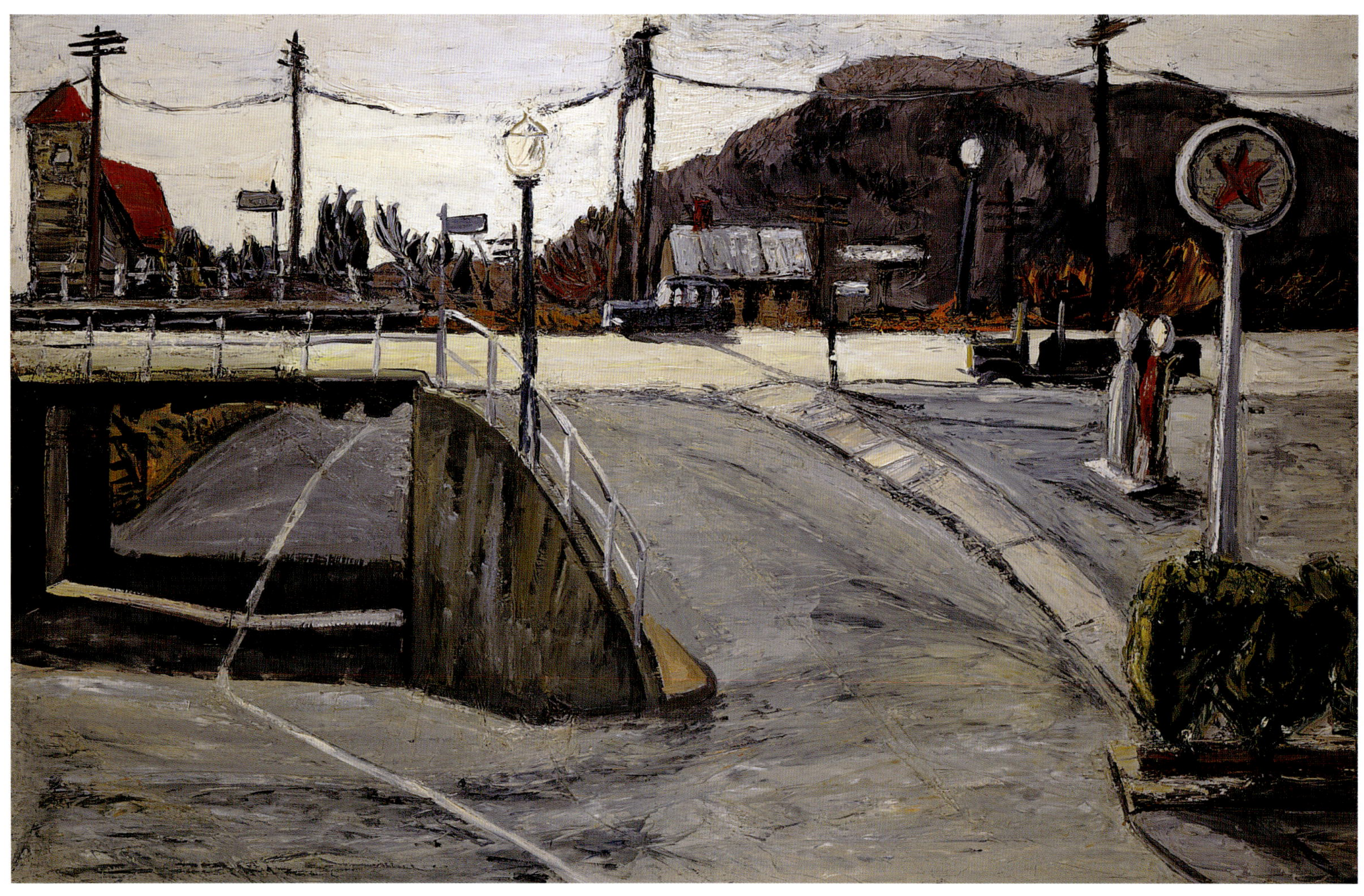

Underpass, c. 1949, oil on canvas, 24 x 36 inches.

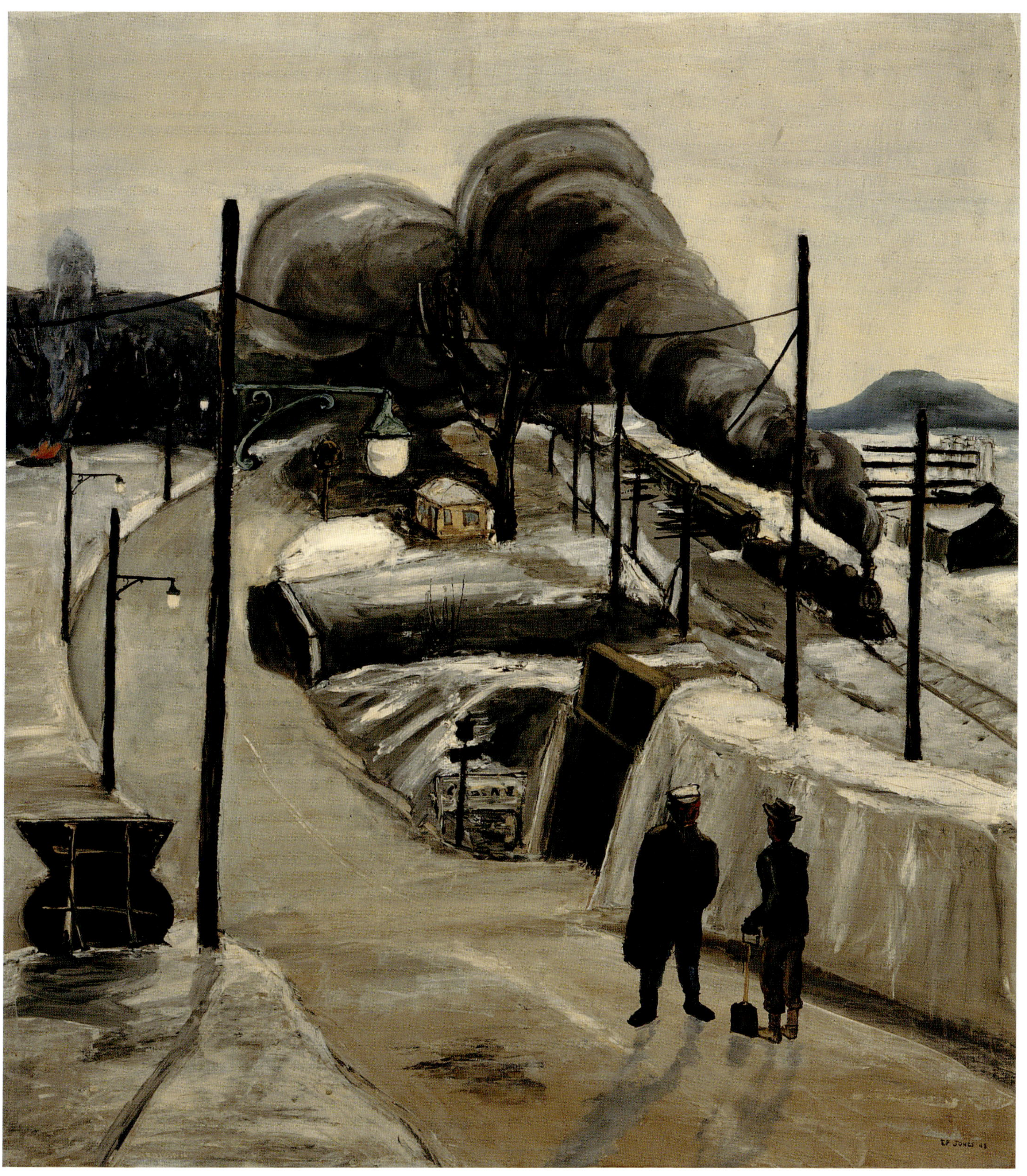

February, 1948, oil on canvas, 35 x 21 inches.

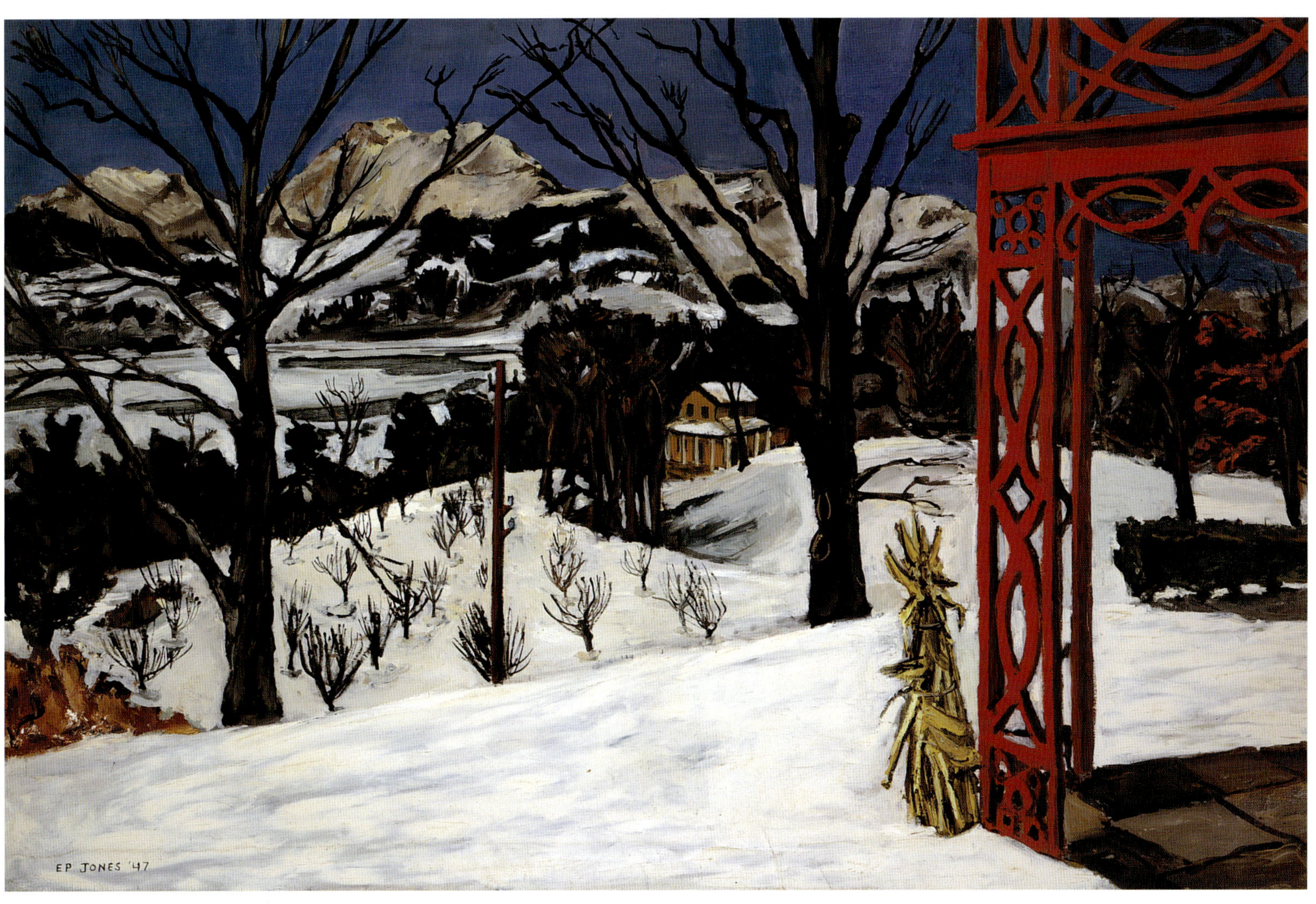

View from Good Hap, 1947, oil on canvas, 40 x 60 inches.

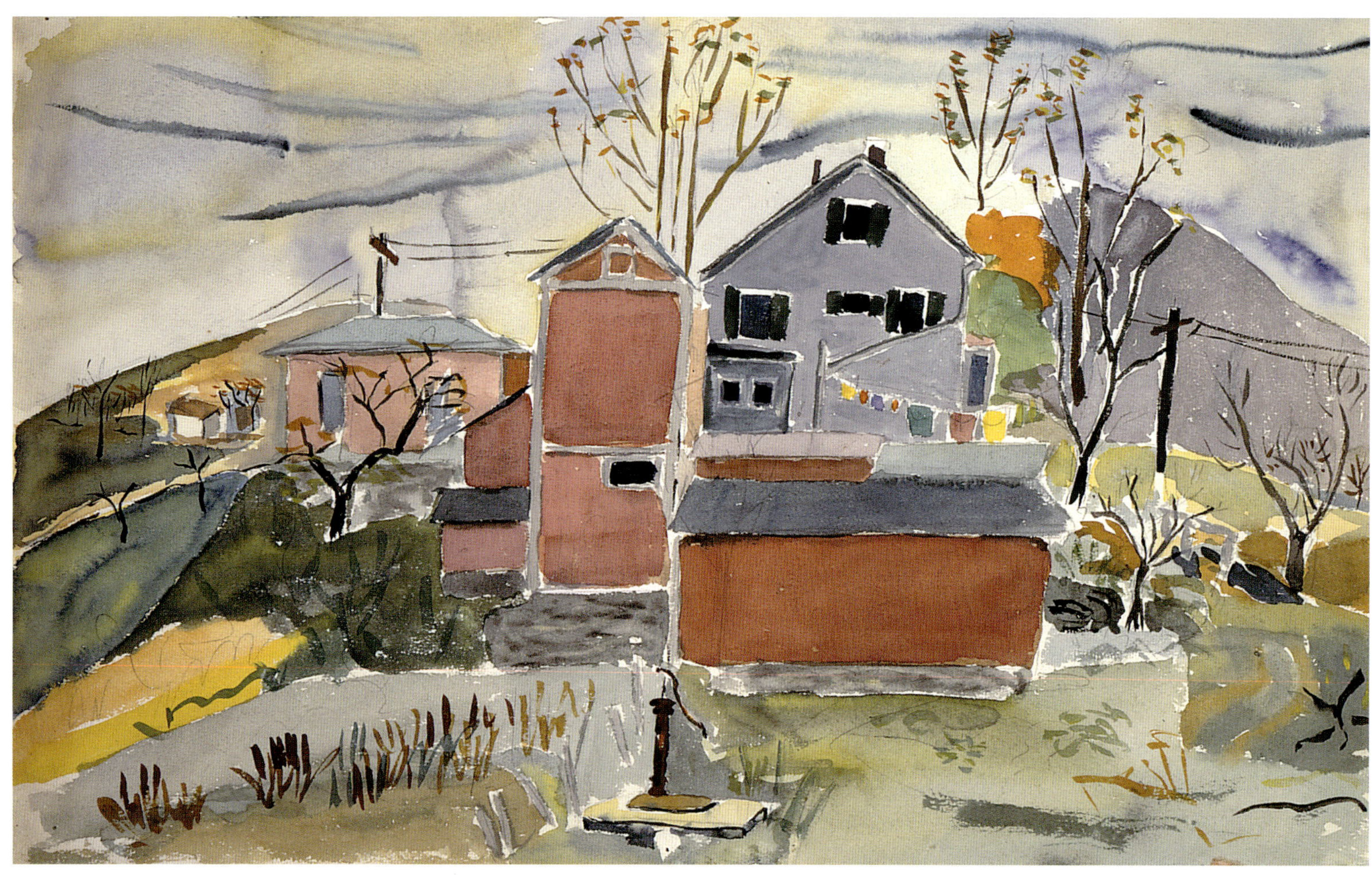

Farm Buildings, 1945, watercolor, 12$\frac{1}{2}$ x 19 inches.

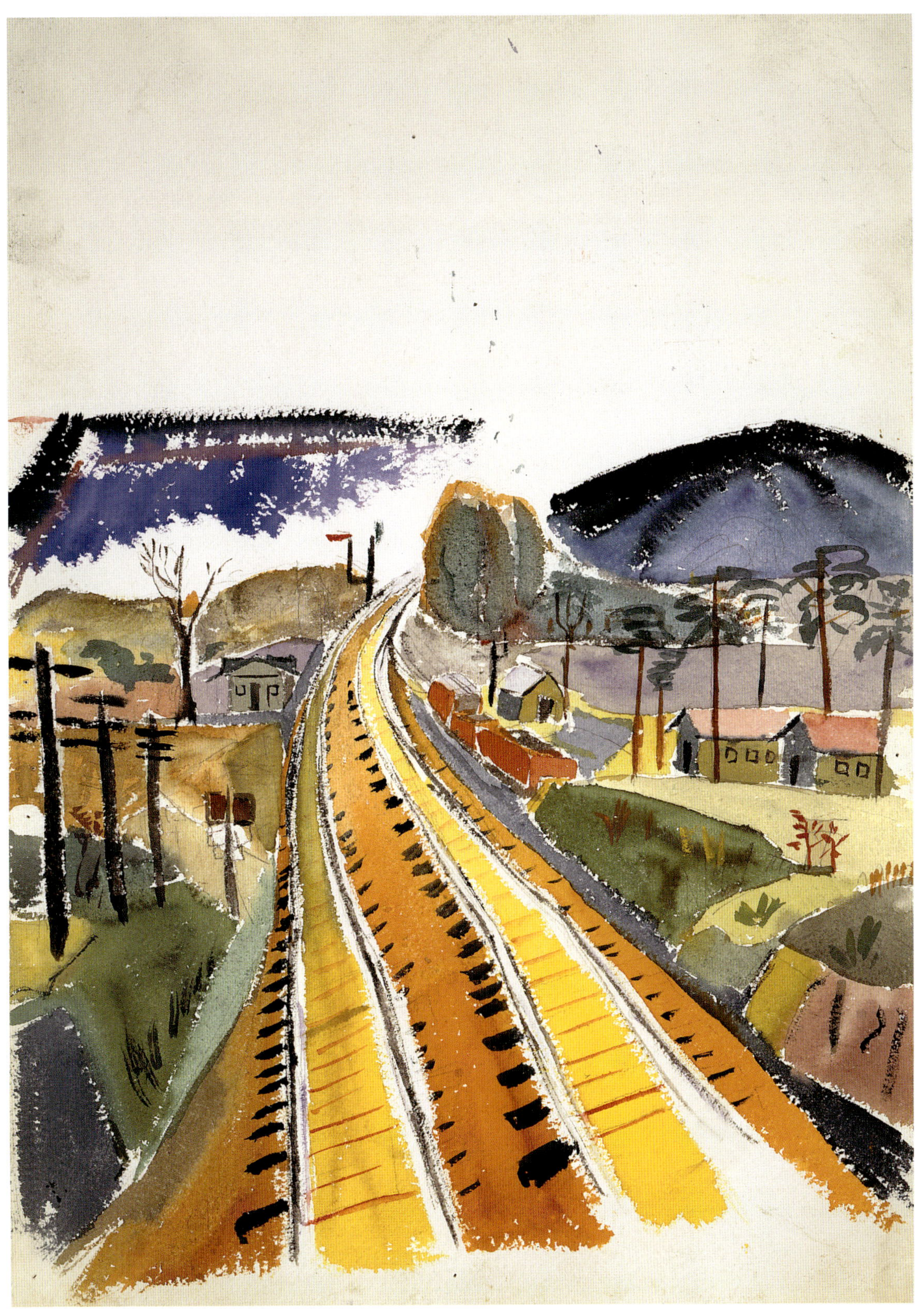

Early Spring, 1945, watercolor, 23 x 15¾ inches.

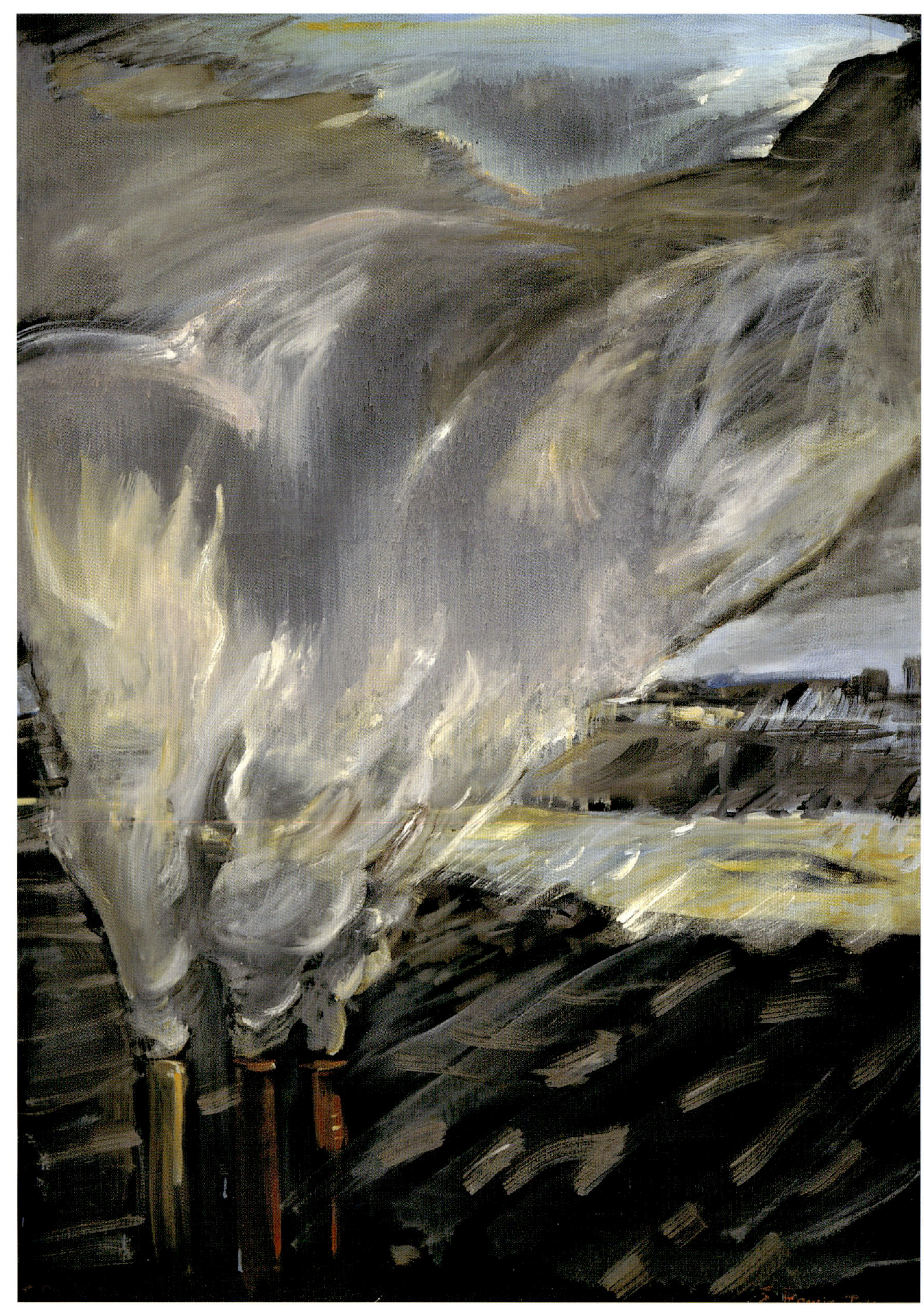

Smoke Stacks, c. 1956, oil on canvas, 38 x 28 inches.

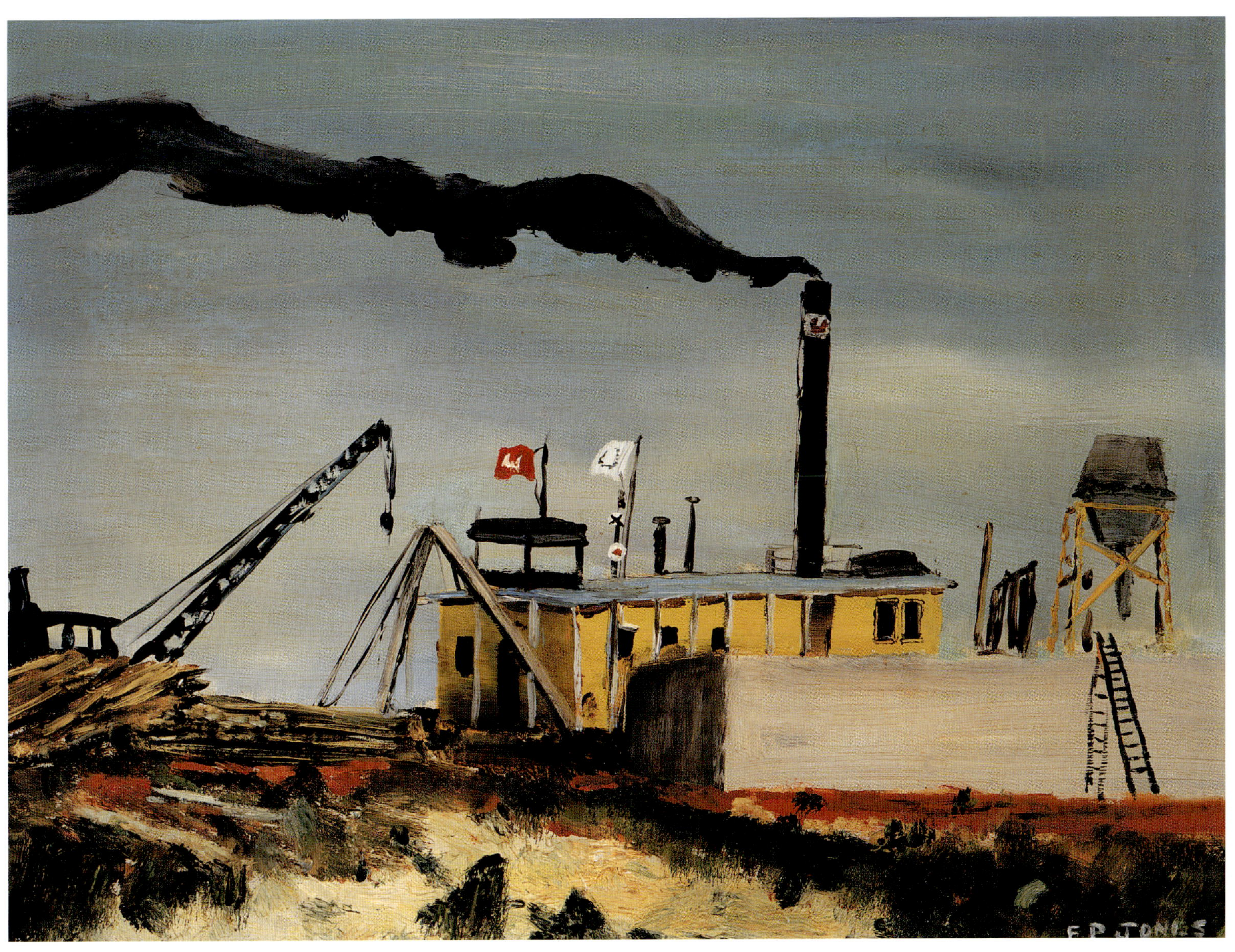

The Dredge, Georgia, 1946, oil on canvas, 15 x 17 inches.

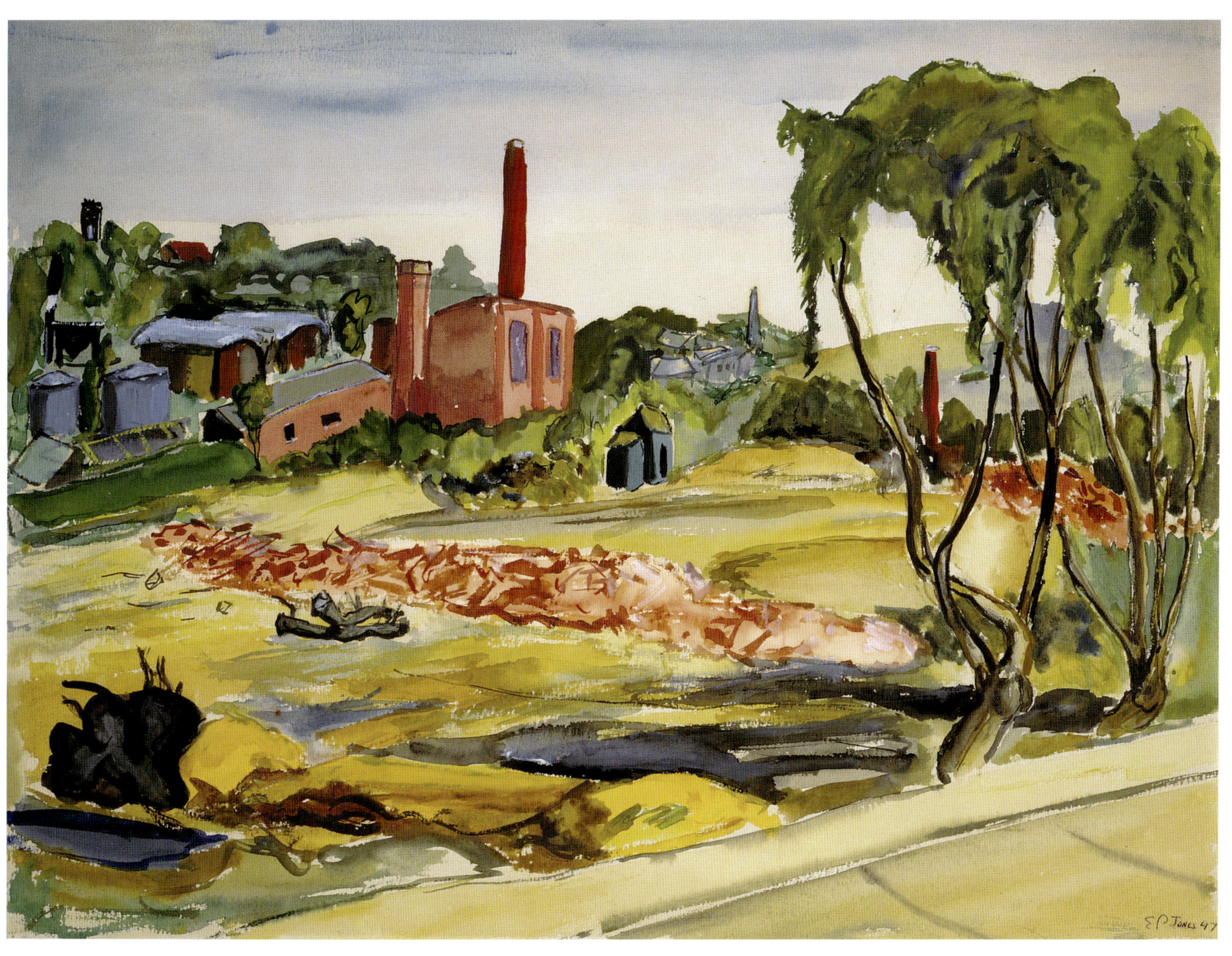

Country Factory, 1947, watercolor, 20 x 25 inches.

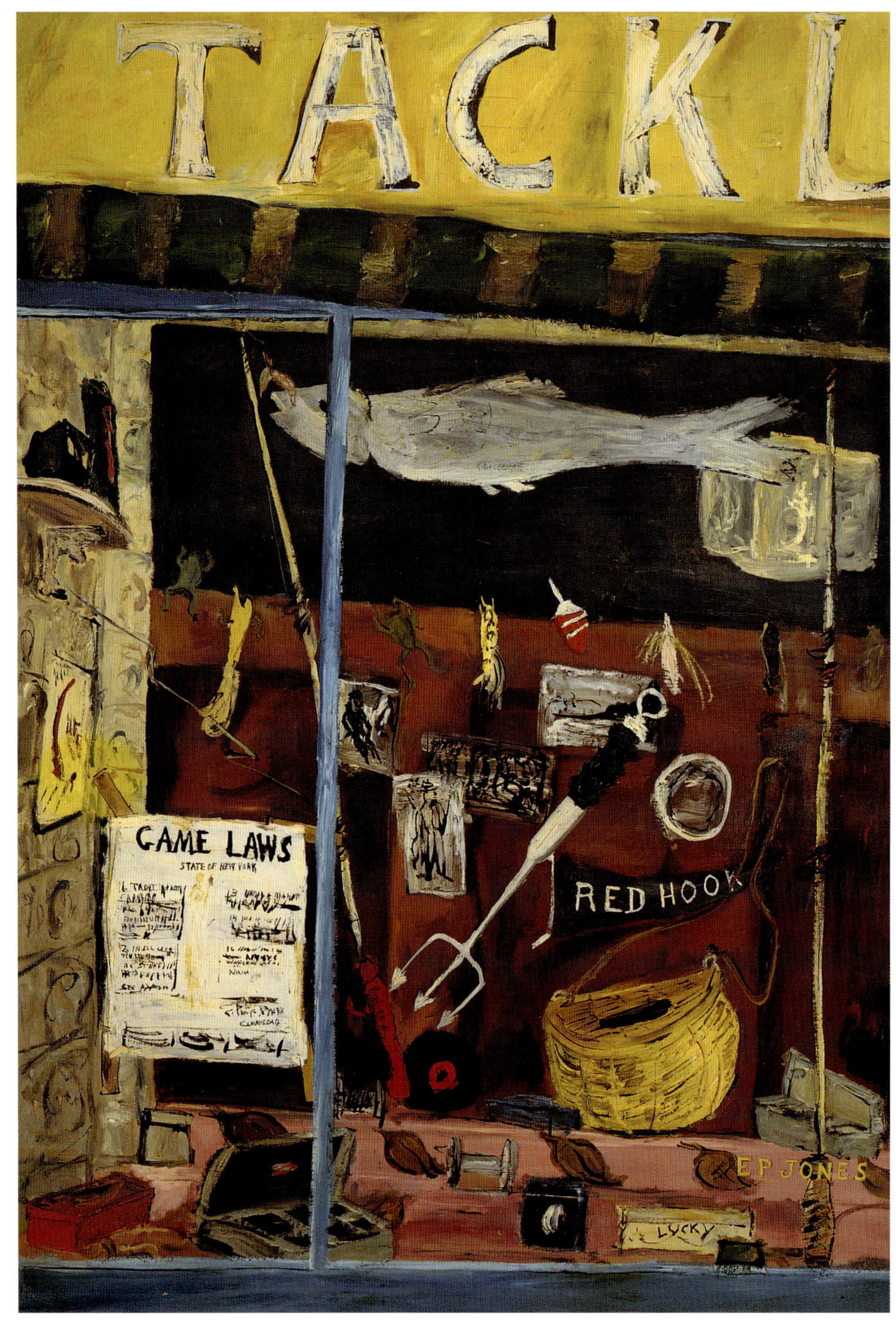

Tackle, 1947, oil on canvas, 60 x 40 inches.

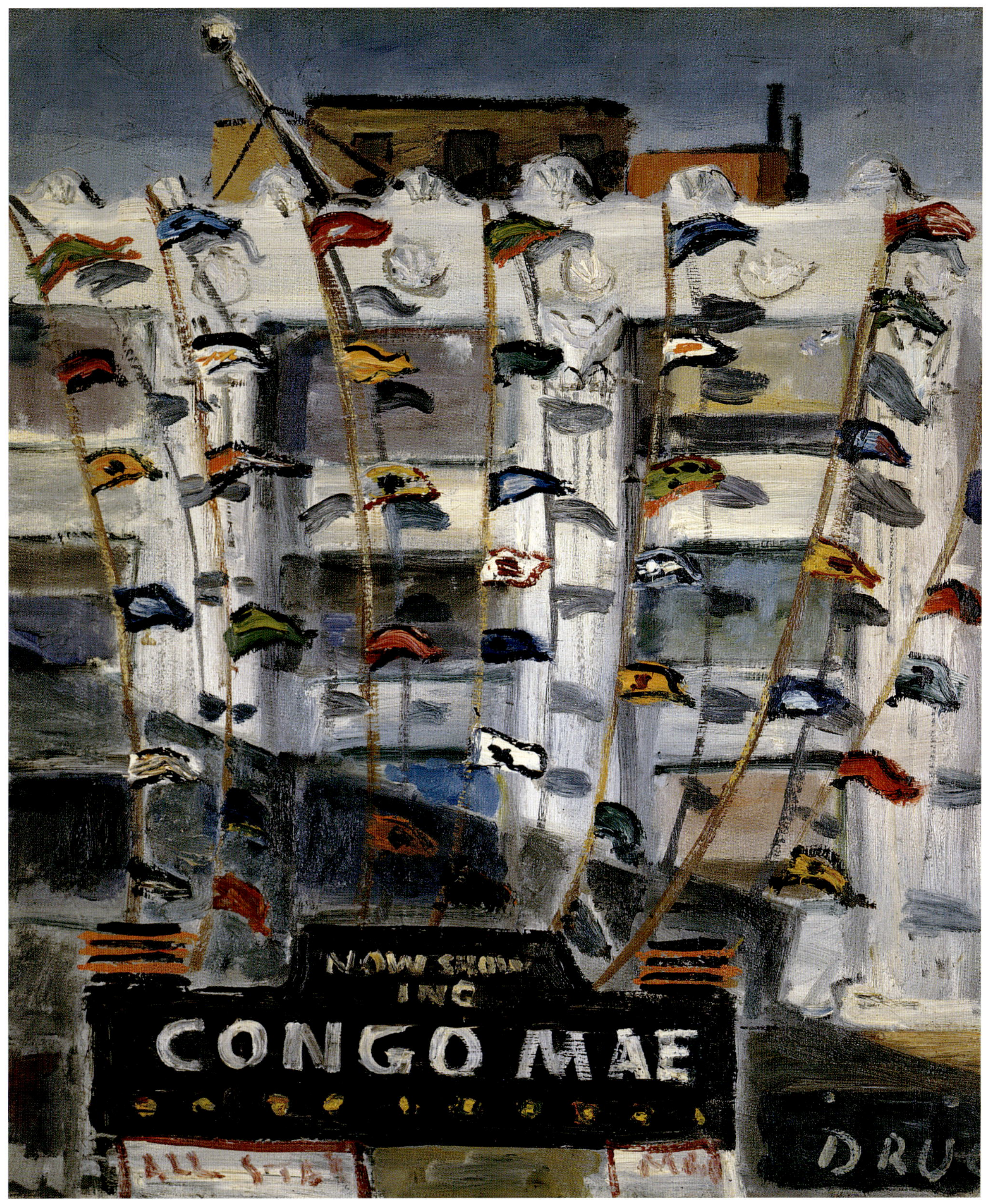

Congo Mae, c. 1938, oil on canvas, 21 x 17 inches.

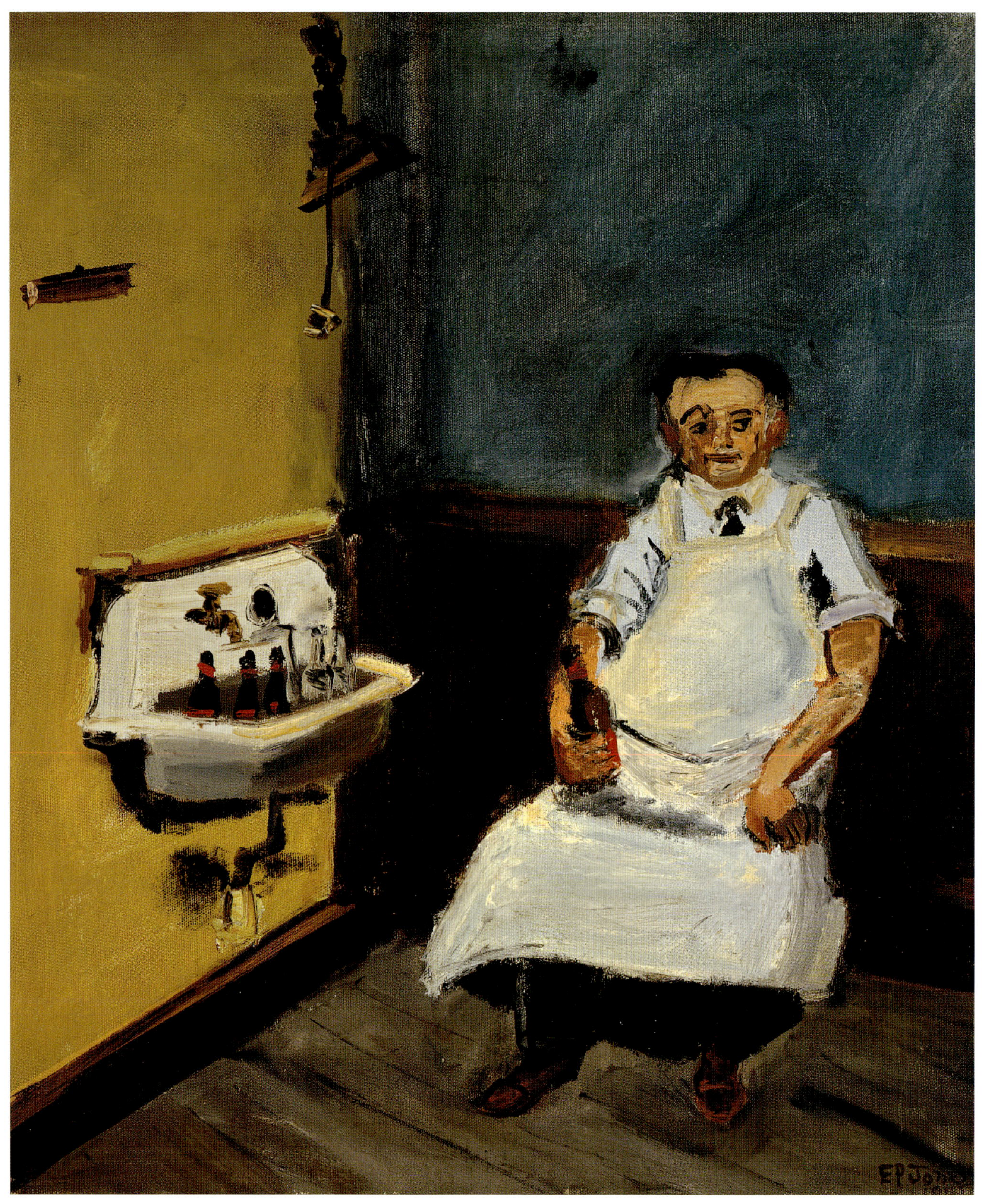

Man with Bottle, 1945, oil on canvas, 22 x 18 inches.

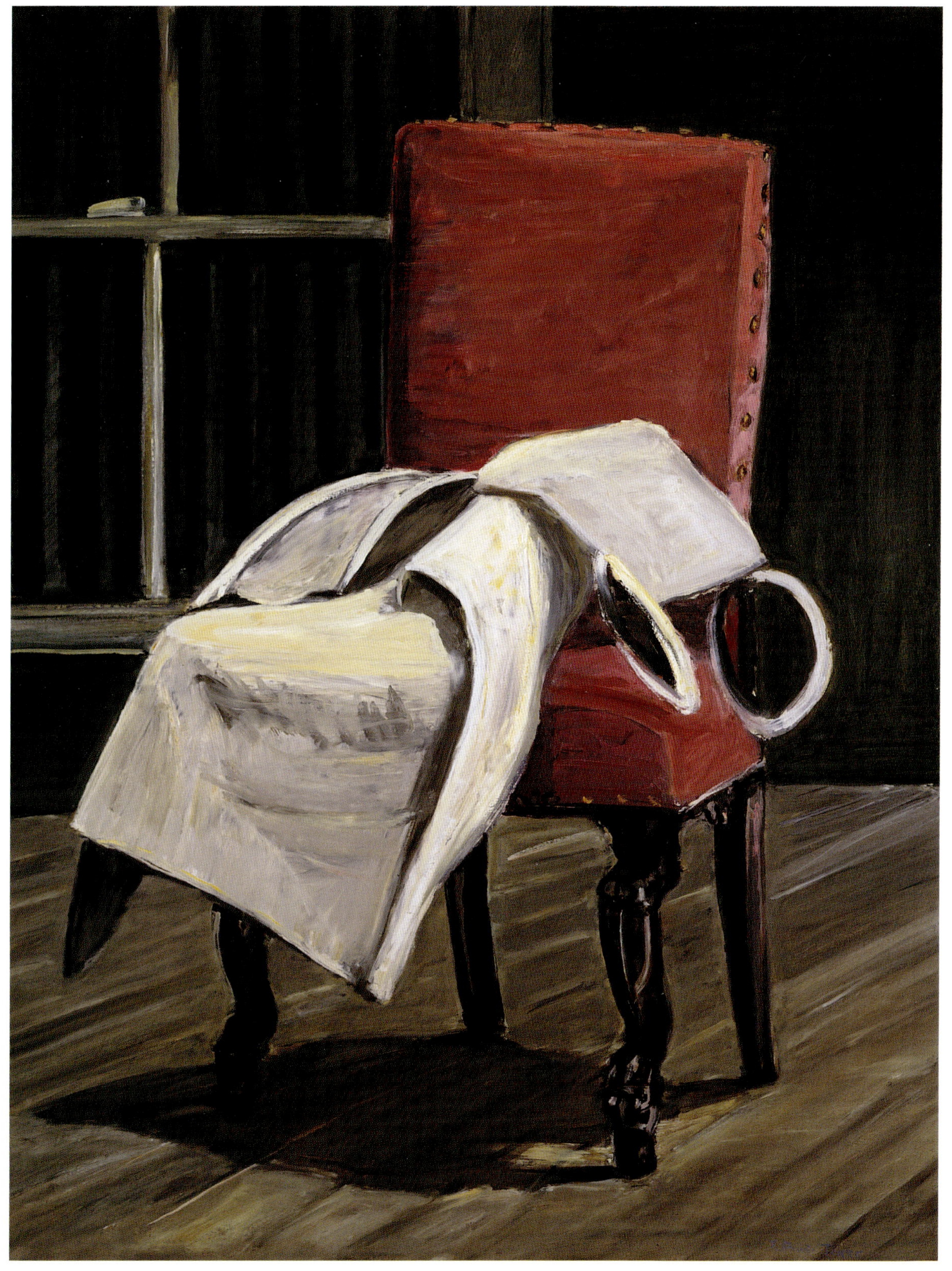

Chair with Etcher's Apron, c. 1957, oil on canvas, 40 x 30 inches.

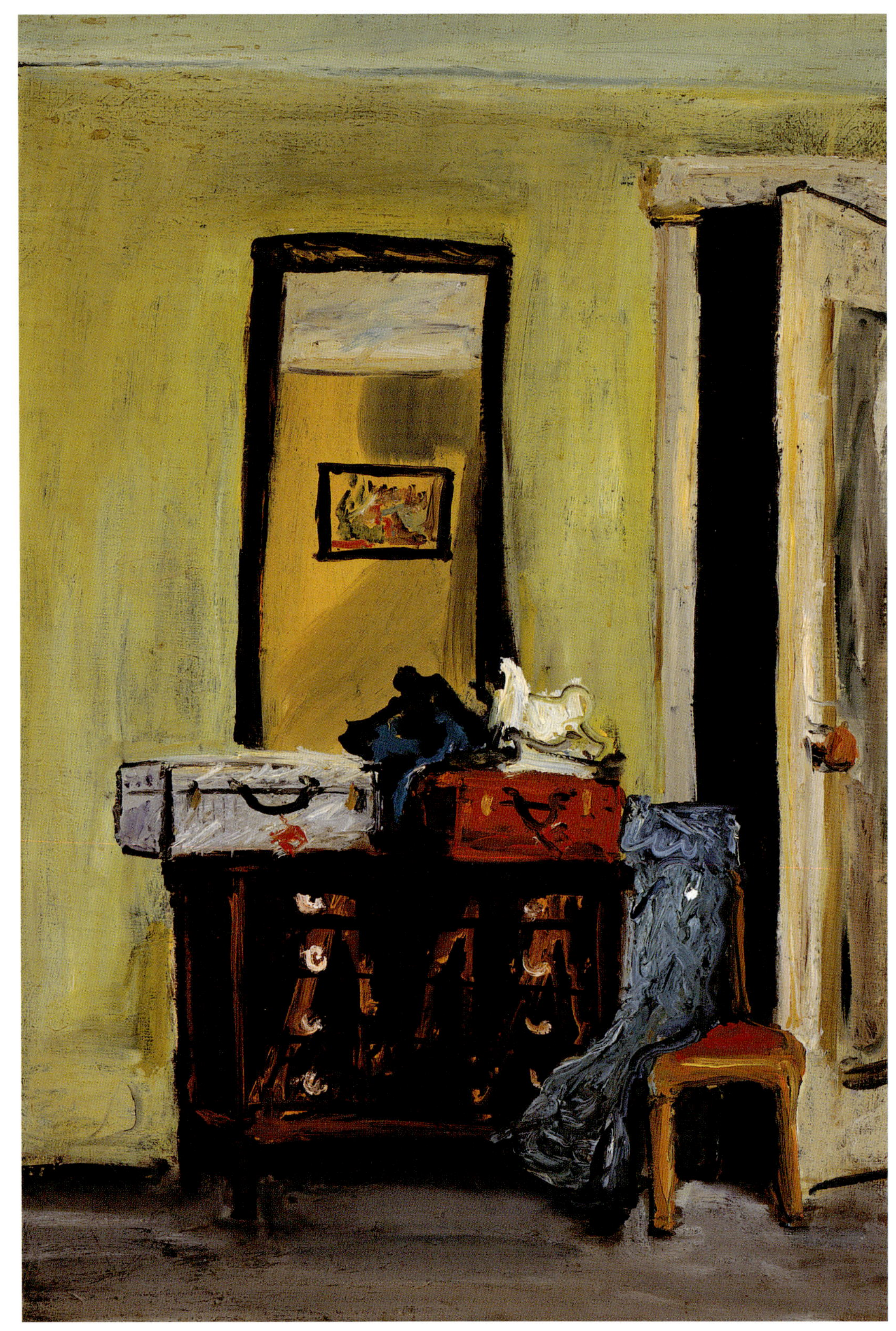

Hotel Room, 1946, oil on canvas, 24 x 16 inches.

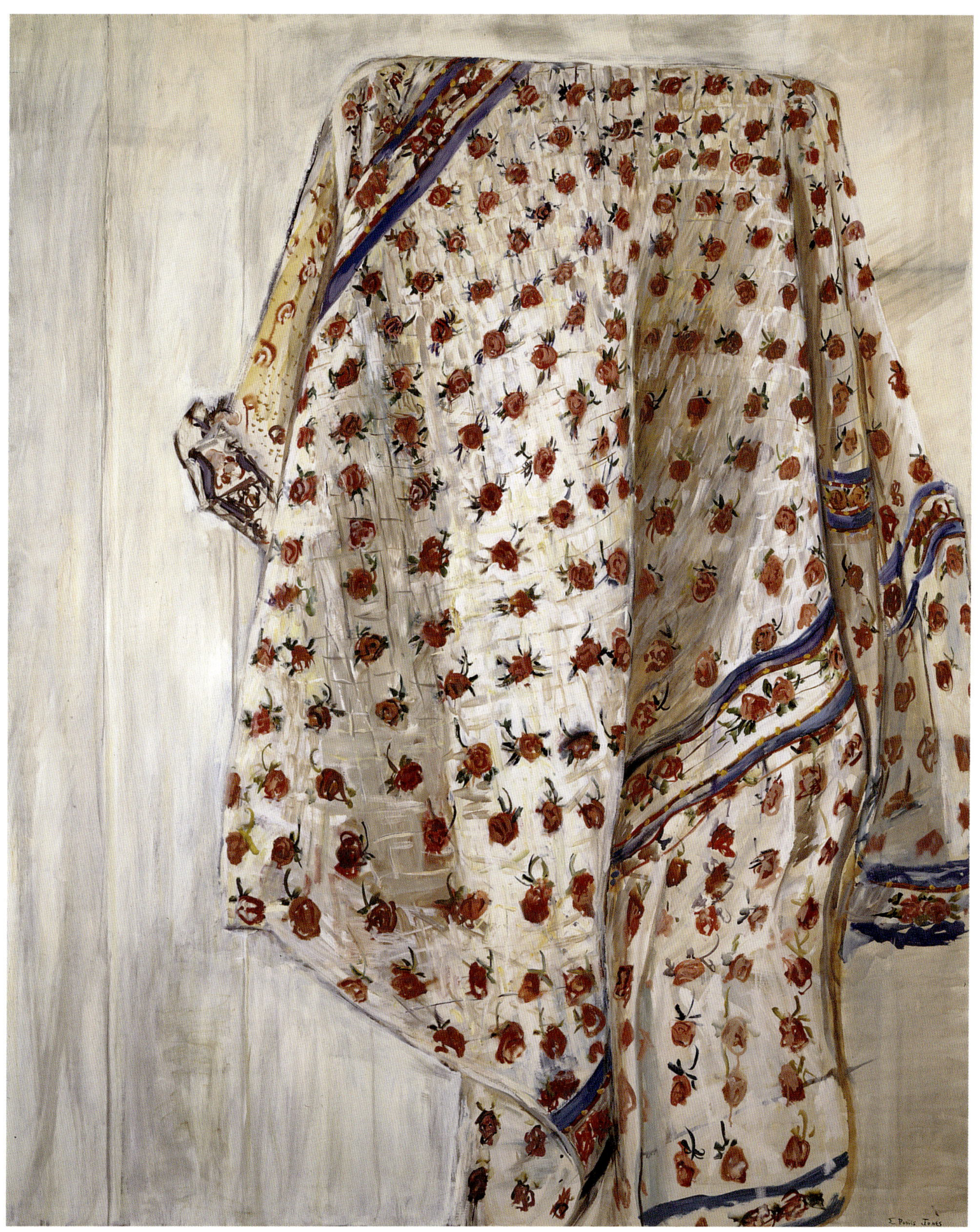

Bedspread, c. 1960, oil on canvas, 64 x 51 inches.

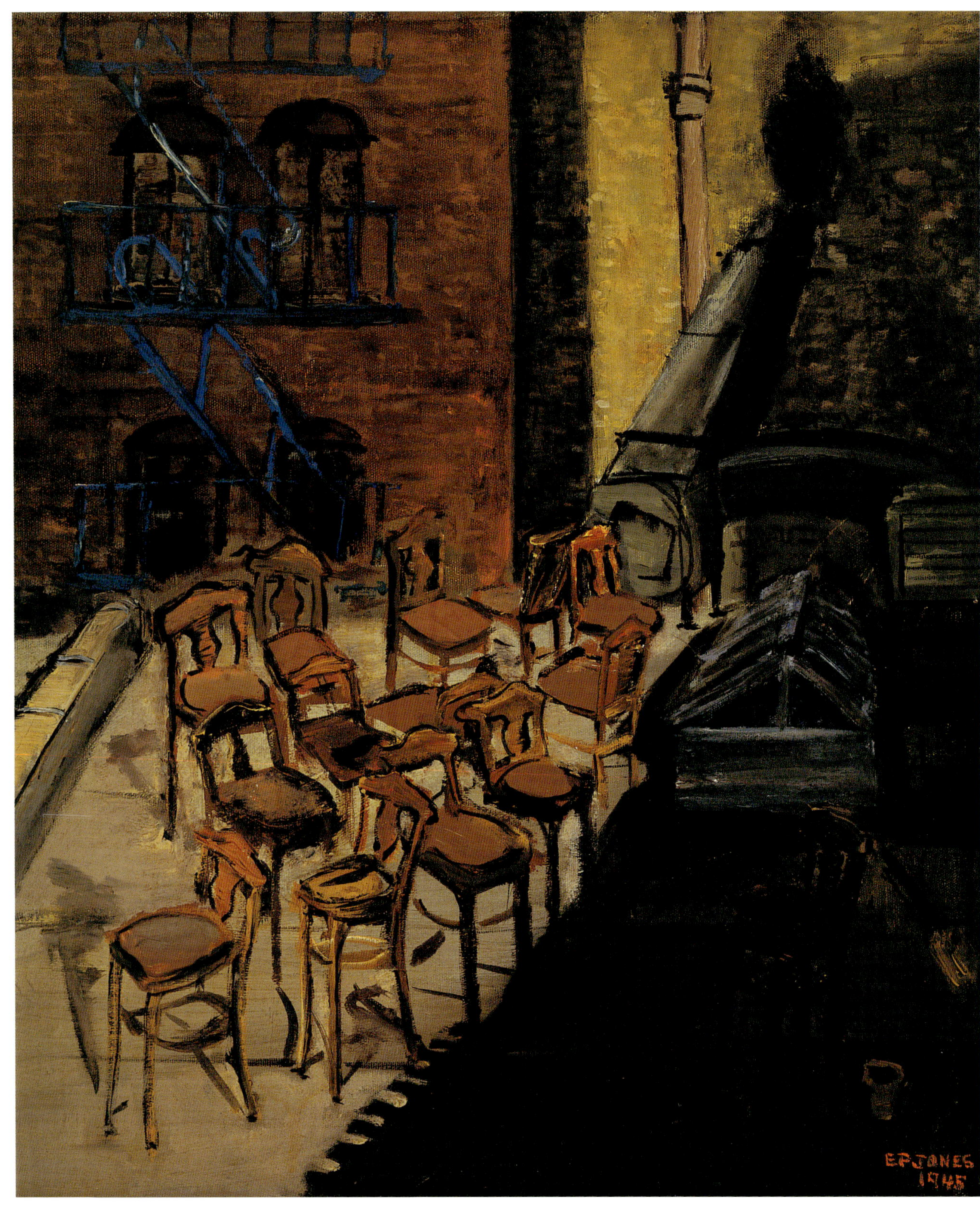

Rooftop Chairs, 1945, oil on canvas, 22 x 18 inches.

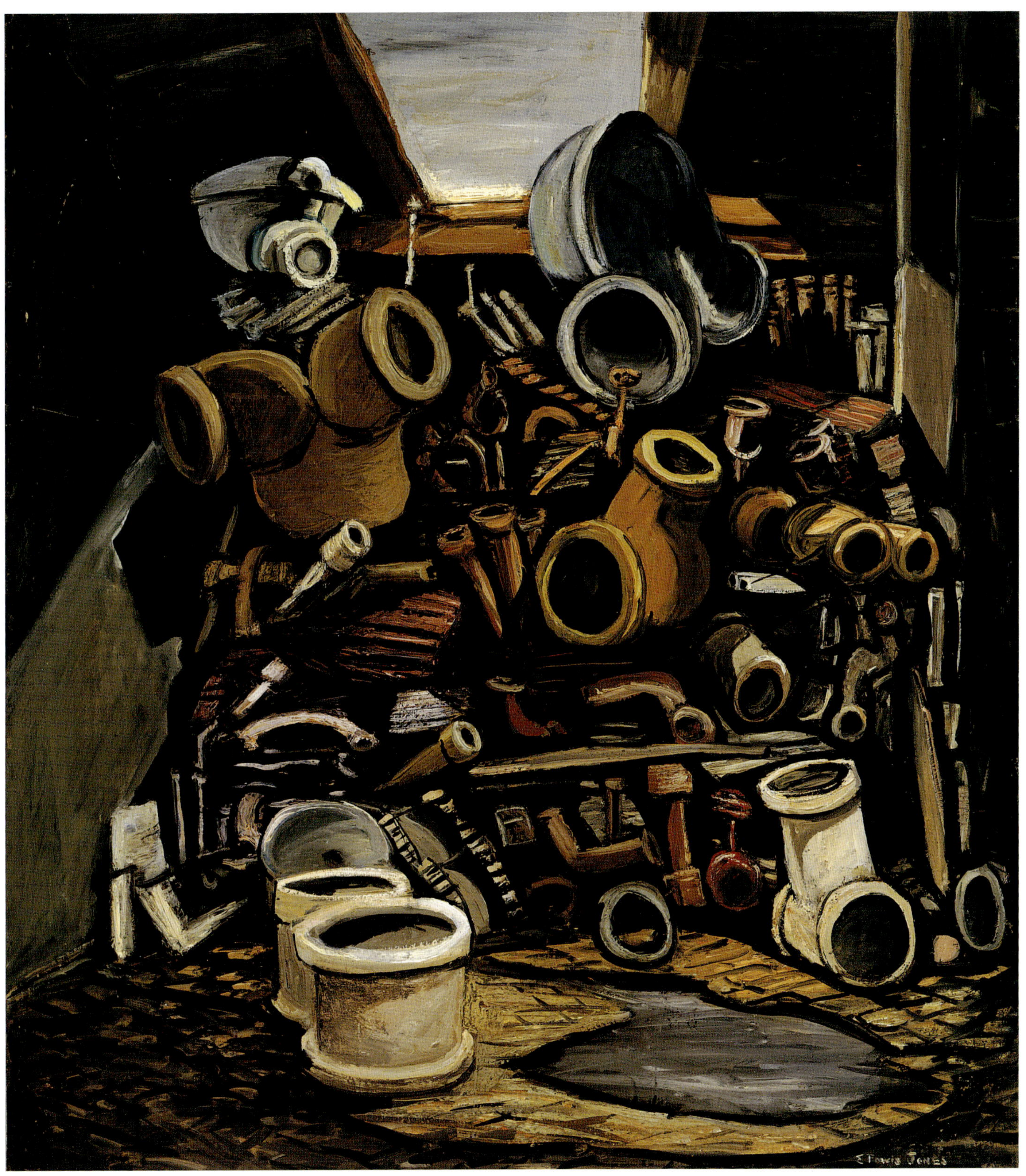

Pipes and Elbows, c. 1950, oil on canvas, 39 x 33 inches.

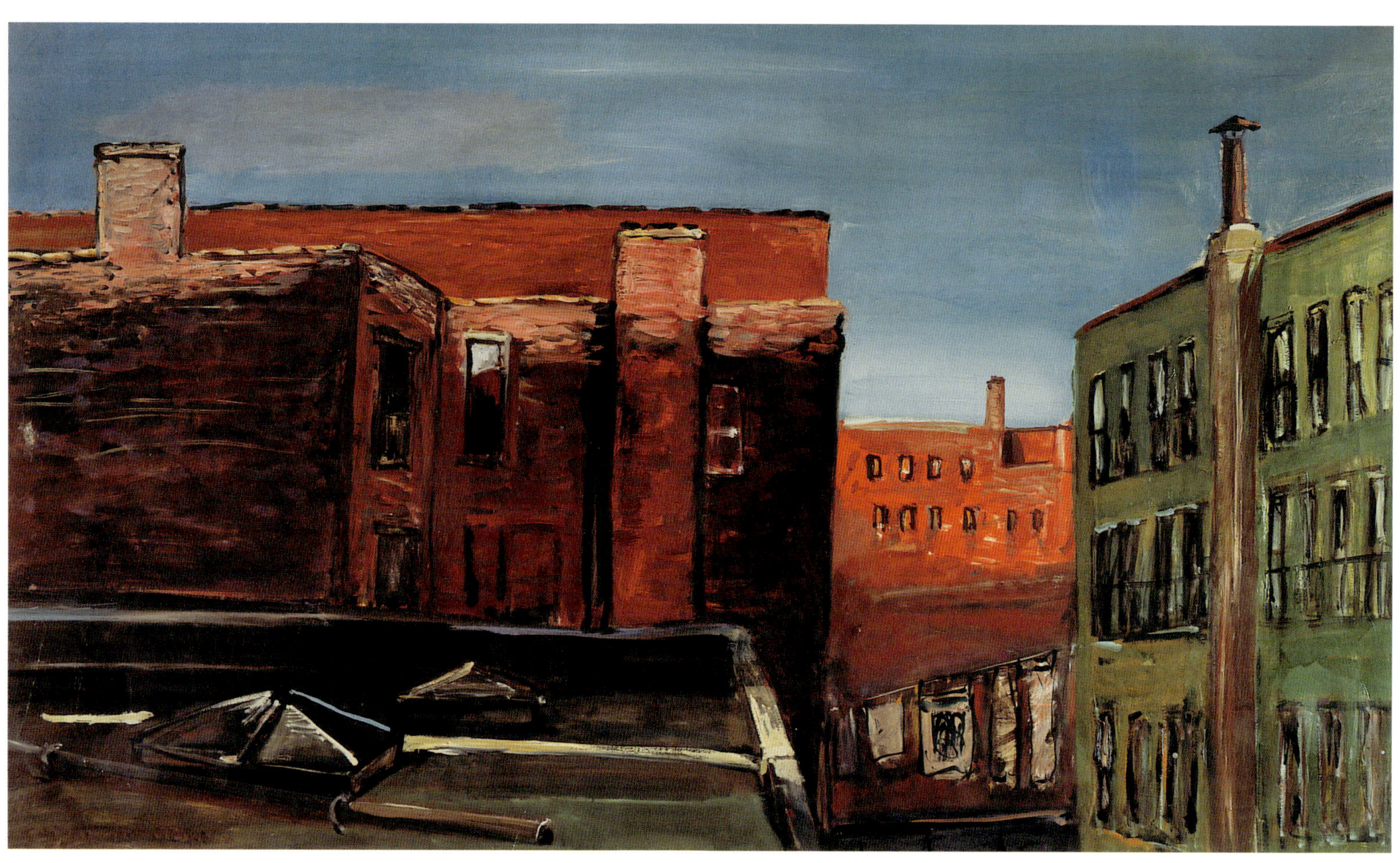

From the Studio, Looking East, c. 1955, oil on canvas, 23 x 39 inches.

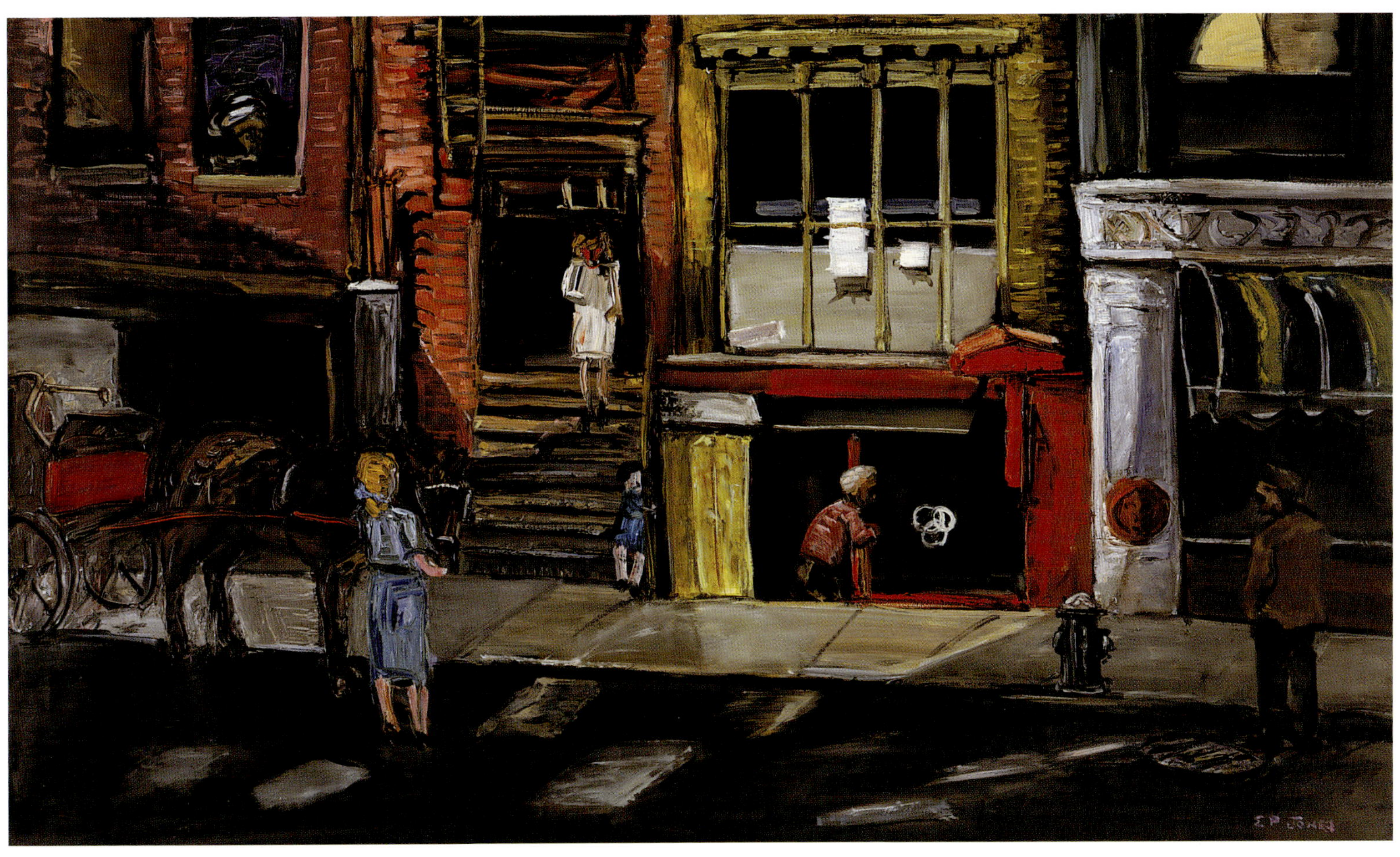

Bleecker Street, c. 1950, oil on canvas, 24 x 40 inches.

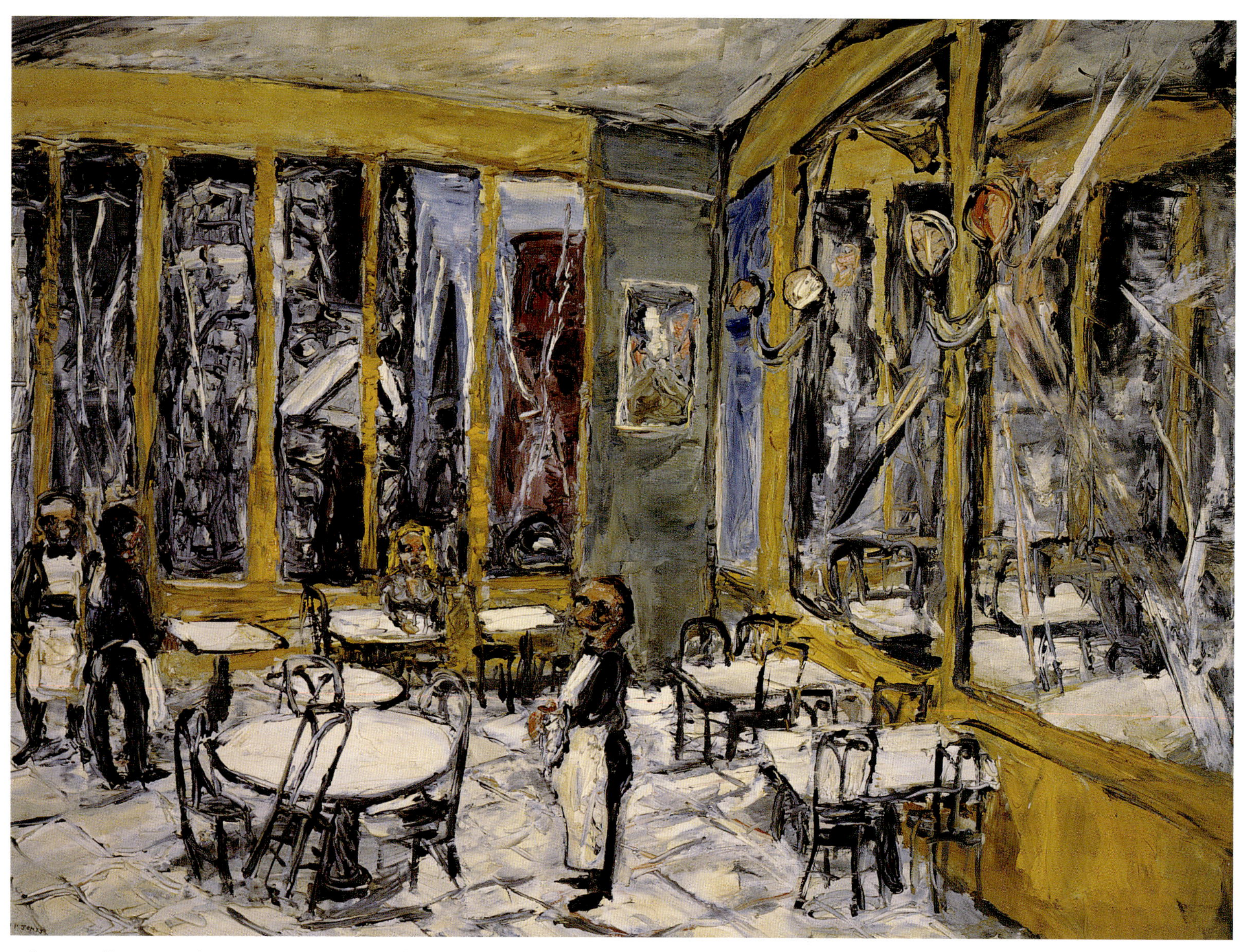

Lafayette Café, 1945, oil on canvas, 24 x 30 inches.

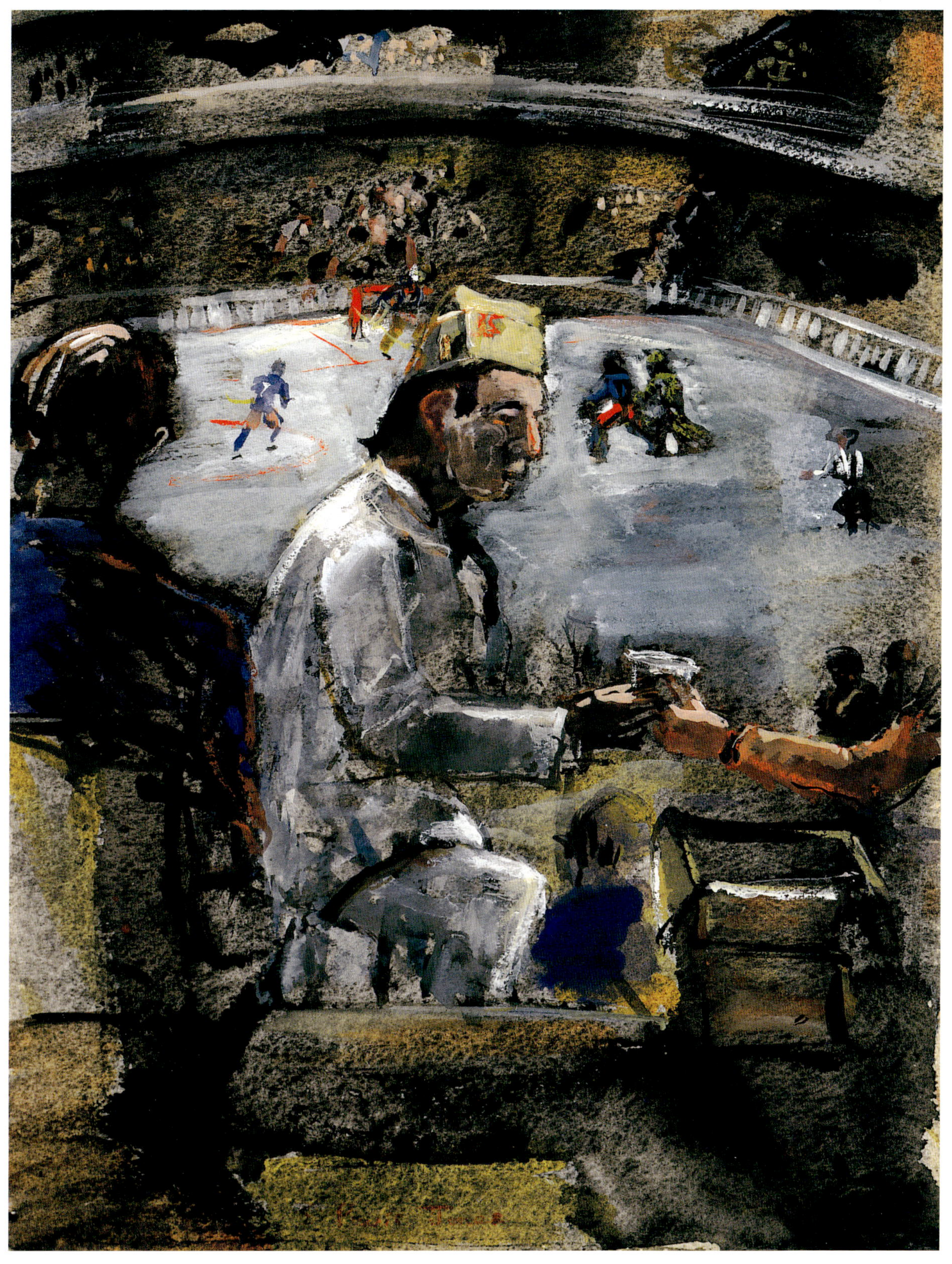

Madison Square Garden, c. 1962, watercolor, 11 x 8 1/2 inches.

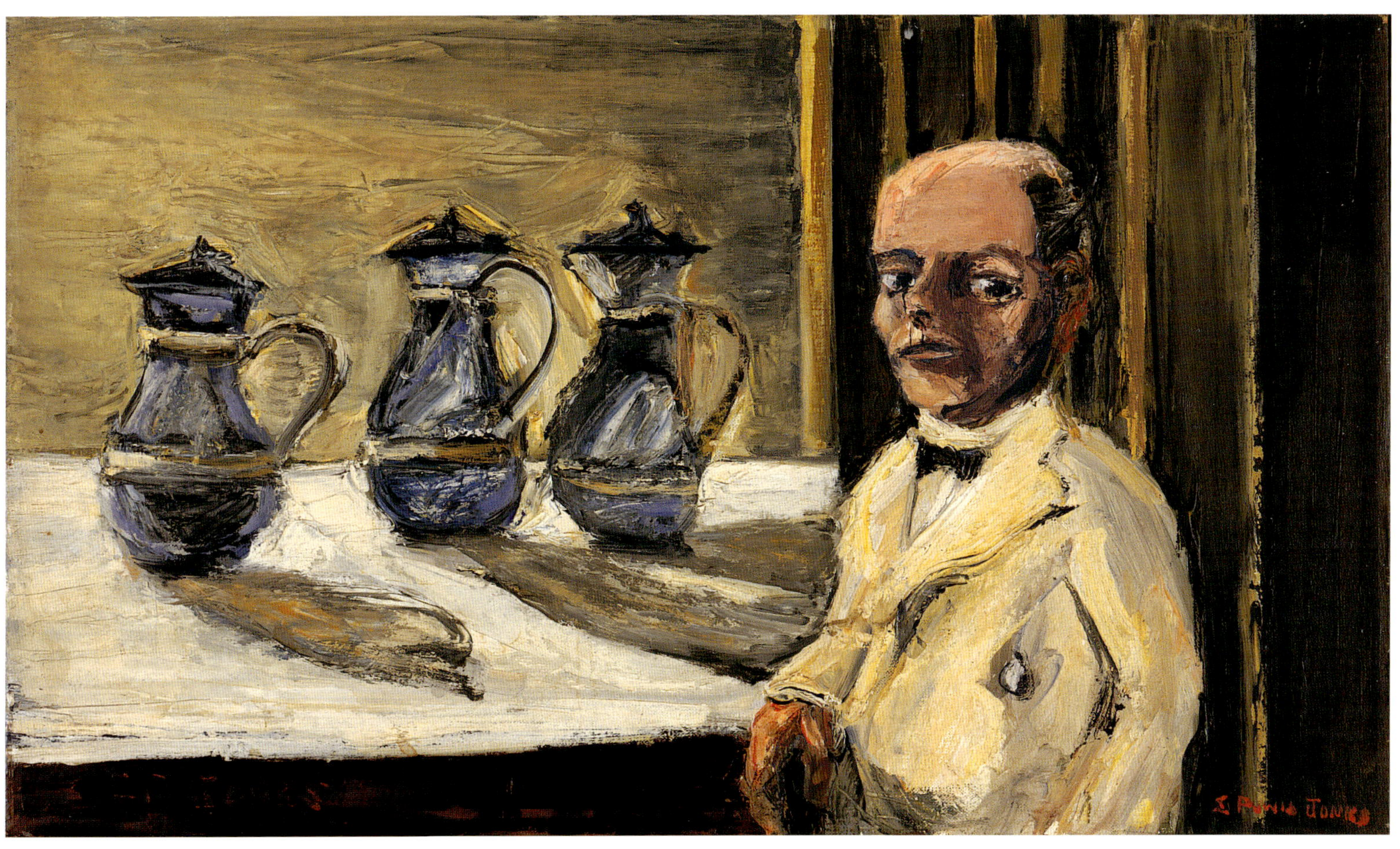

The Waiter, c. 1948, oil on canvas, 9 x 15 inches.

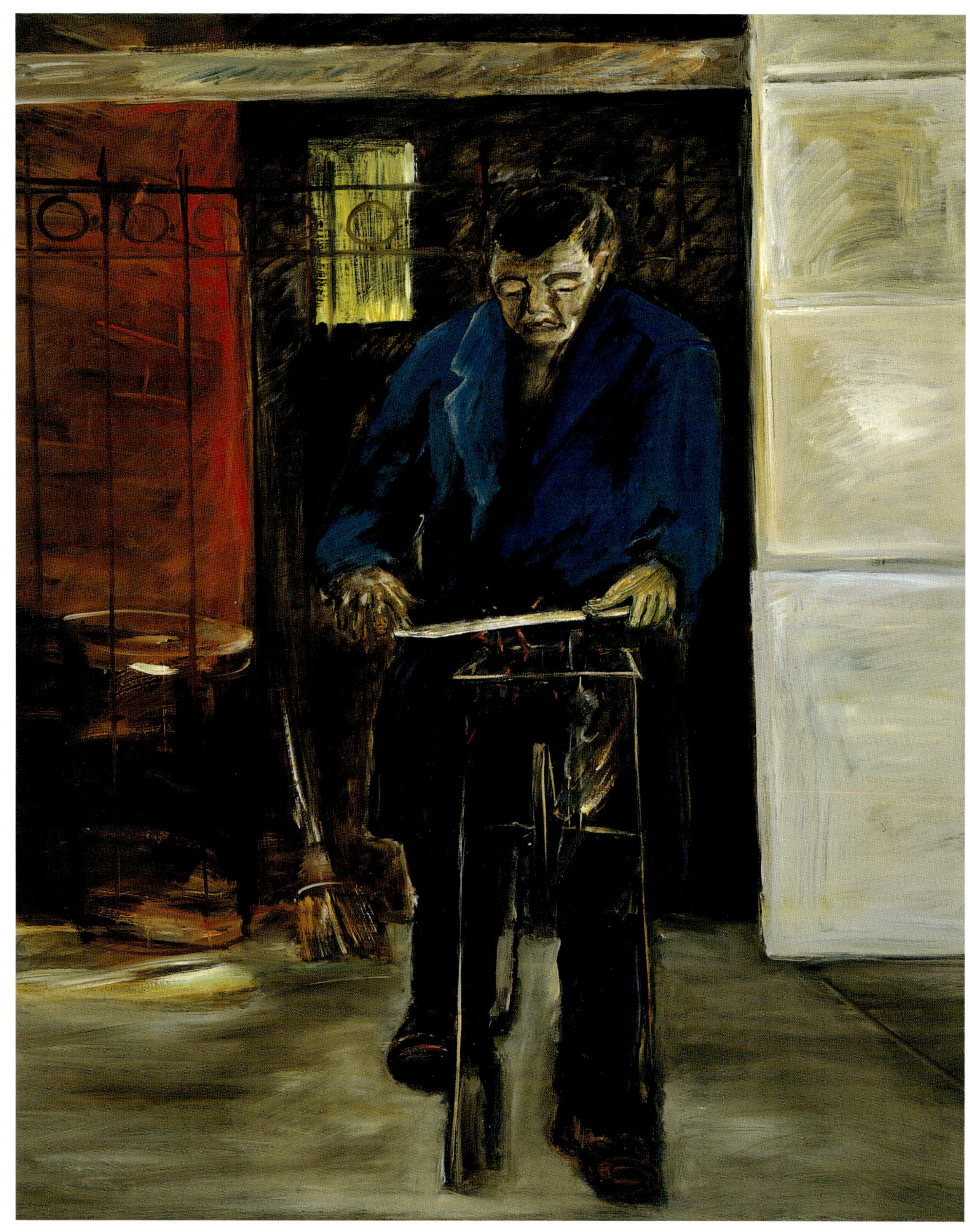

The Knife Grinder, c. 1955, oil on canvas, 60 x 48 inches.

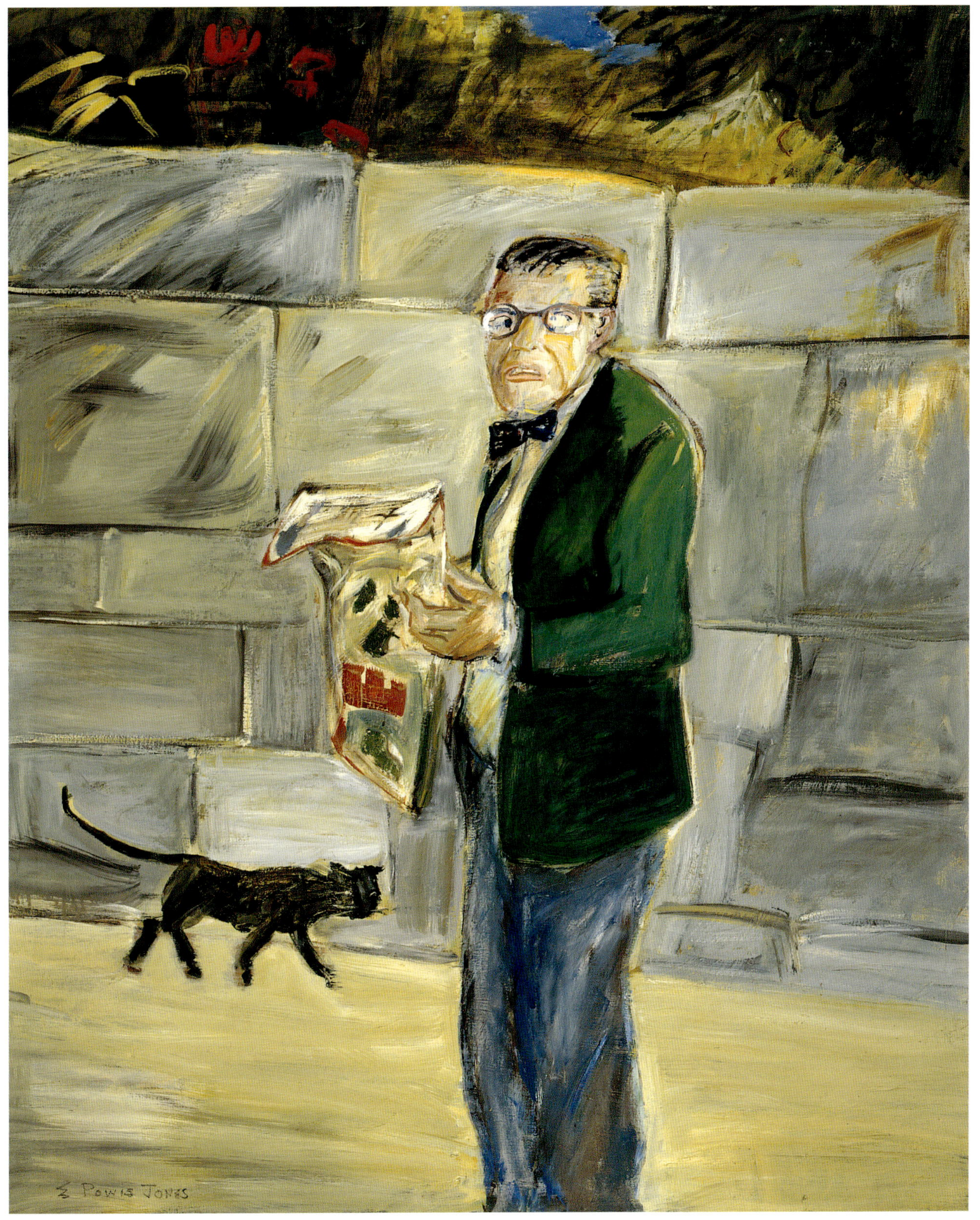

Portrait of Sam Crowther, c. 1953, oil on canvas, 60 x 48 inches.

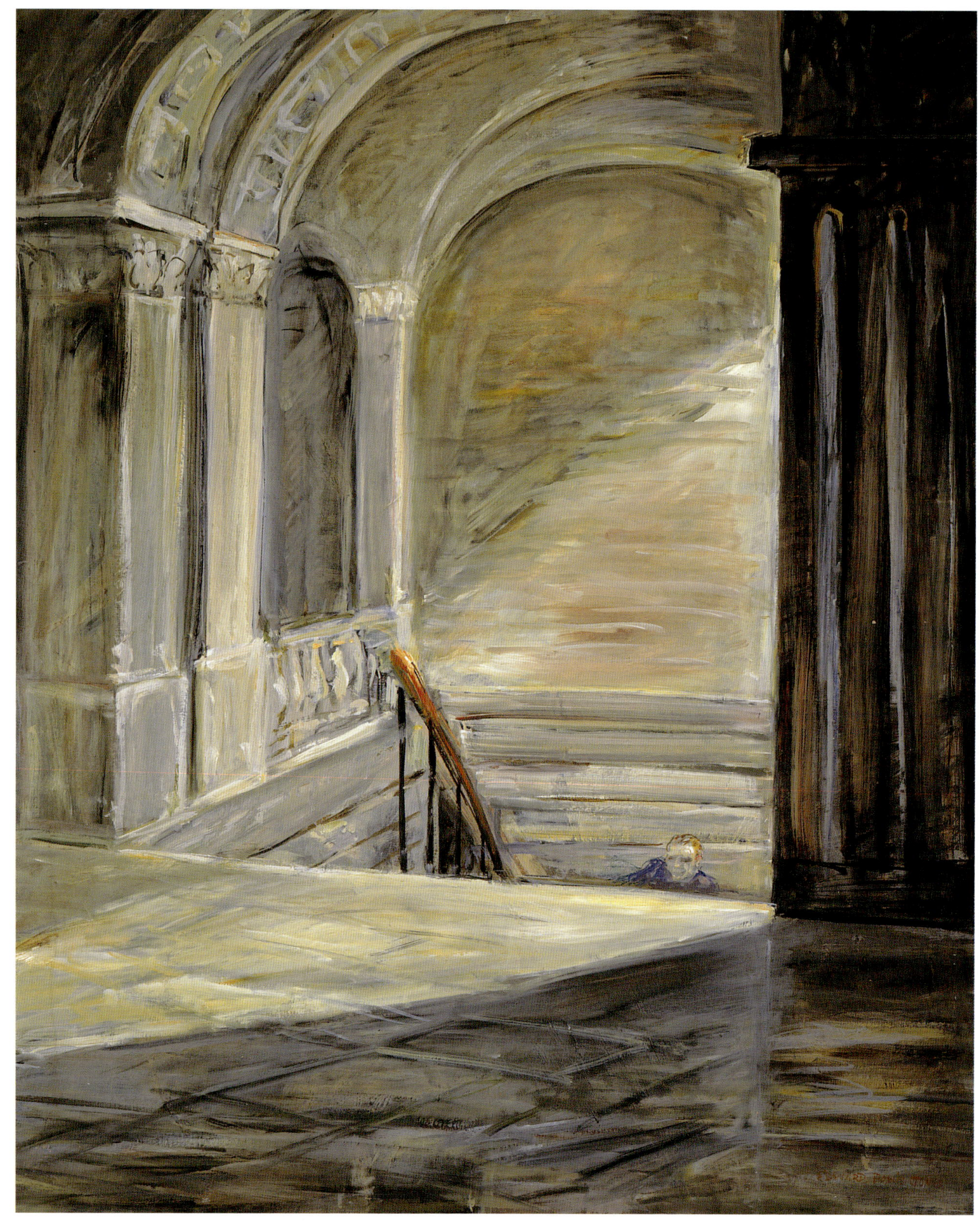

New York Public Library, c. 1960, oil on canvas, 48 x 38 inches.

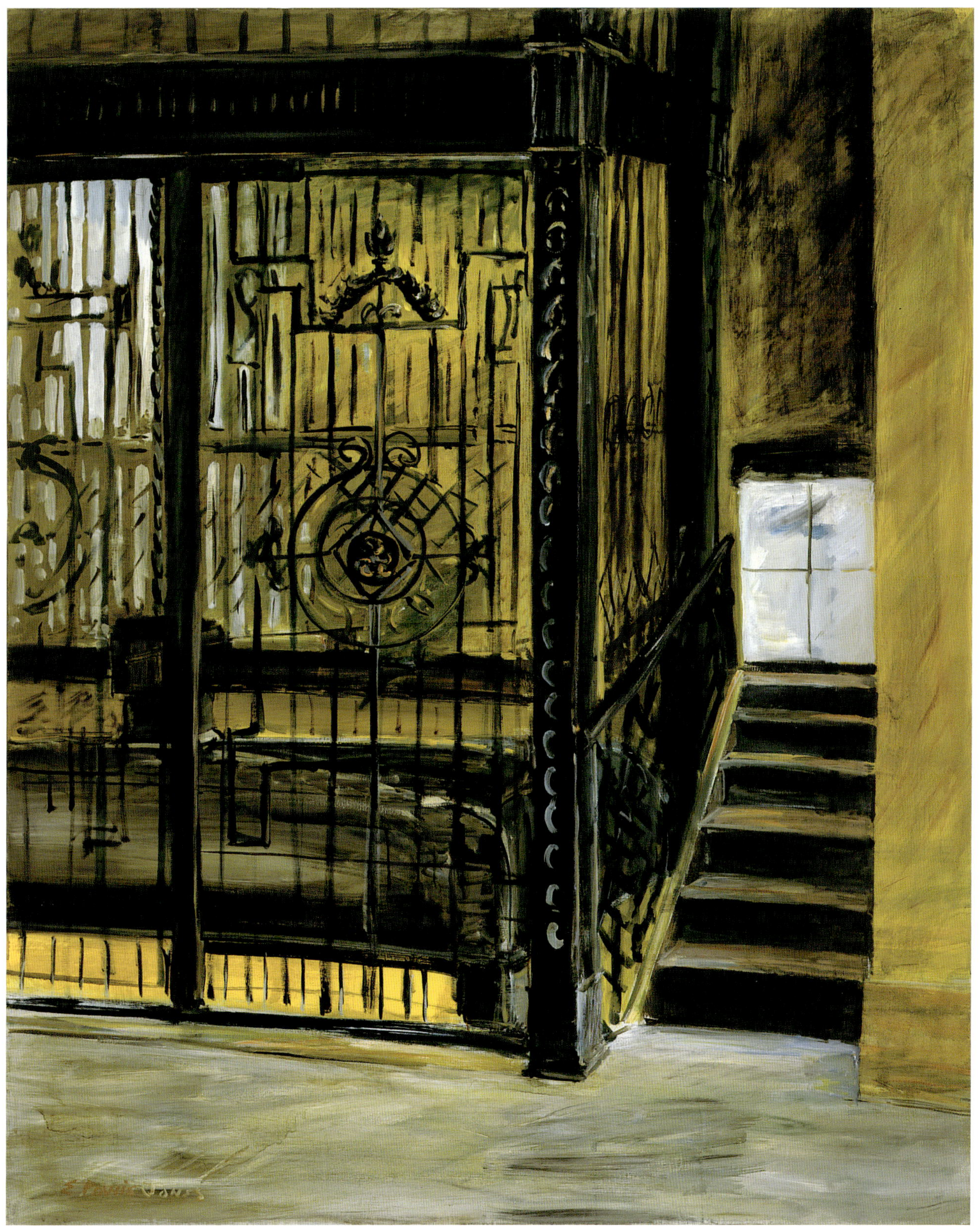

Birdcage Elevator, c. 1965, oil on canvas, 59 x 47 inches.

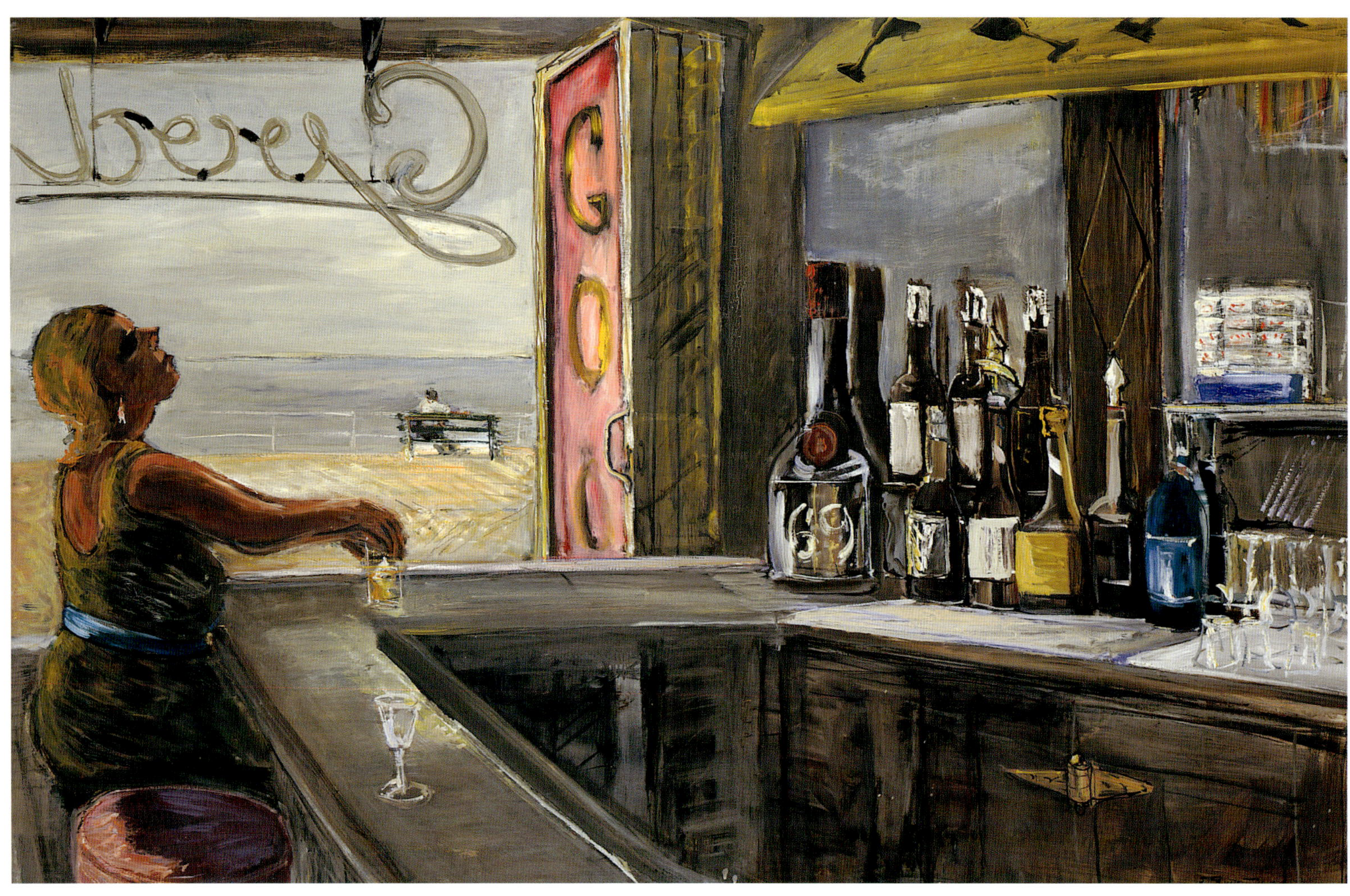

Goodie's, c. 1959, oil on canvas, 46 1/2 x 60 inches.

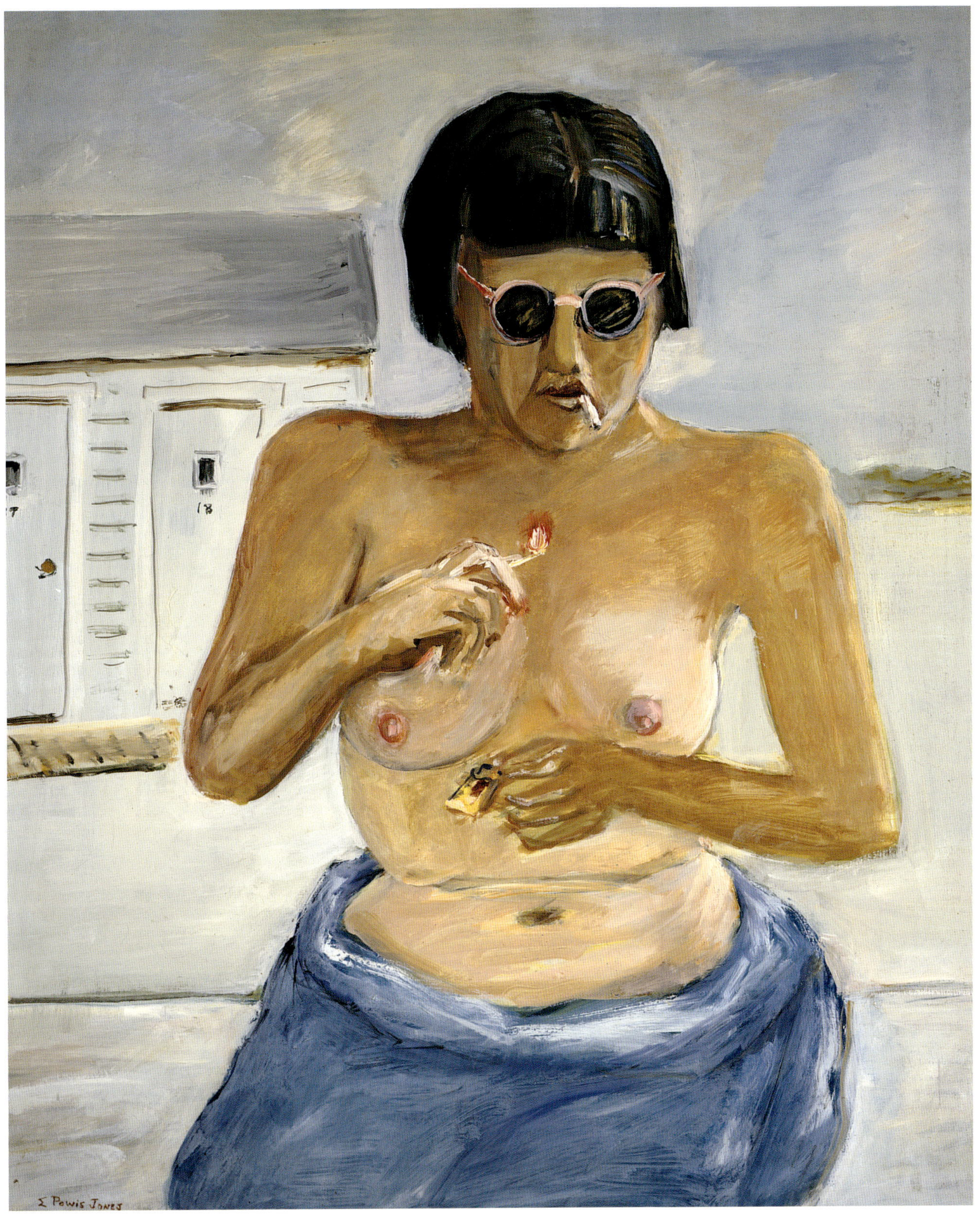

Lighting Up, c. 1953, oil on canvas, 29 1/2 x 24 inches.

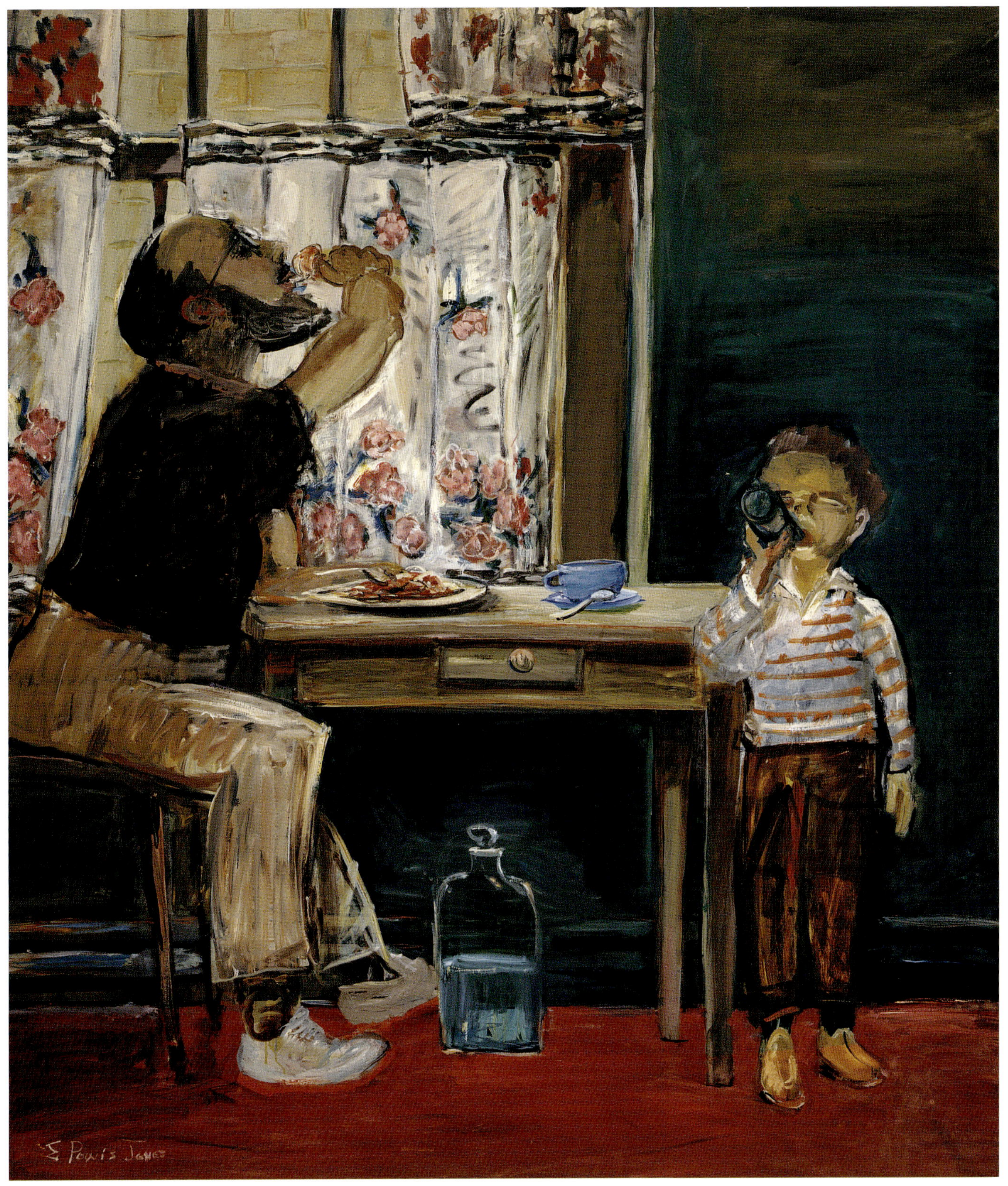

Studio Lunch, 1956, oil on canvas, 60 x 50 inches.

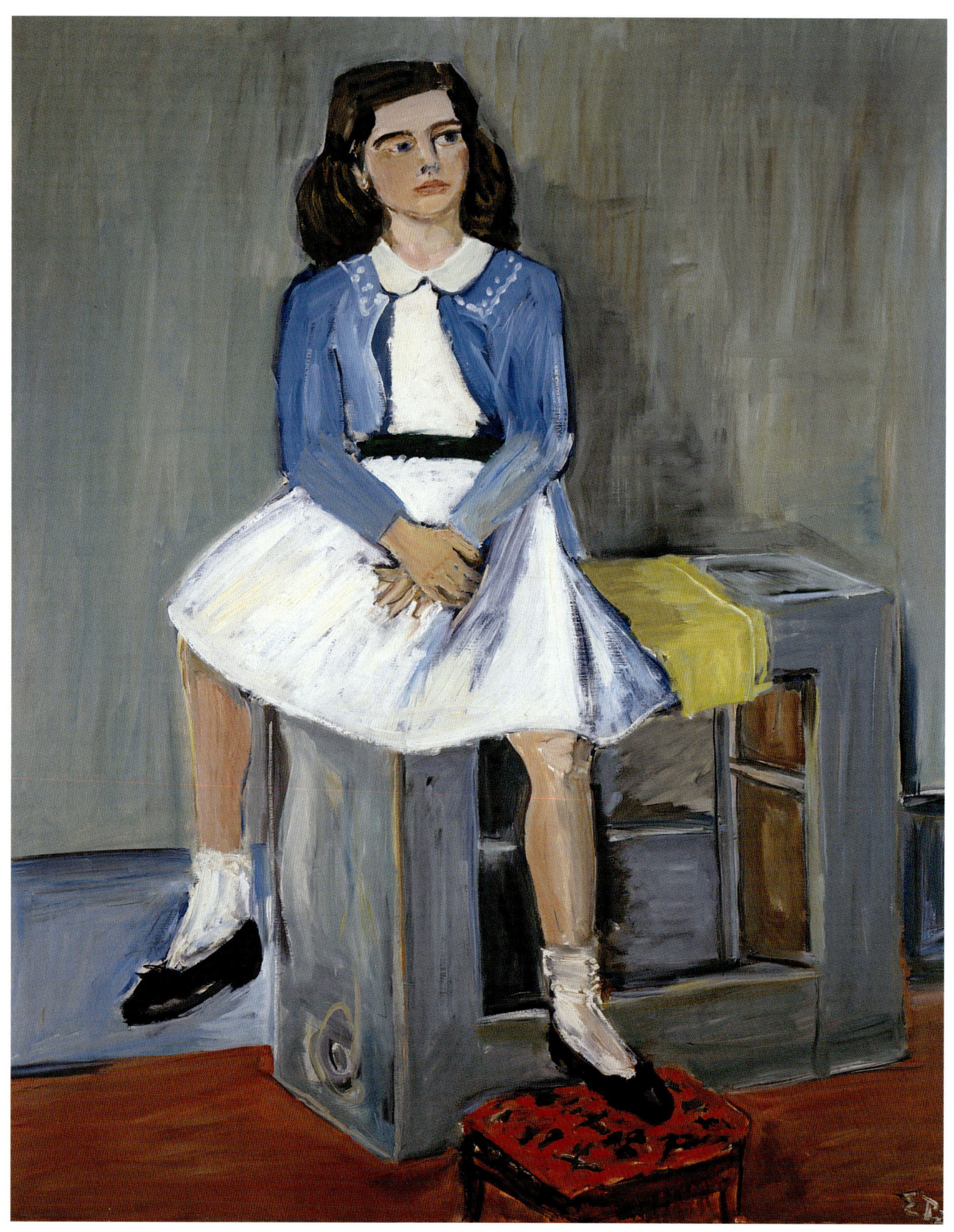

Portrait of Elizabeth, 1958, oil on canvas, 48 x 38 inches.

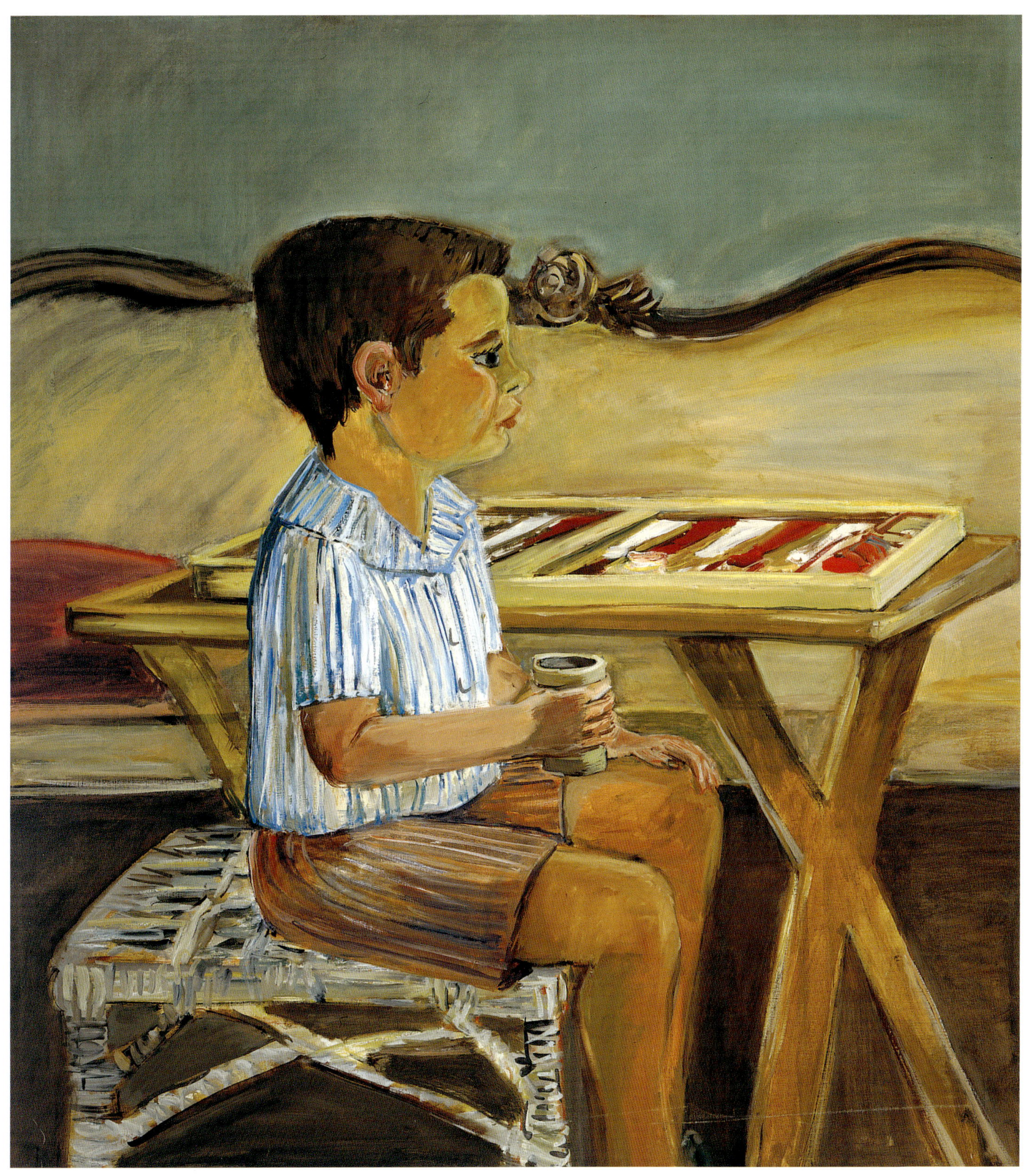

Peter at the Backgammon Board, c. 1956, oil on canvas, 351/2 x 311/2 inches.

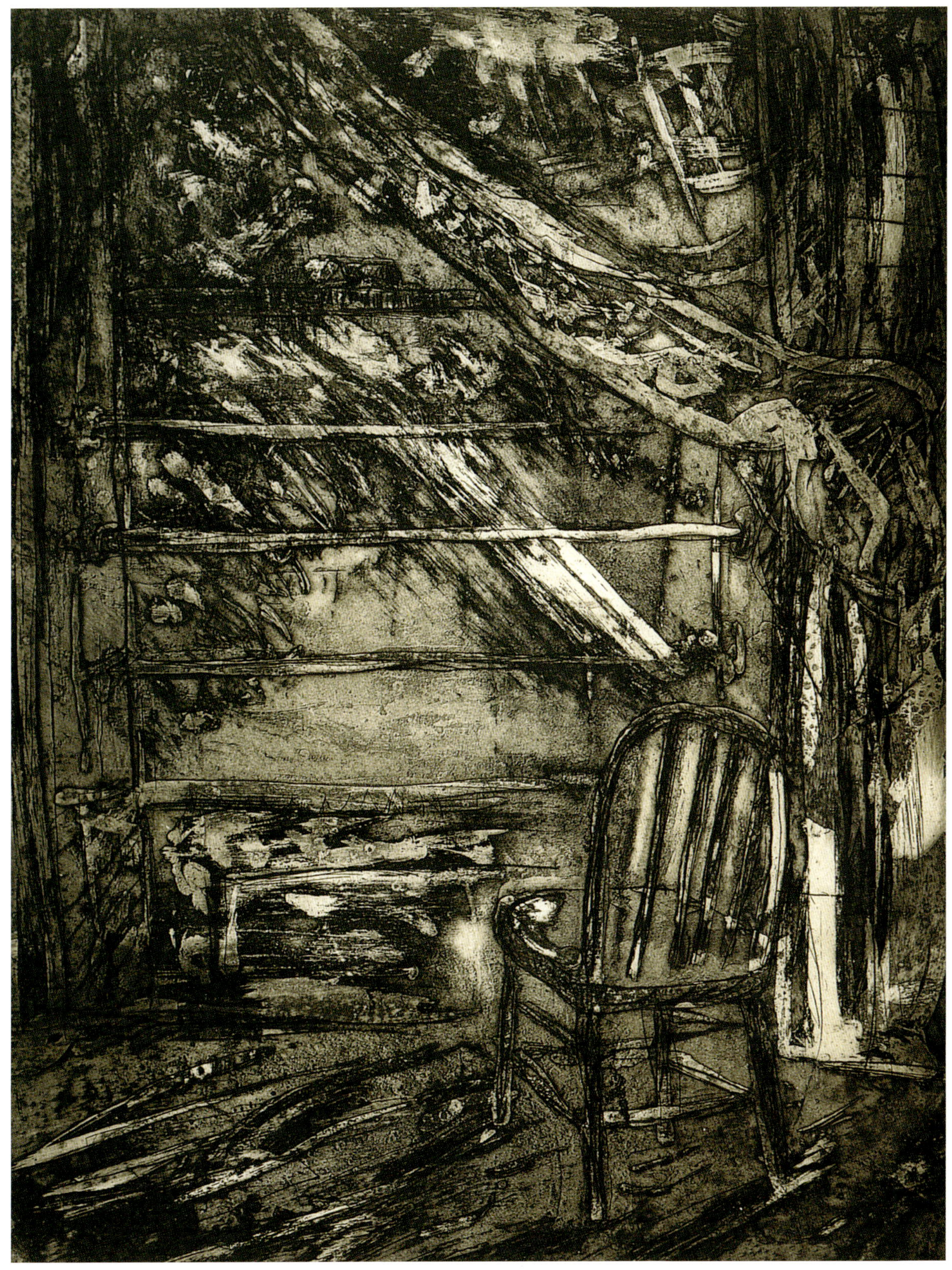

Chair by an Open Window, c. 1963, etching and aquatint, 13 x 9 1/2 inches.

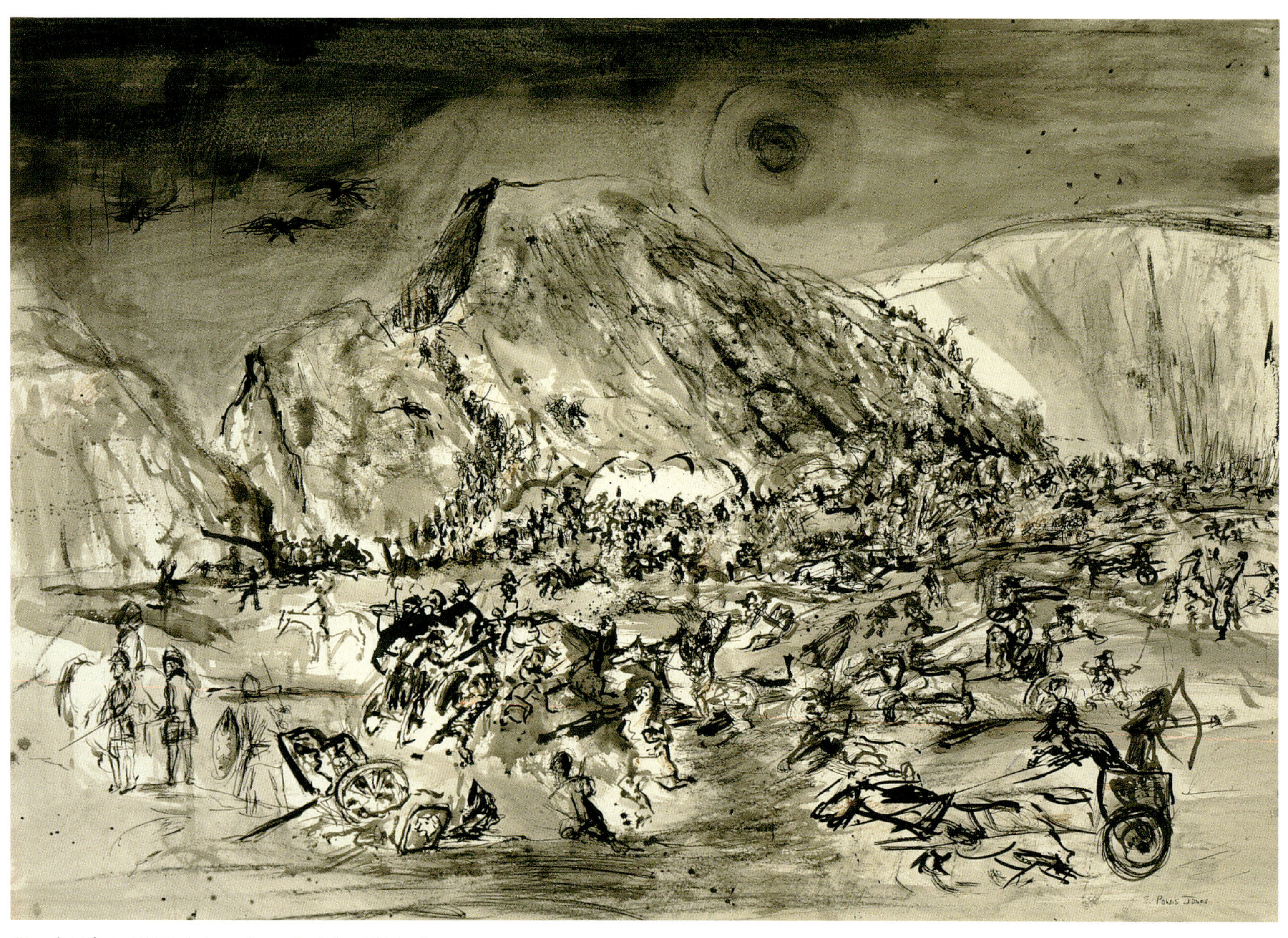

Sisera's Defeat, 1958, ink and wash, 20 x 28 inches.

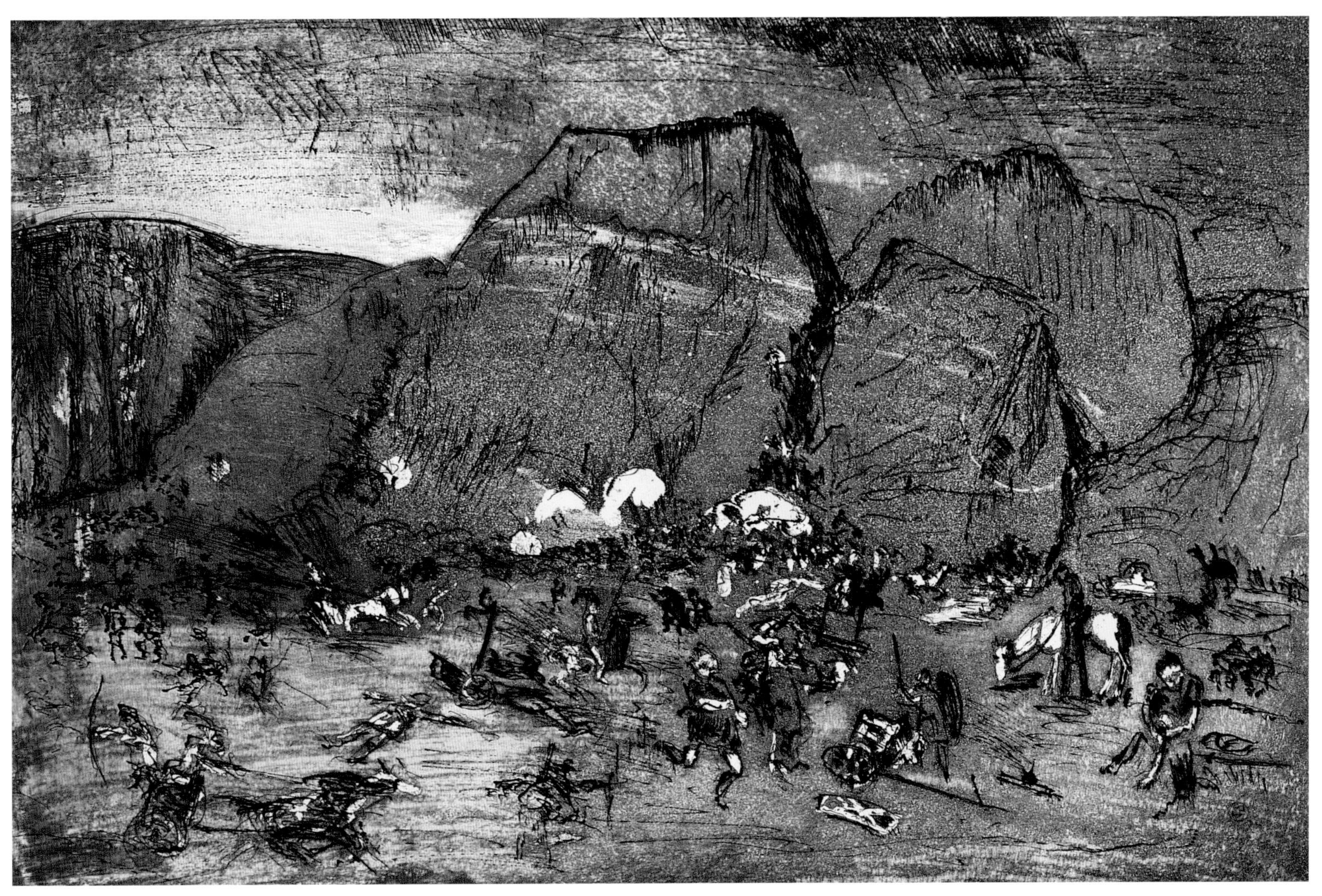

Sisera's Defeat, 1958, etching and aquatint, 12 x 17 1/2 inches (plate).

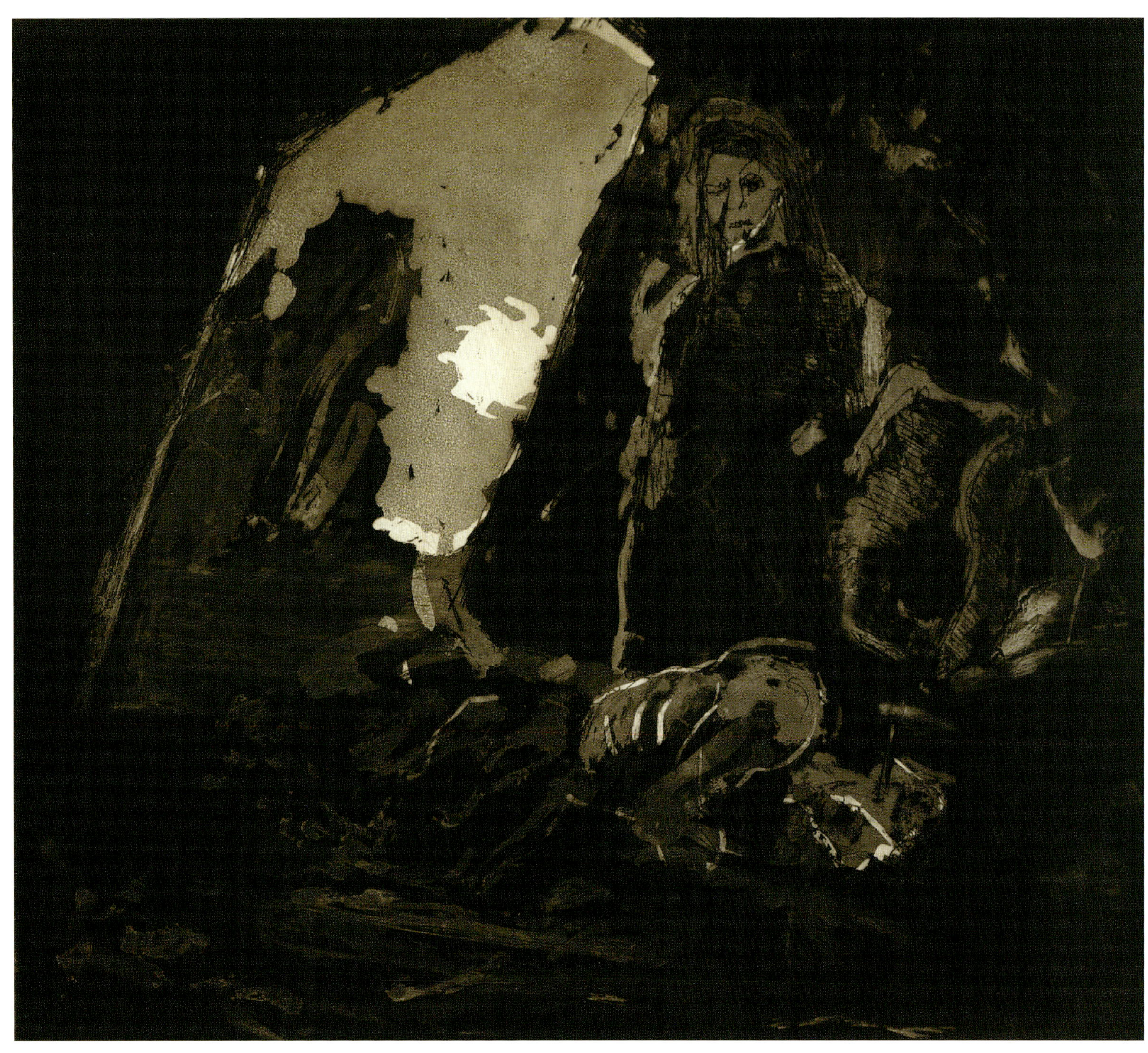

The Death of Sisera, c. 1962, etching and aquatint, printed in brown, 15³/₄ x 17¹/₂ inches (plate).

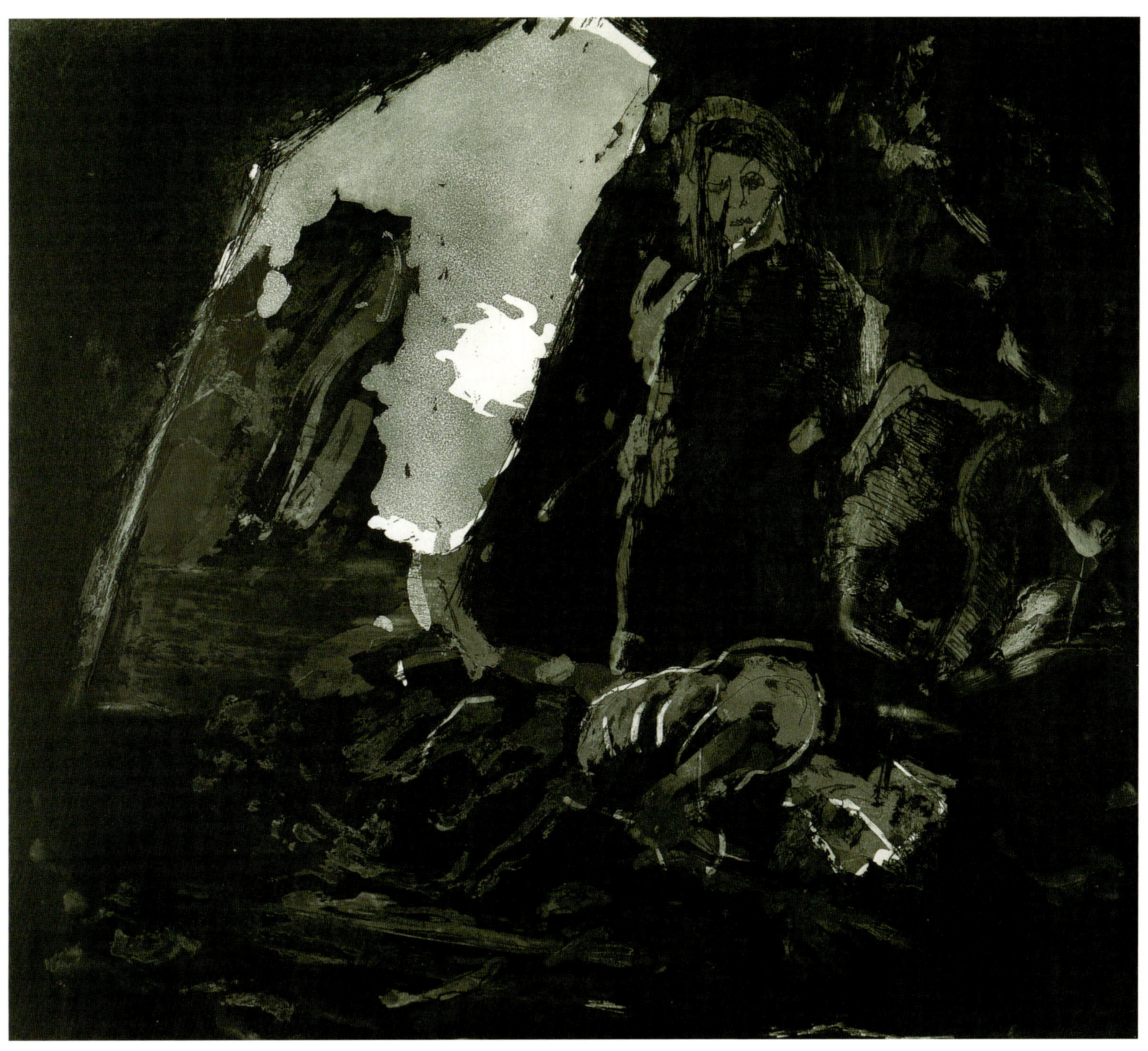

The Death of Sisera, c. 1962, etching and aquatint, printed in green, 15 3/4 x 17 1/2 inches (plate).

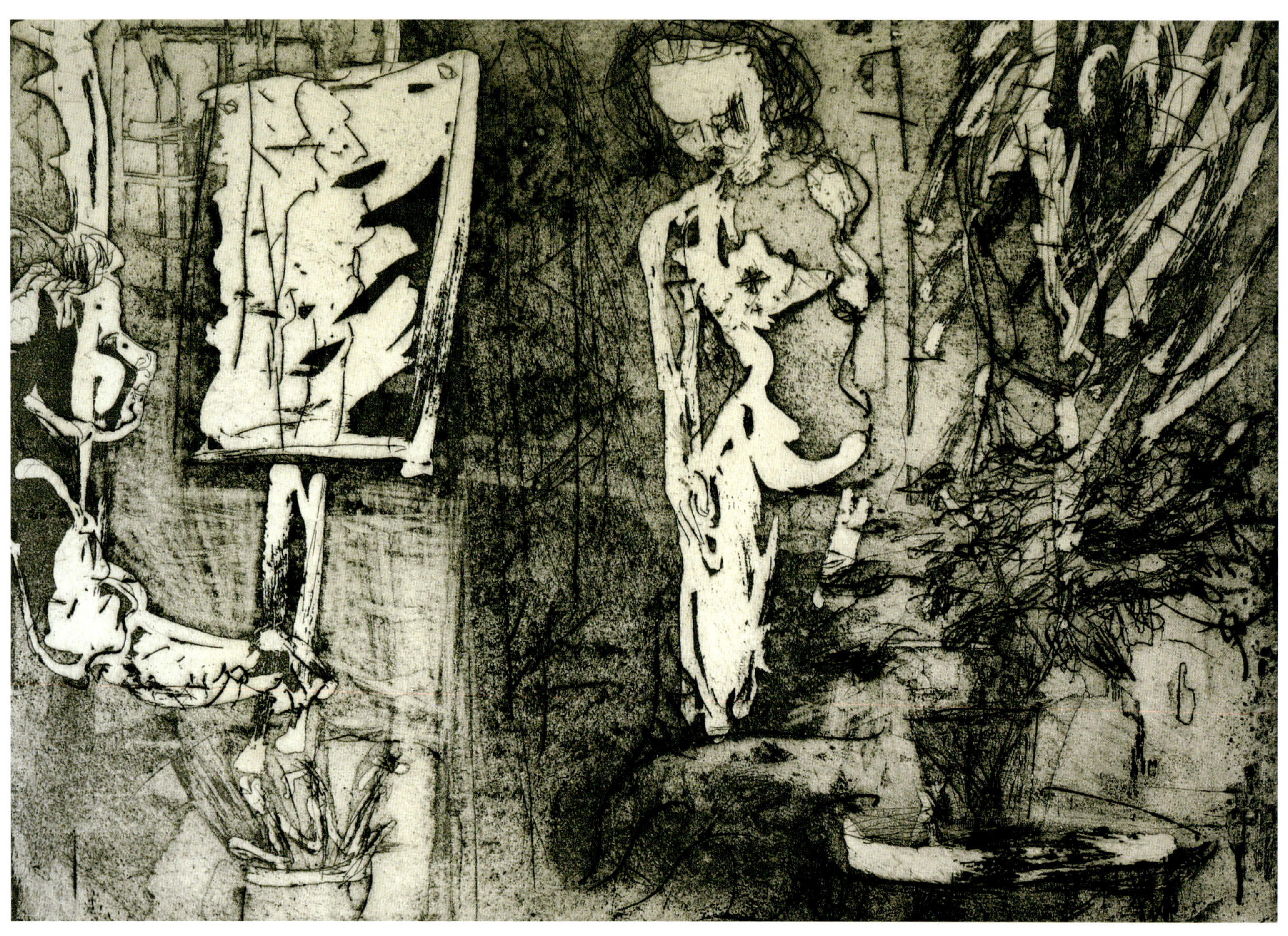

Artist and Model, c. 1963, etching and aquatint, 9 1/2 x 13 inches (plate).

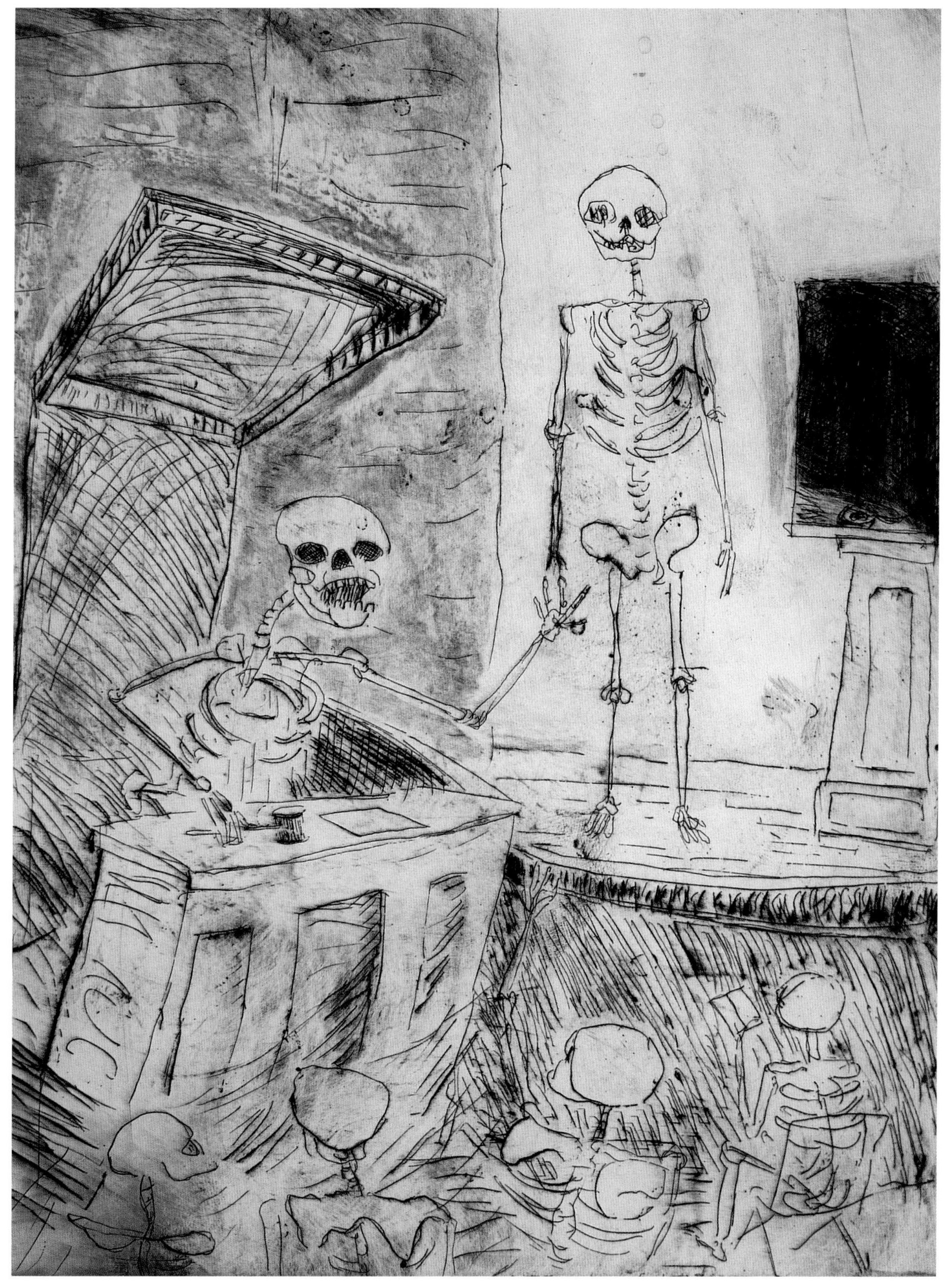

Auctioneer, c. 1963, etching, 13 x 9 1/2 inches (plate).

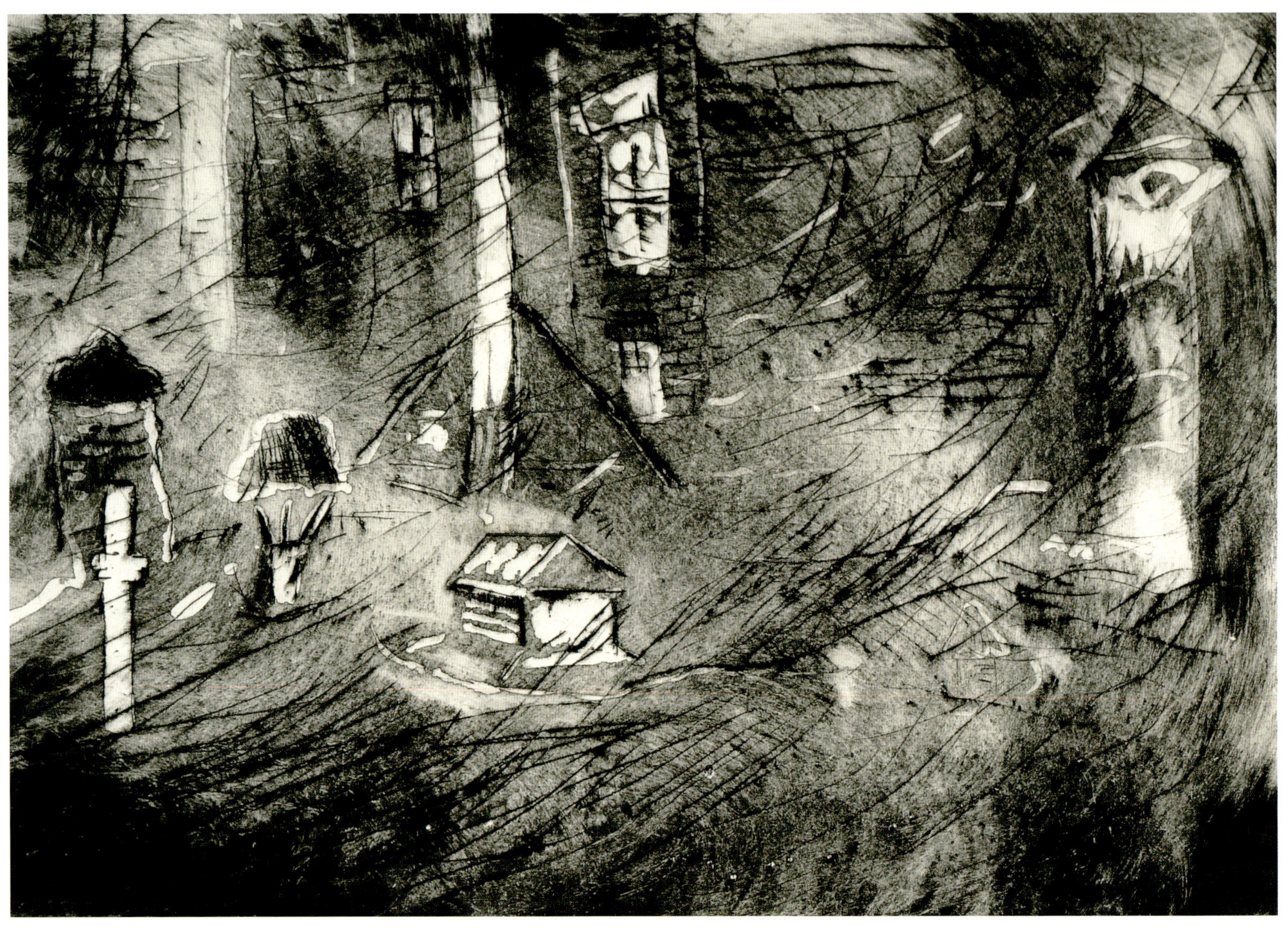

Roof in a Storm, c. 1965, etching and aquatint, printed in black on white paper, 9 1/4 x 12 3/4 inches (plate).

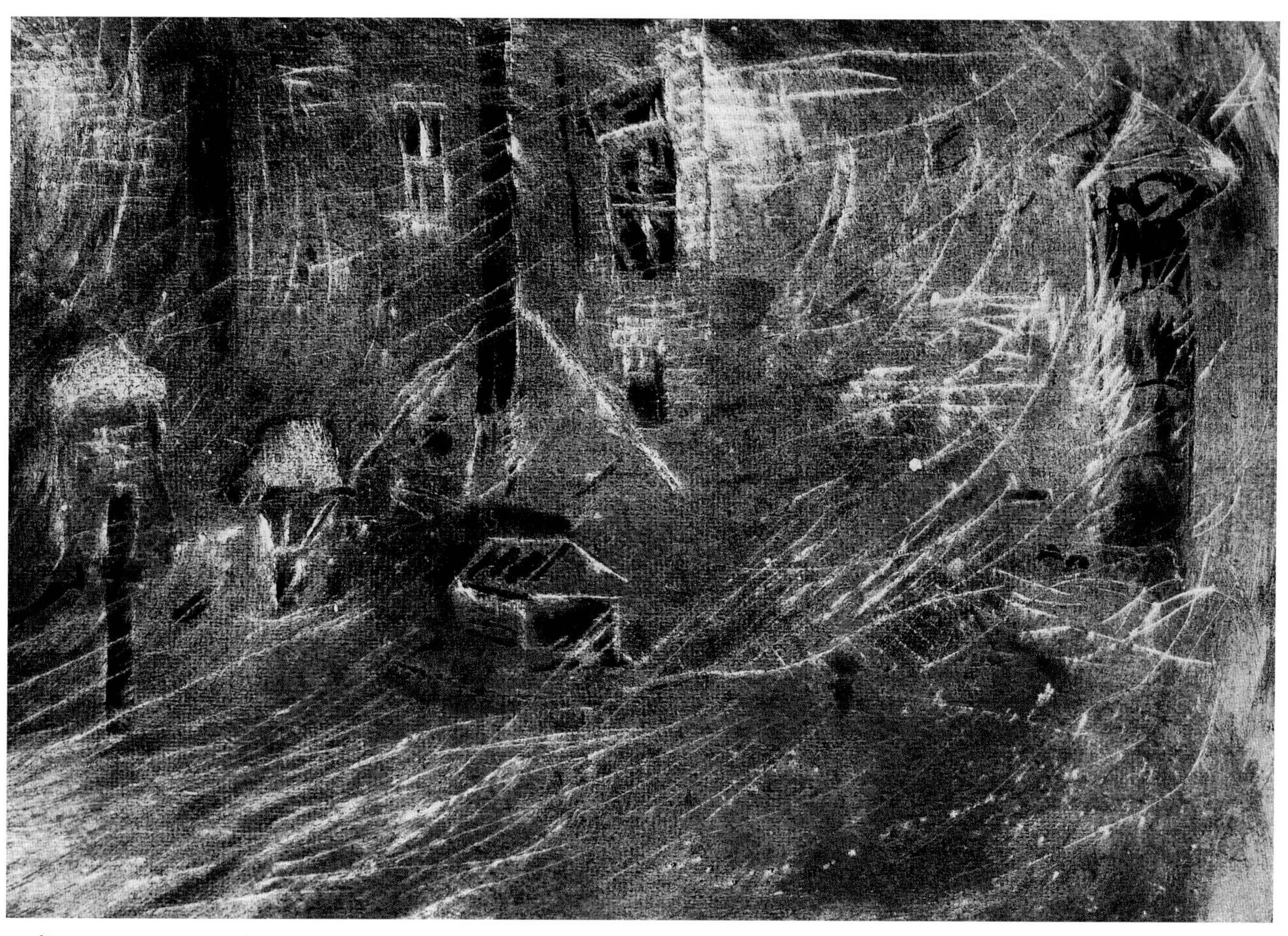

Roof in a Storm, c. 1965, etching and aquatint, printed in white on black paper, 9 1/4 x 12 3/4 inches (plate).

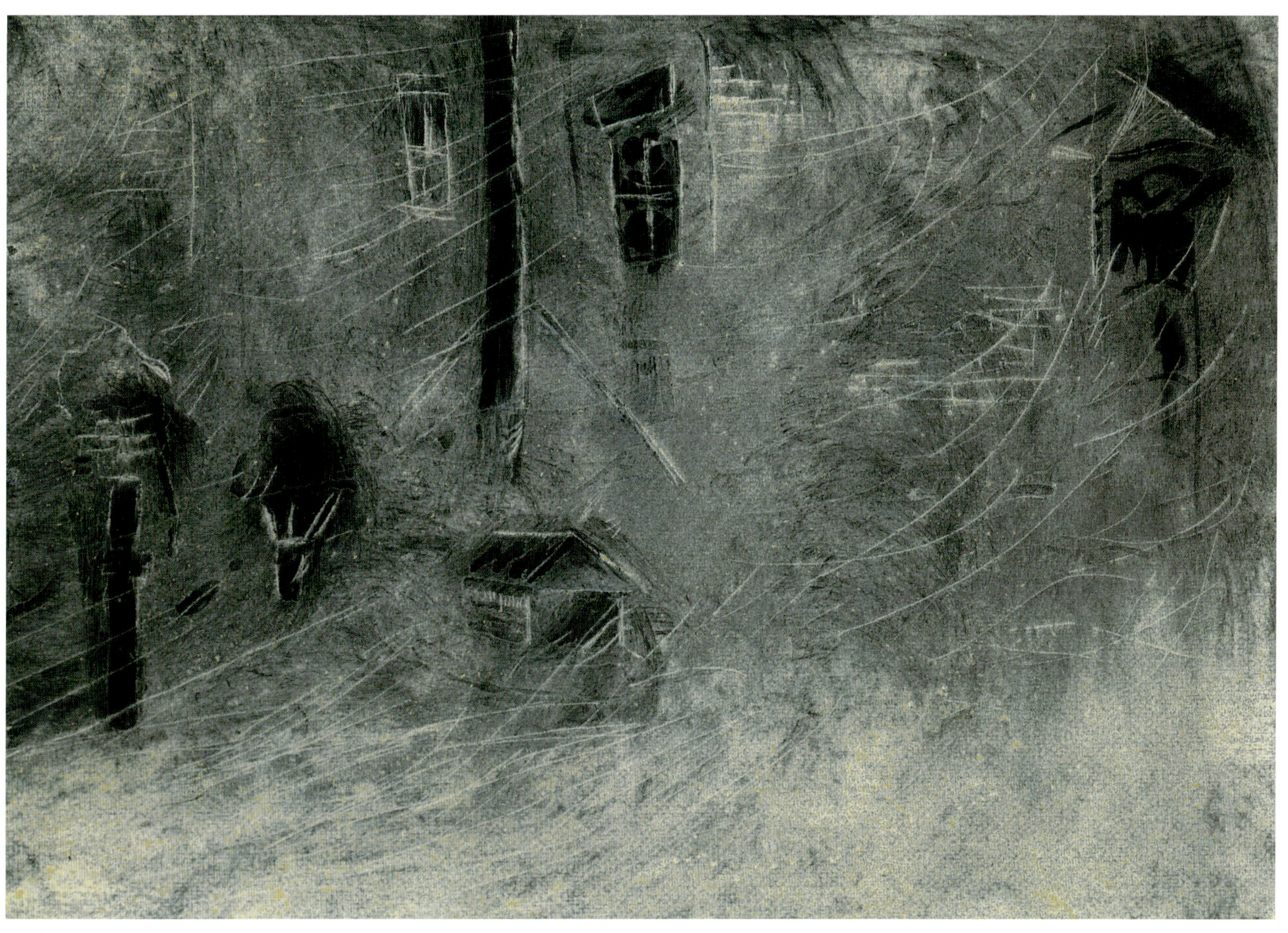

Roof in a Storm, c. 1965, etching and aquatint, printed in white on black paper, 9 1/4 x 12 3/4 inches (plate).

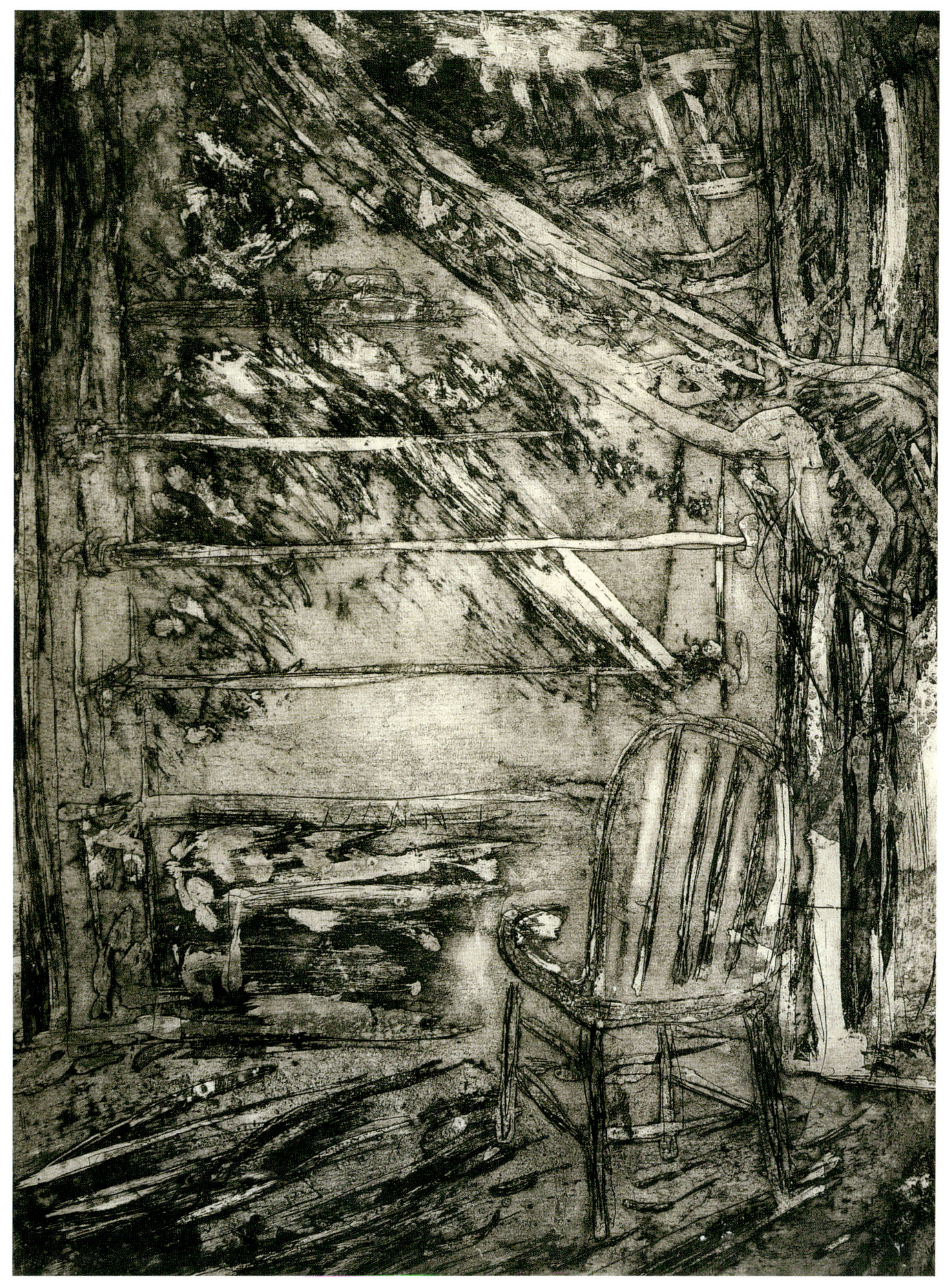

Chair by an Open Window, c. 1963, etching and aquatint, 9¼ x 12¾ inches (plate).

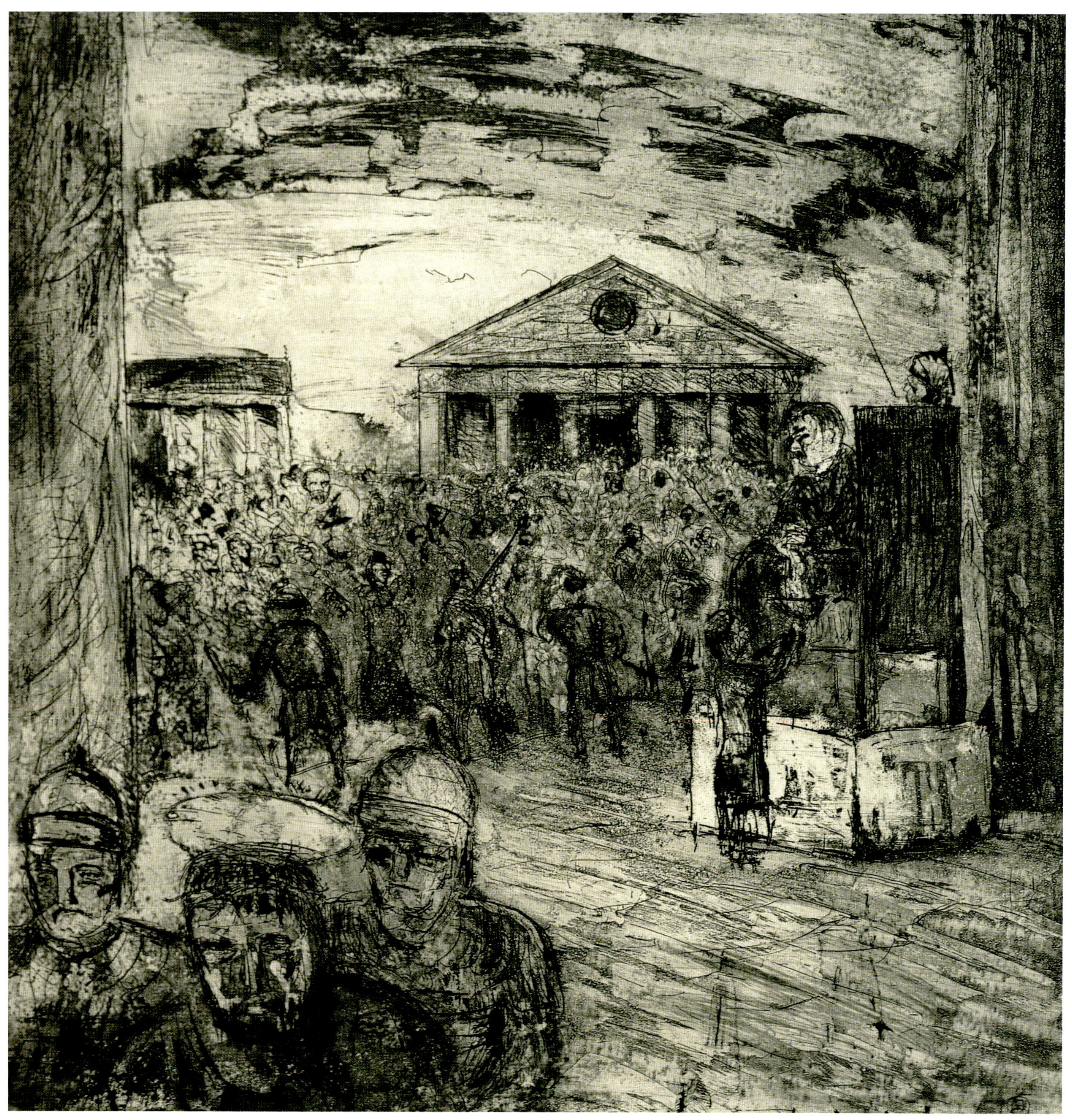

Stations of the Cross I, Jesus is Condemned to Death, 1960, etching and aquatint, 17$1/2$ x 16 inches.

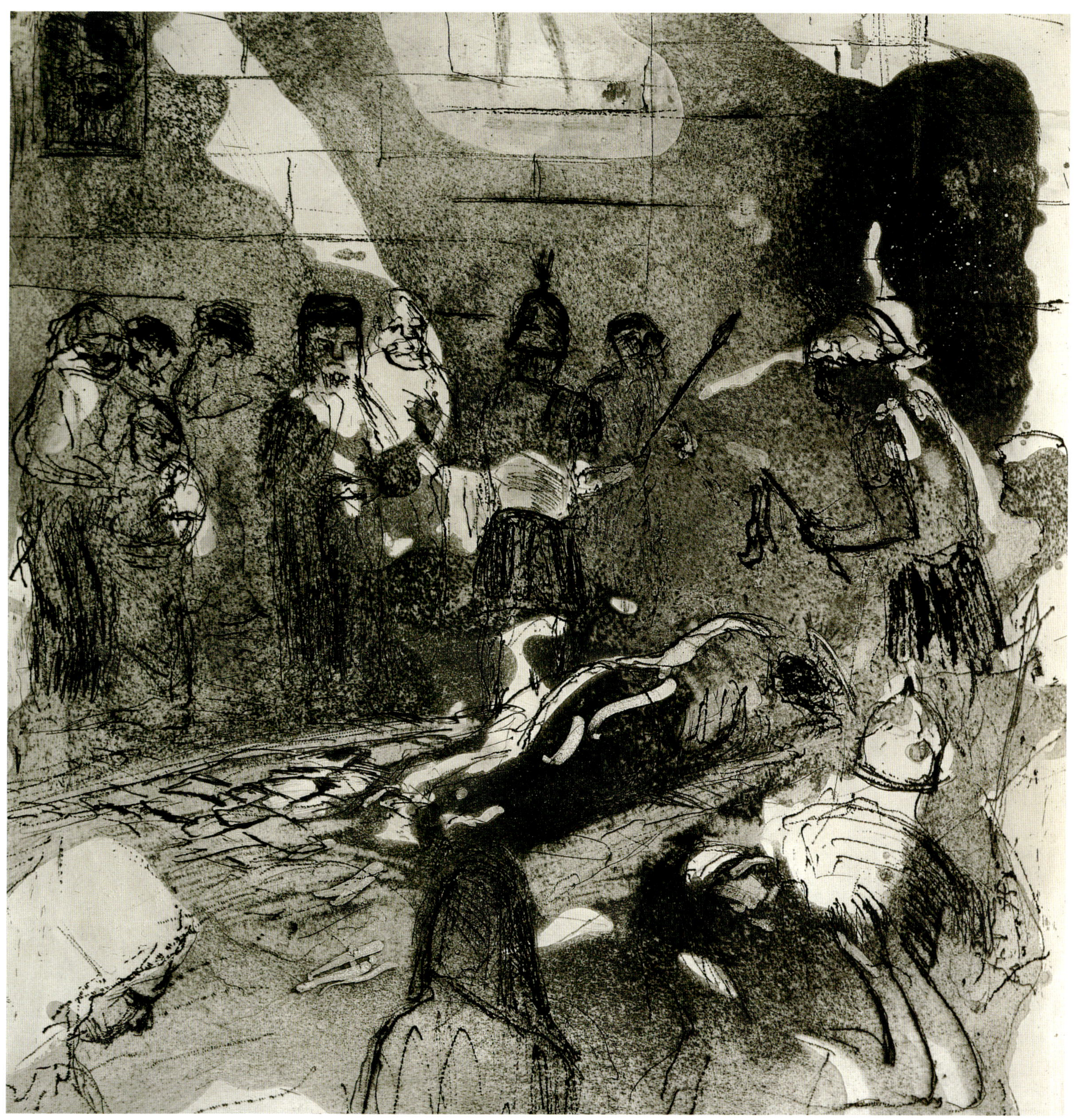

Stations of the Cross VIII, The Women of Jerusalem Mourn for Jesus, 1960, etching and aquatint, 17 1/2 x 16 inches.

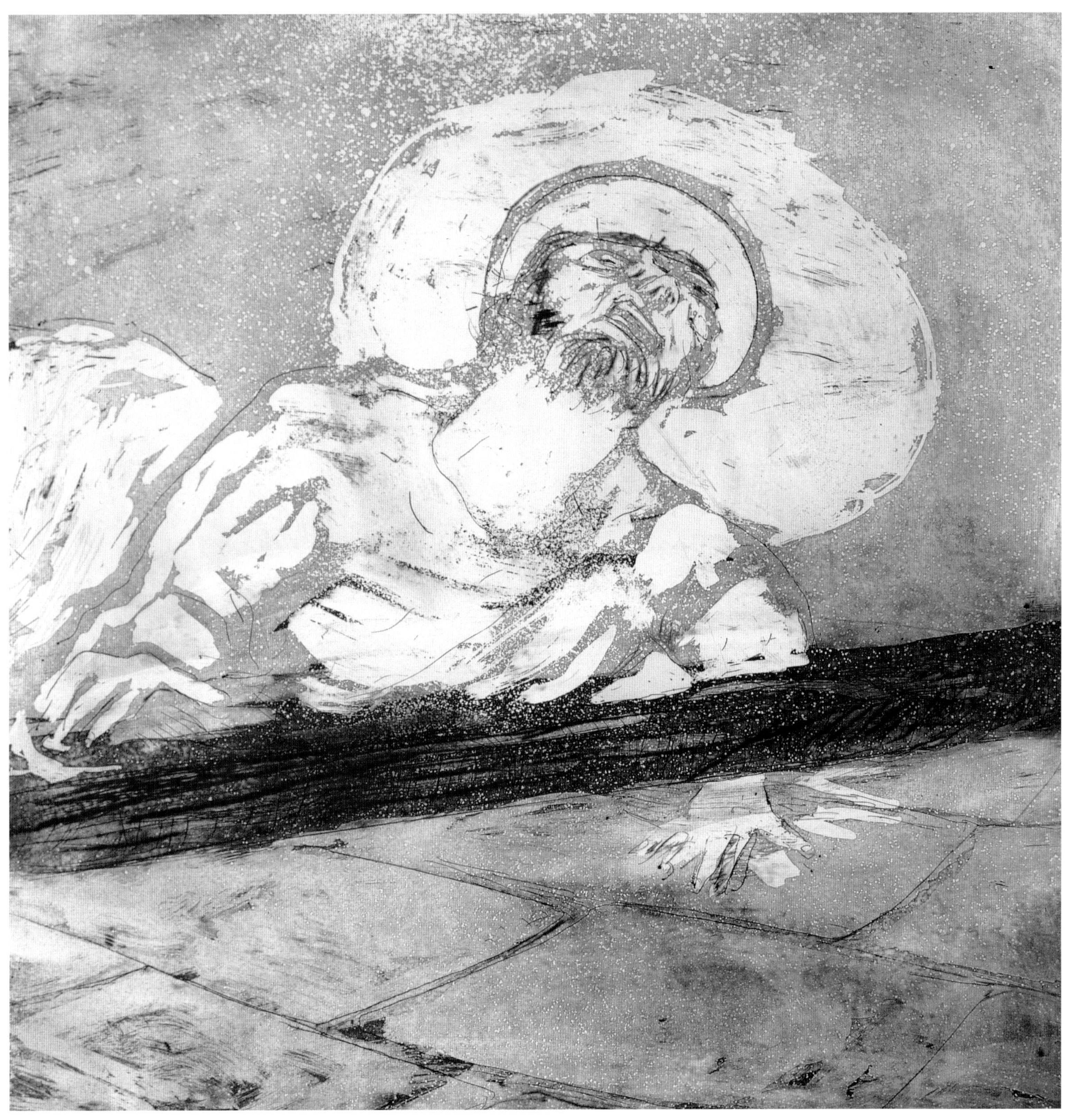

Stations of the Cross III, Jesus Falls for the First Time, 1960, etching and aquatint, 17 1/2 x 16 inches.

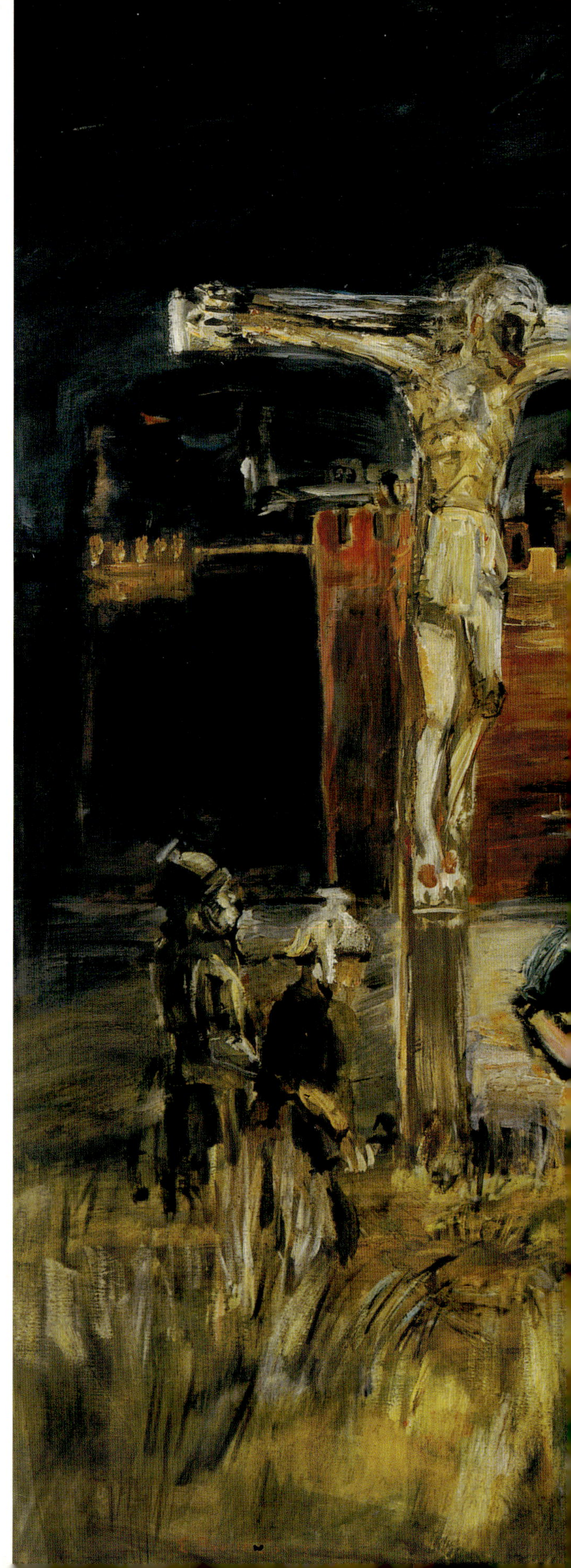

Crucifixion, c. 1963, oil on canvas, 48 x 60 inches.

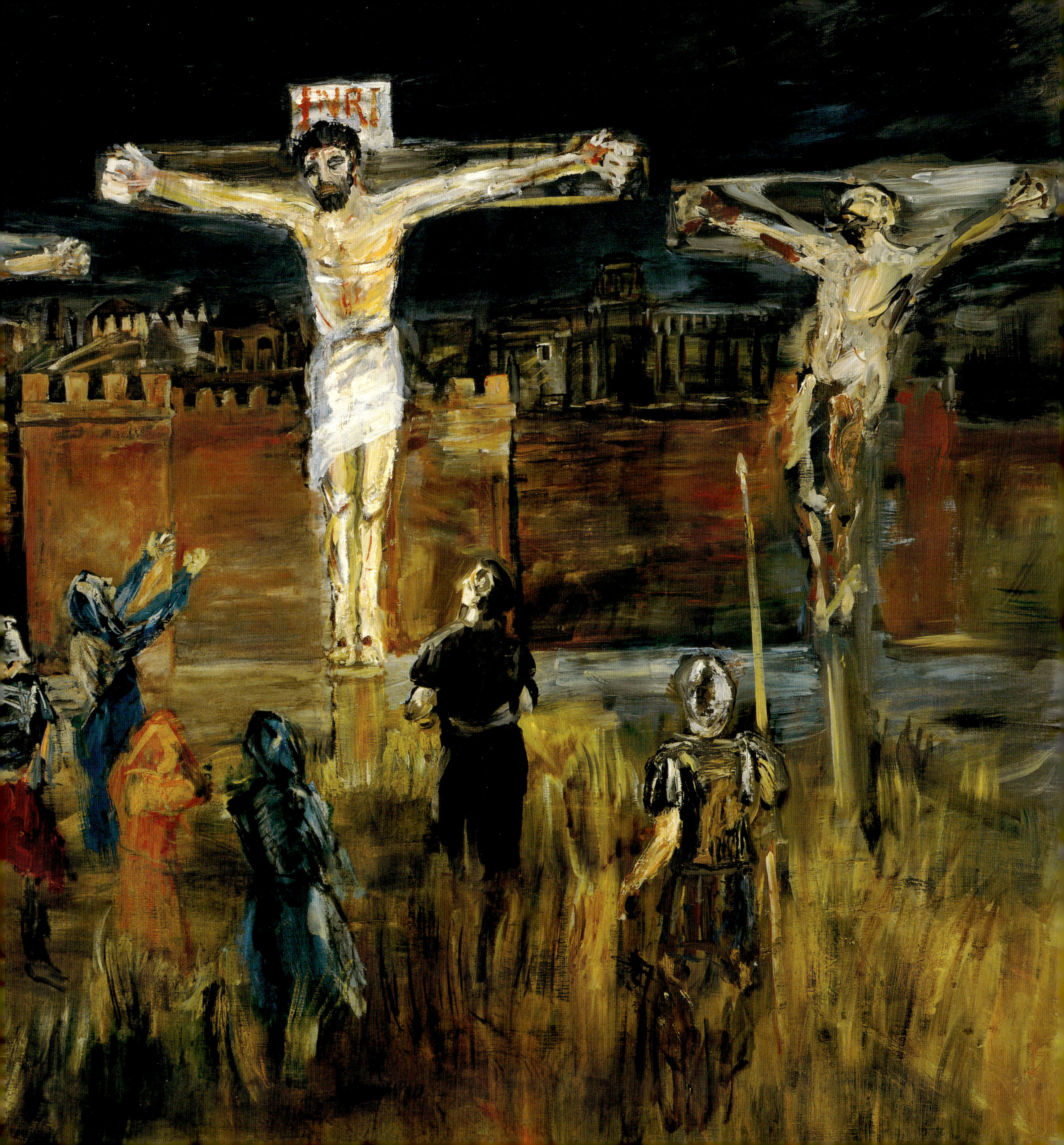

INRI

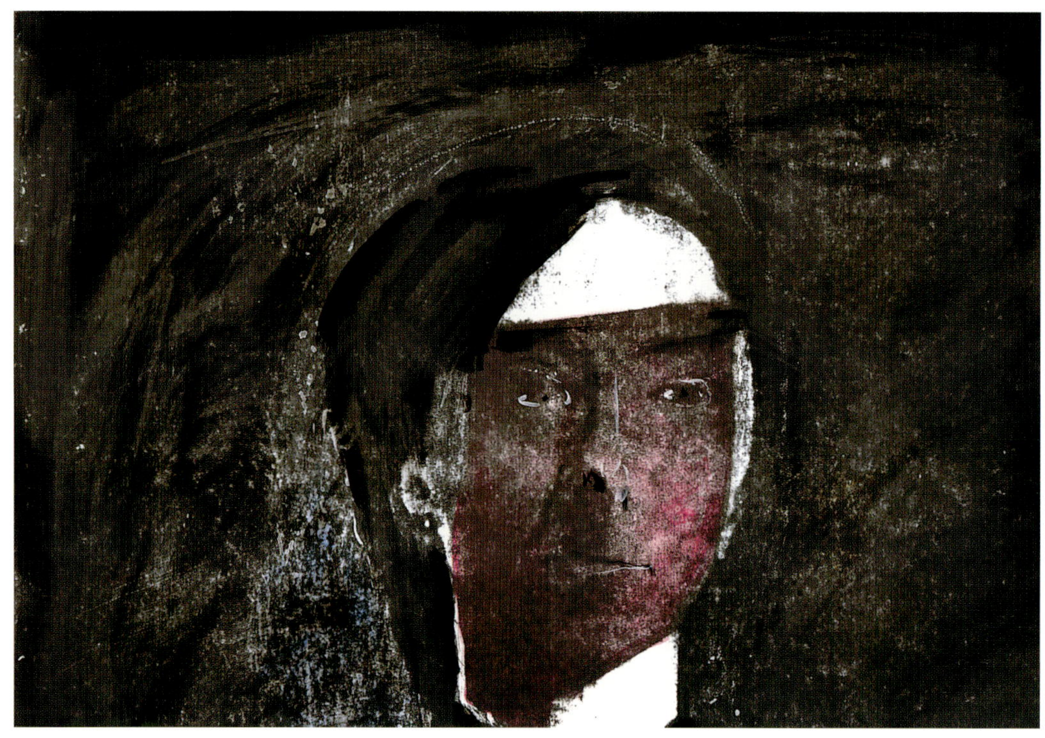

19 x 26³/4 inches.

Variations on a Self-Portrait by Gwen John
In London during the summer of 1980, I began to randomly distort images by using various copier machines. The resultant effects created by a combination of causes, some of which were beyond my control, had qualities and interest of an unexpected nature. The selection of images also owes a good deal to chance. This machine process, in a sense, is akin to that of the use of automatic or subconscious action, which has been part of the process of painting and drawing for a long time. My images deliberately ranged from minor variations to a realistic piece to that of the totally abstract. The humanity expressed in the superb *Self-Portrait* by Gwen John made it a most stimulating subject for these transformations. Beautiful in itself, a creation of remarkable sensitivity, it always retained a special strength and excitement. Distortion in form and color to a point close to obliteration of the picture did not destroy its great qualities but produced new forms for comparison and thought. These conquests of the conscious by the unseen hand have the most tenuous relationship to the original picture but they increase our frame of vision and form a foundation for even further projection.
EPJ

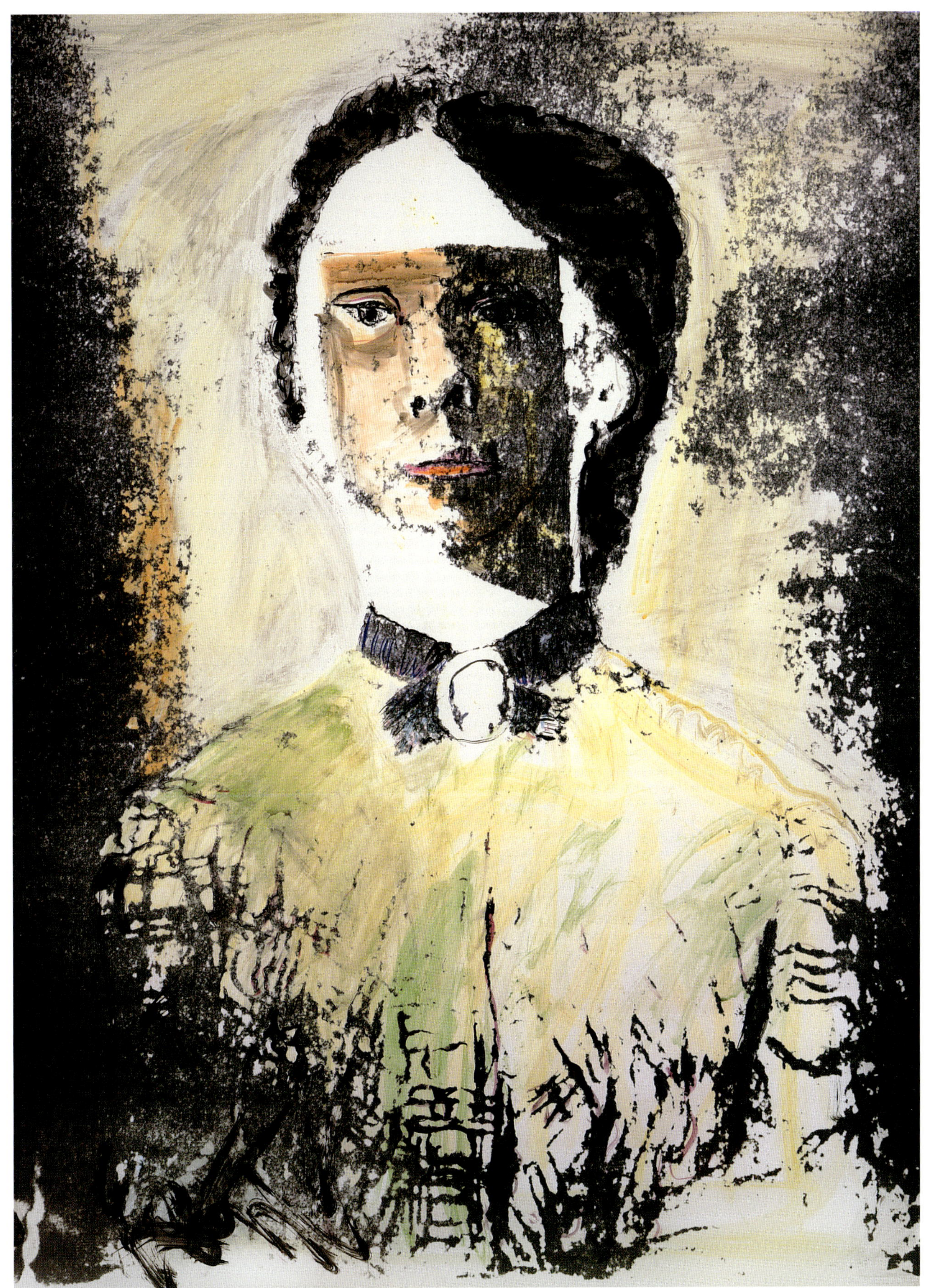

36 x 26 3/4 inches.

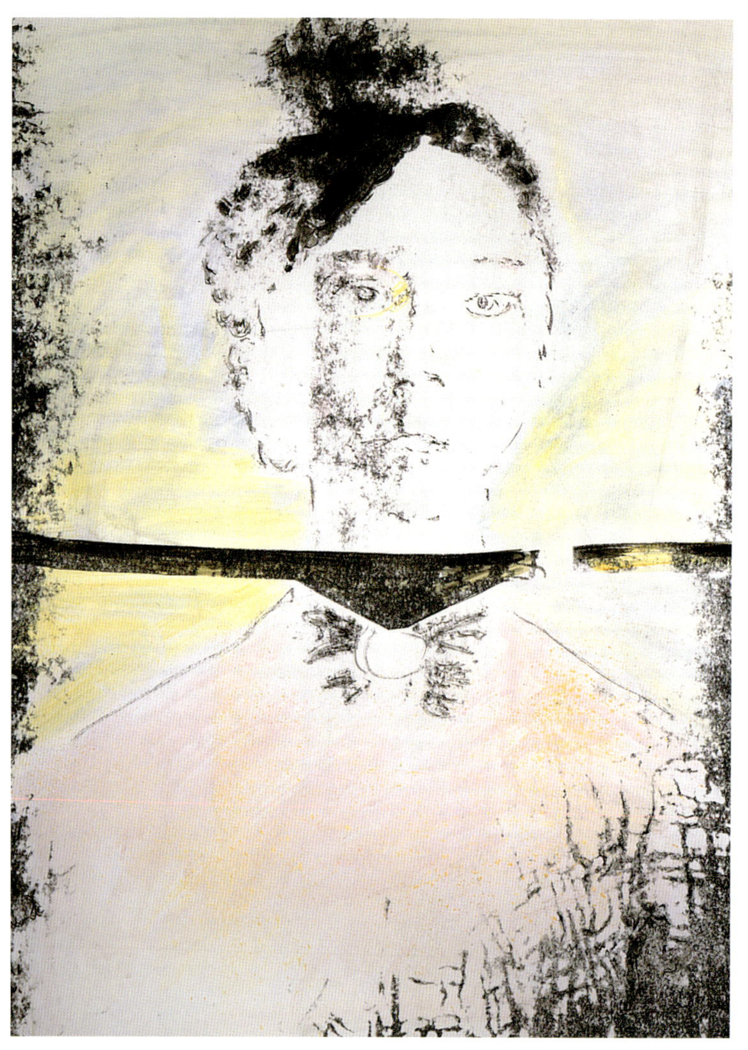

36 x 271/2 inches.

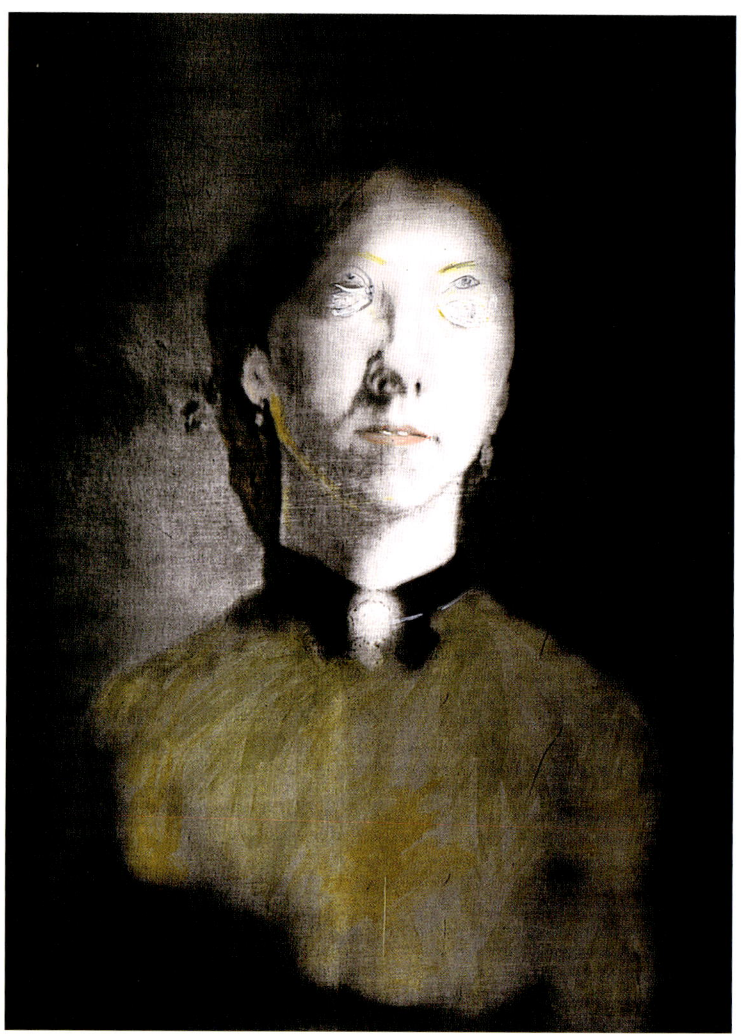

381/2 x 291/2 inches.

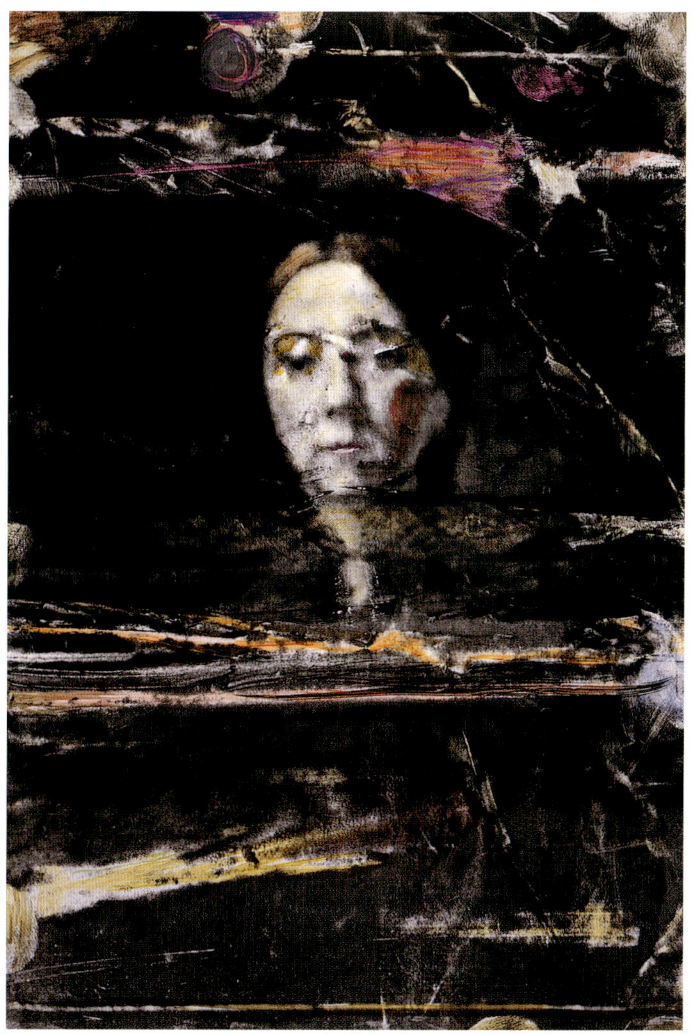

40 1/2 x 27 1/4 inches.

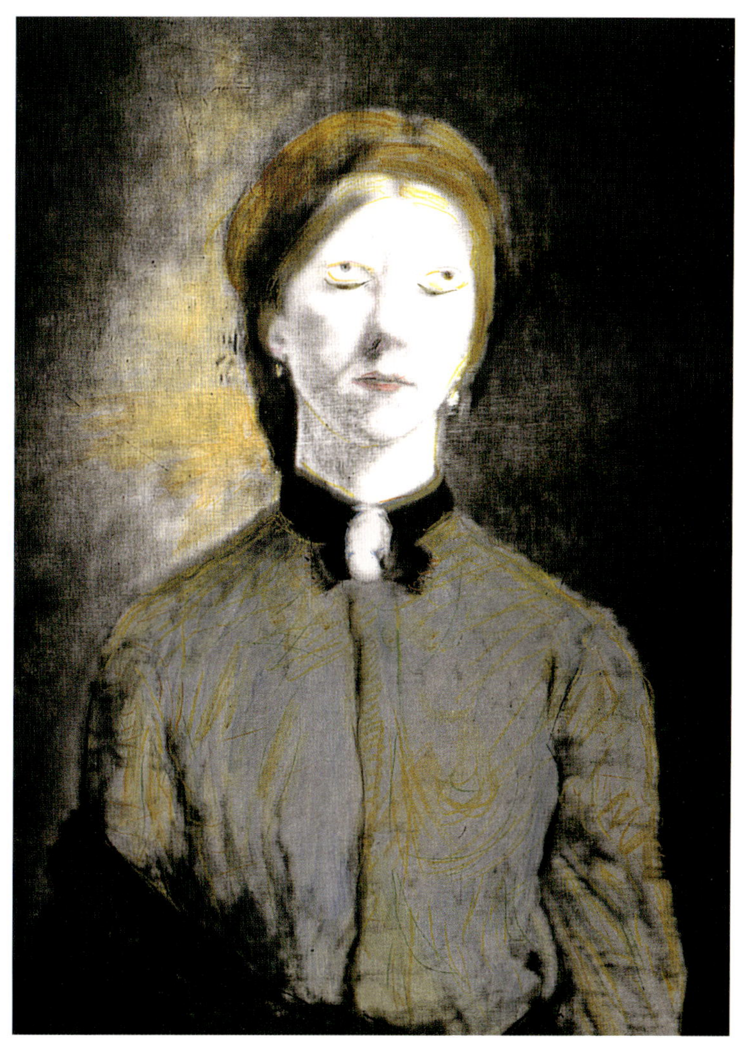

39 1/4 x 30 inches.

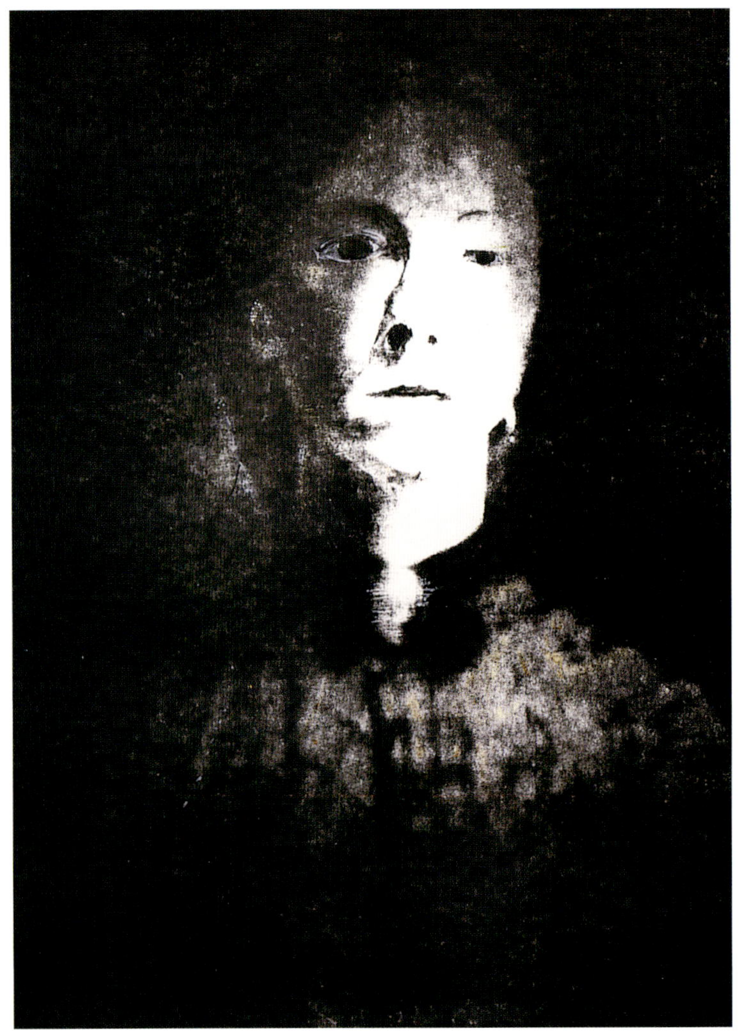

40 x 29 1/2 inches.

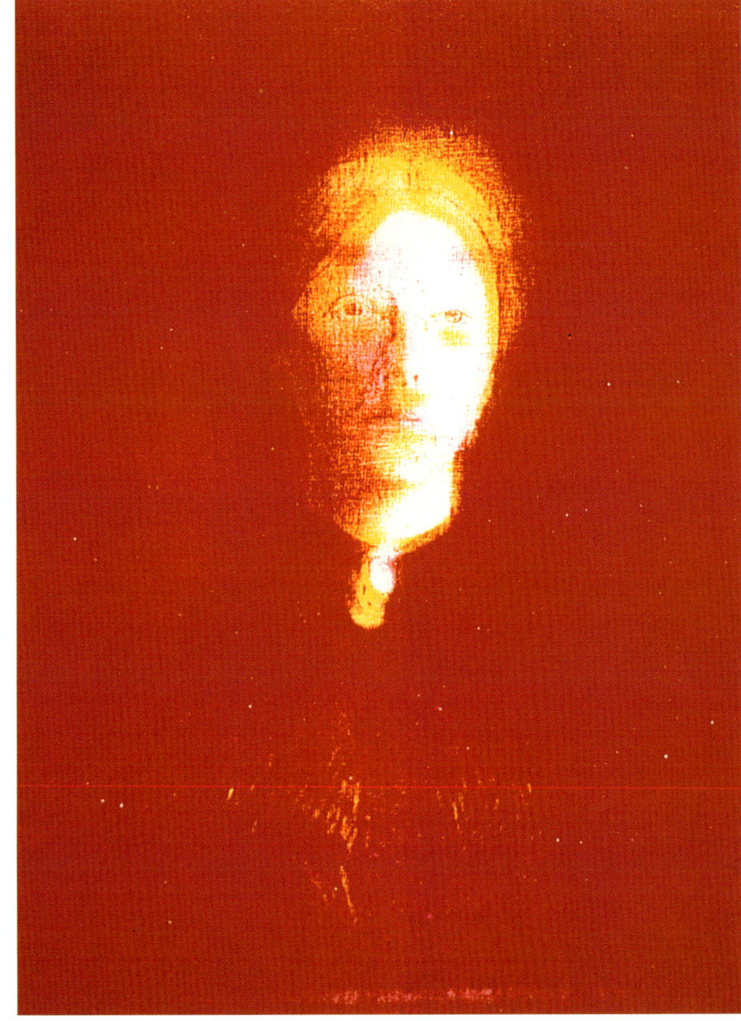

40 x 29 3/4 inches.

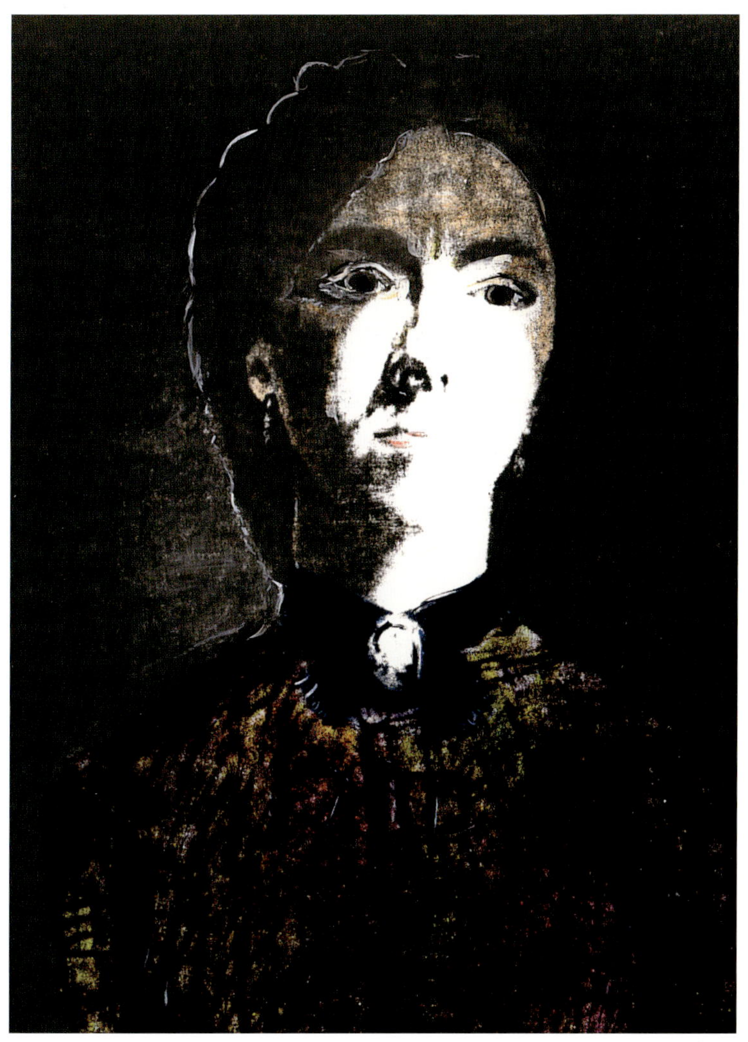

40 x 29 inches.

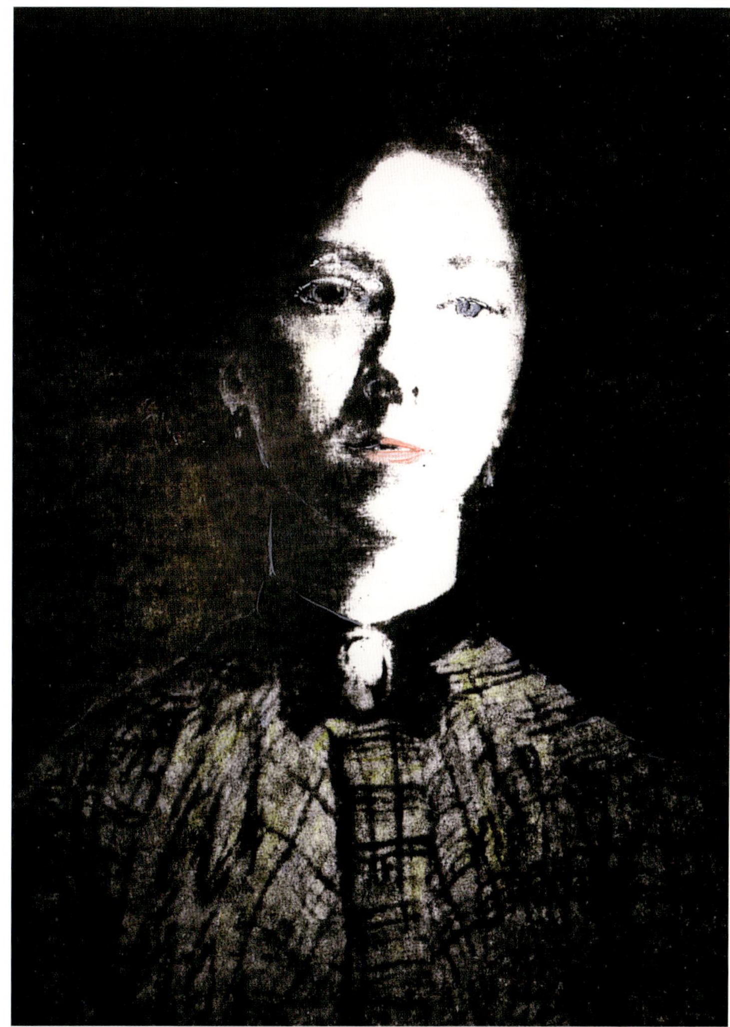

40 x 30 inches.

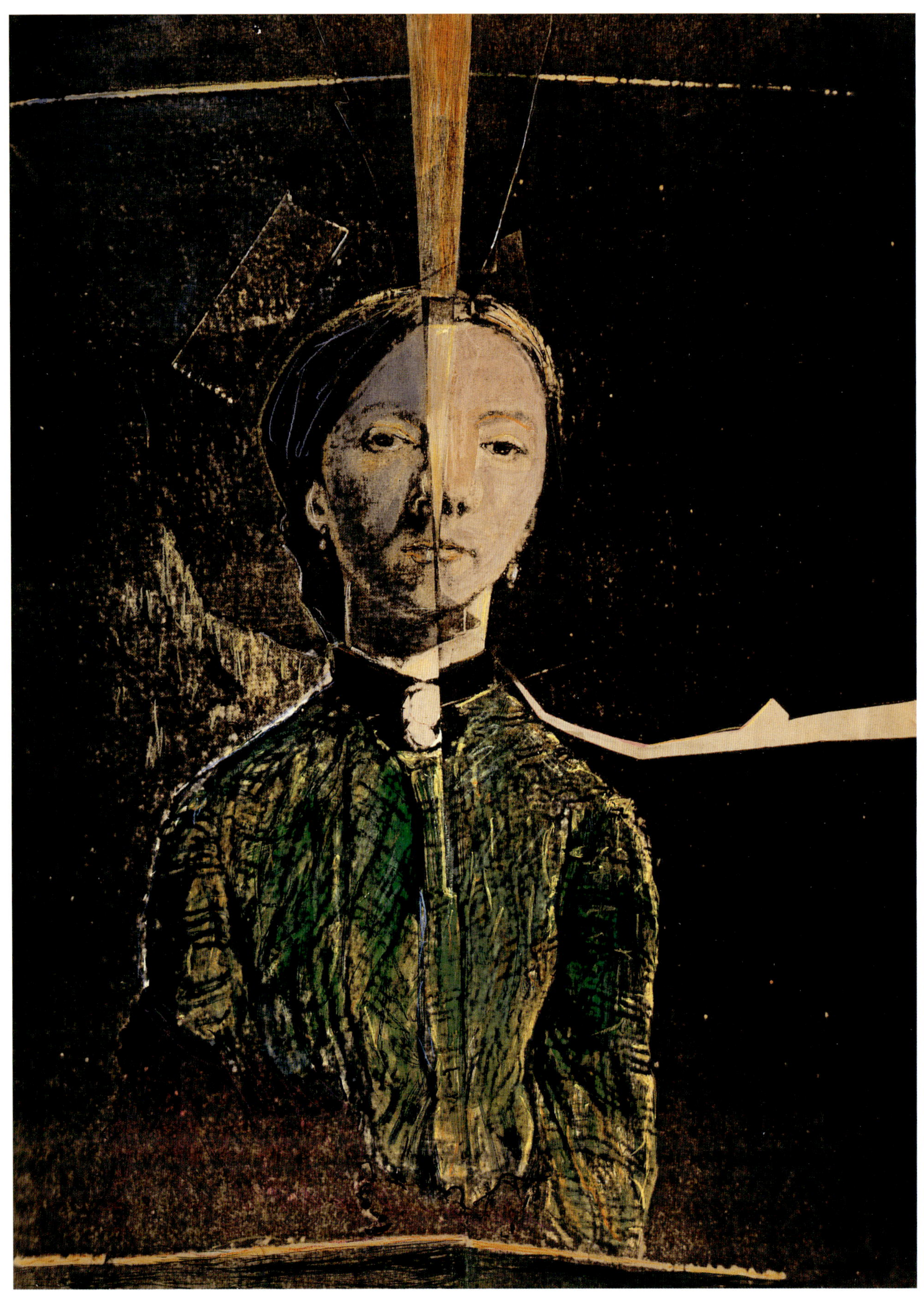

36 x 24 inches.

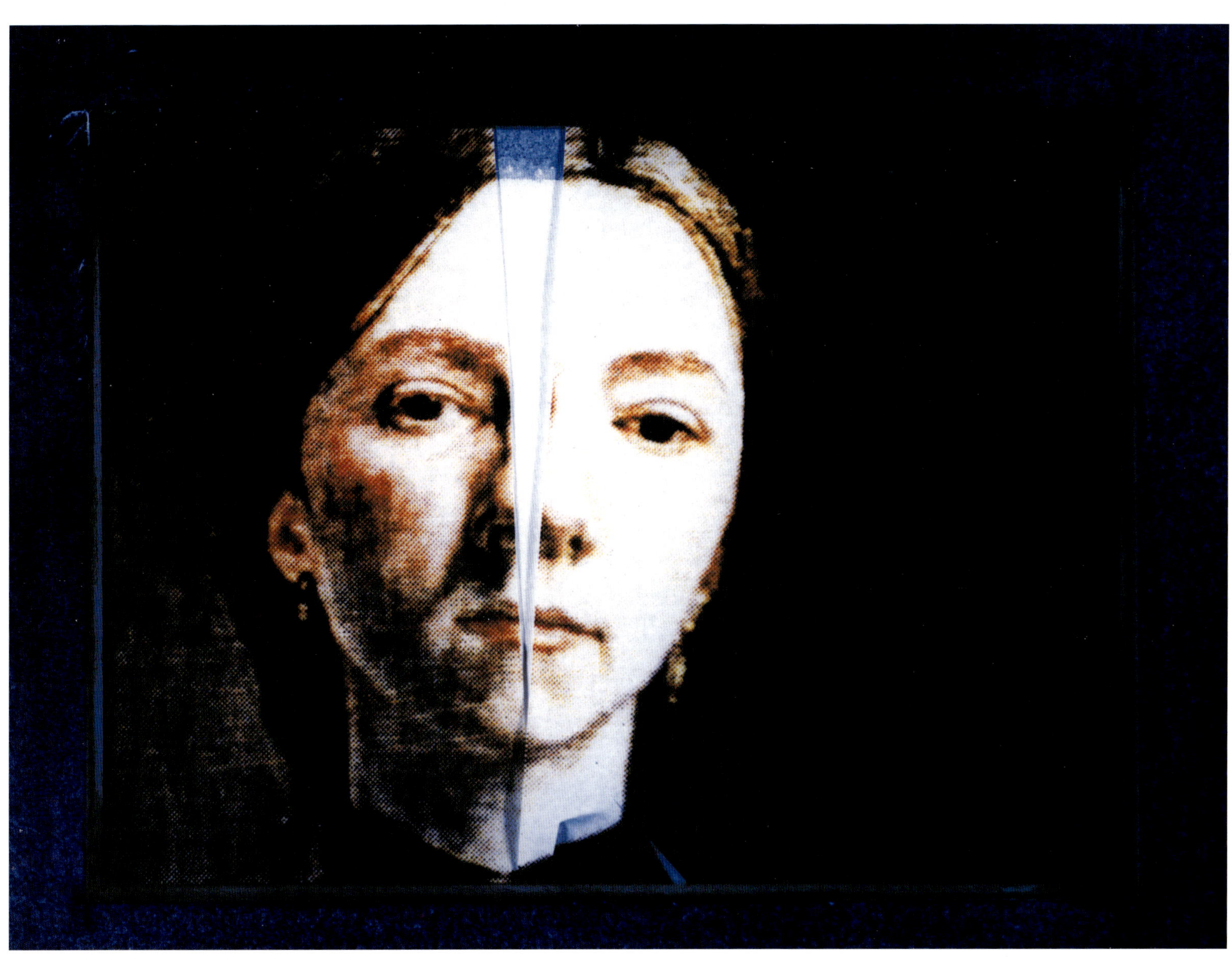

1986, color photograph, 11 x 14 inches.

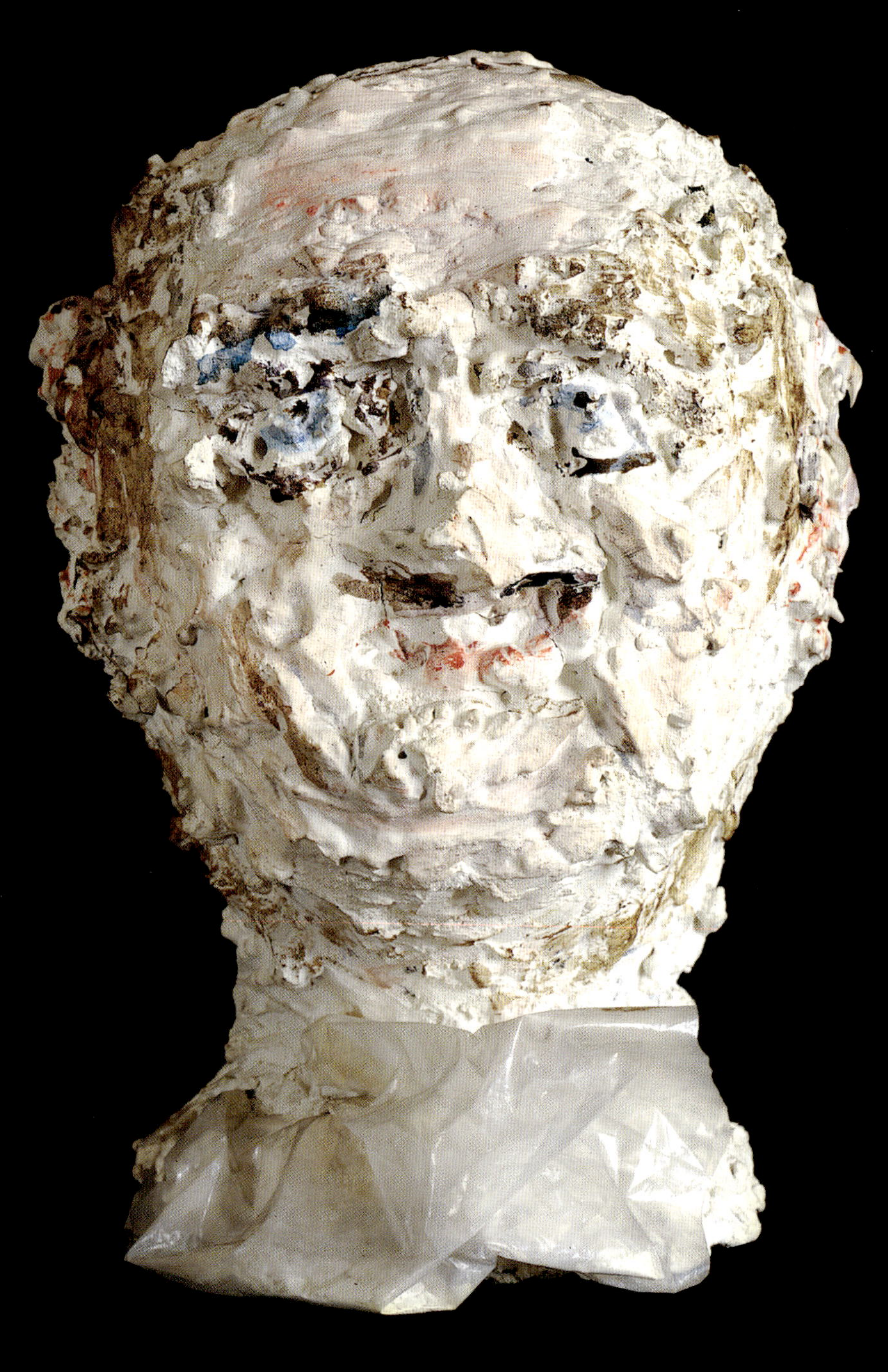

Truman Capote, c. 1980, painted plaster over styrofoam, 9 inches high.

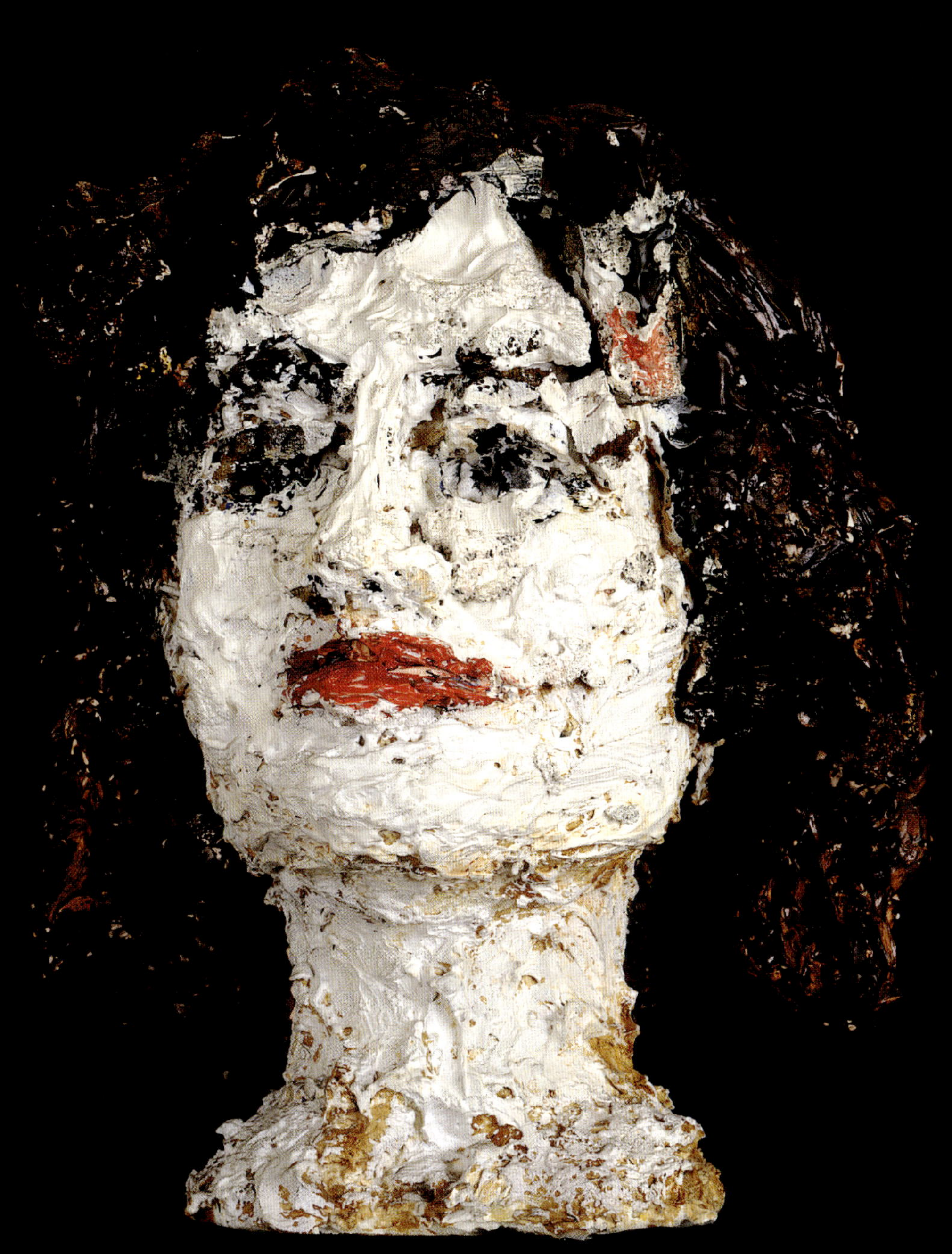

Jackie O, c. 1980, painted plaster over styrofoam, 13 inches high.

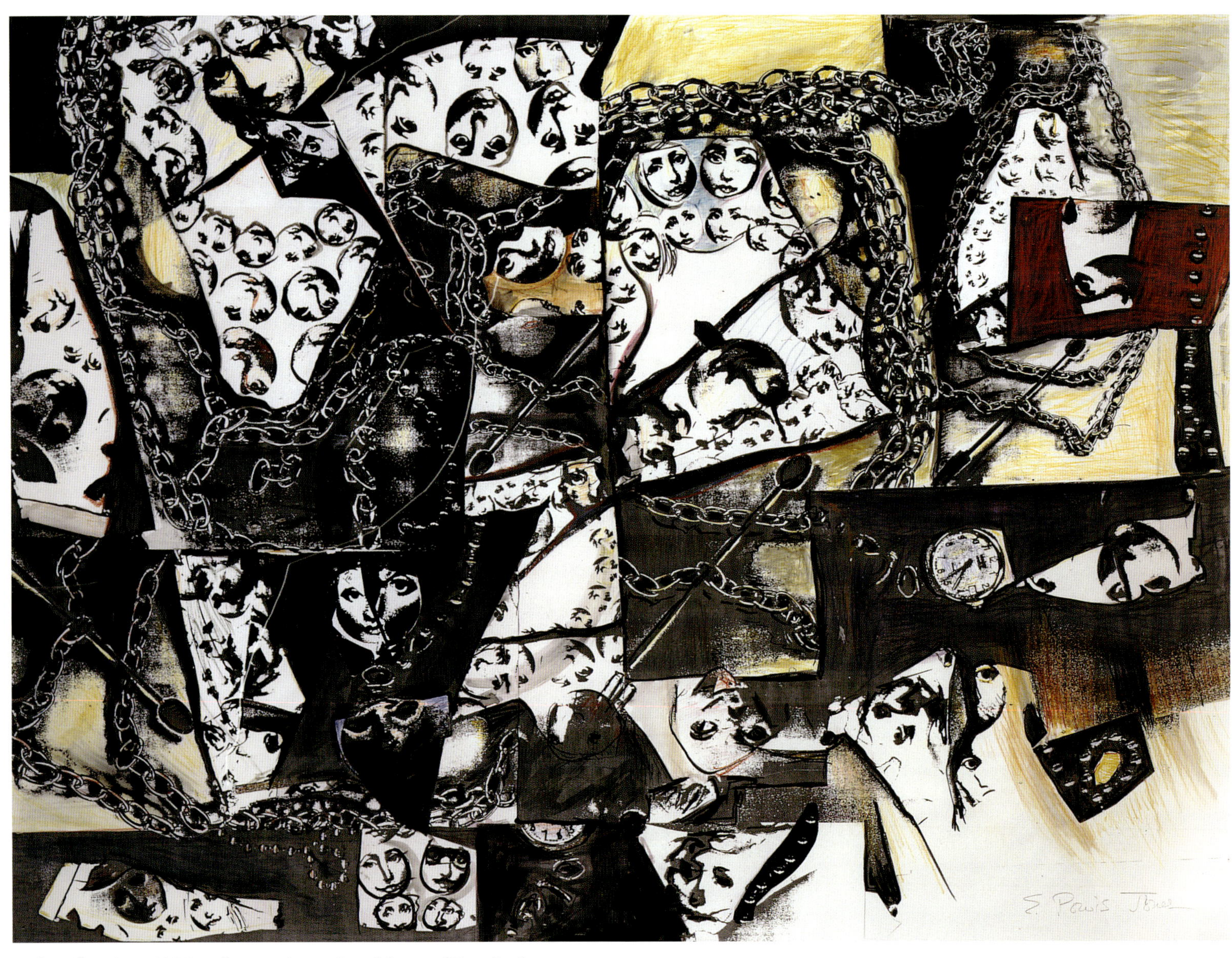

Broken Plate 1, c. 1985, color copier print, 29 3/4 x 37 3/4 inches.

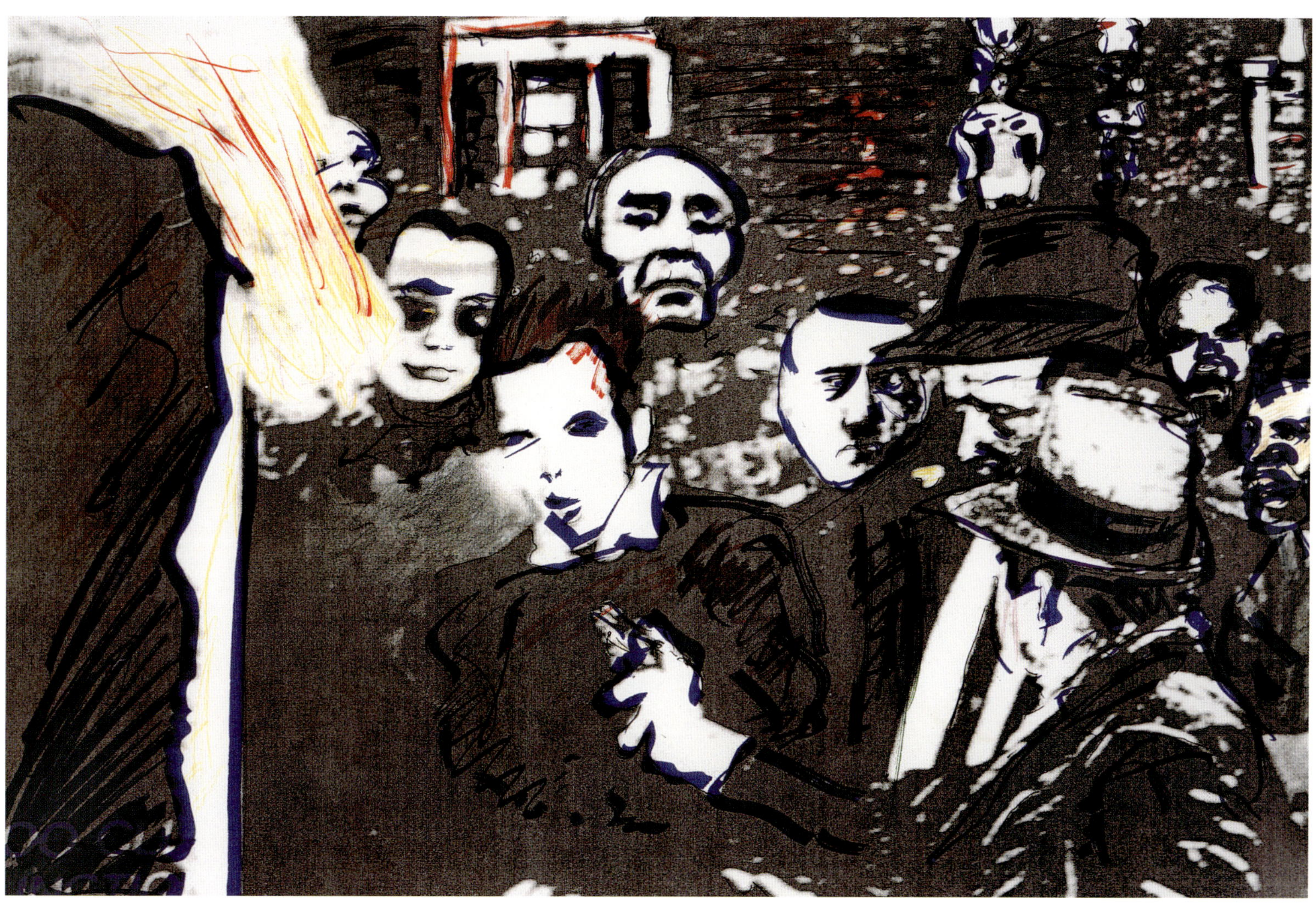

Dictators, c. 1980, copier print, color added, 10 3/4 x 15 3/4 inches.

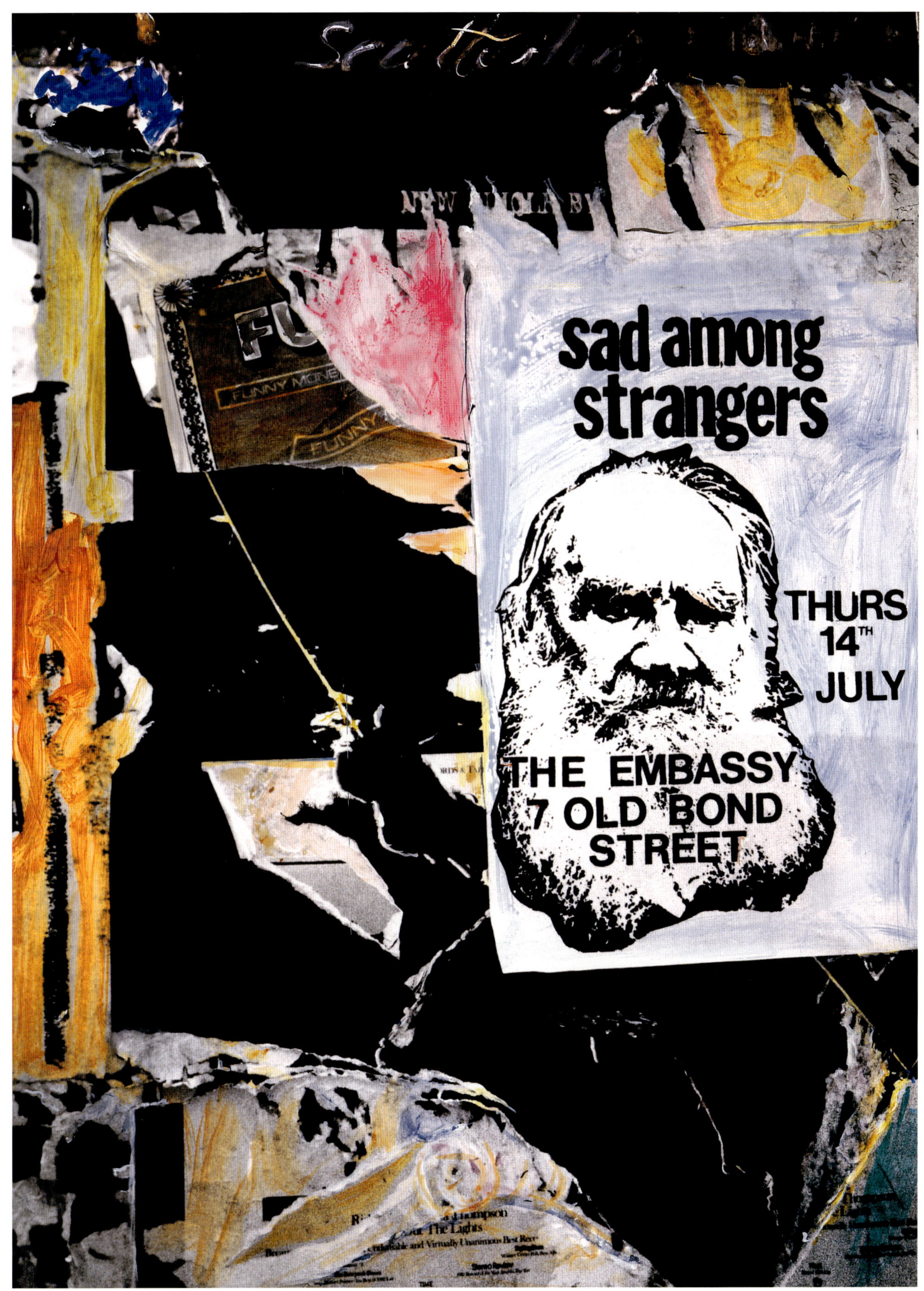

Sad Among Strangers,
c.1982,
copier print, color added,
32 x 23 1/4 inches.

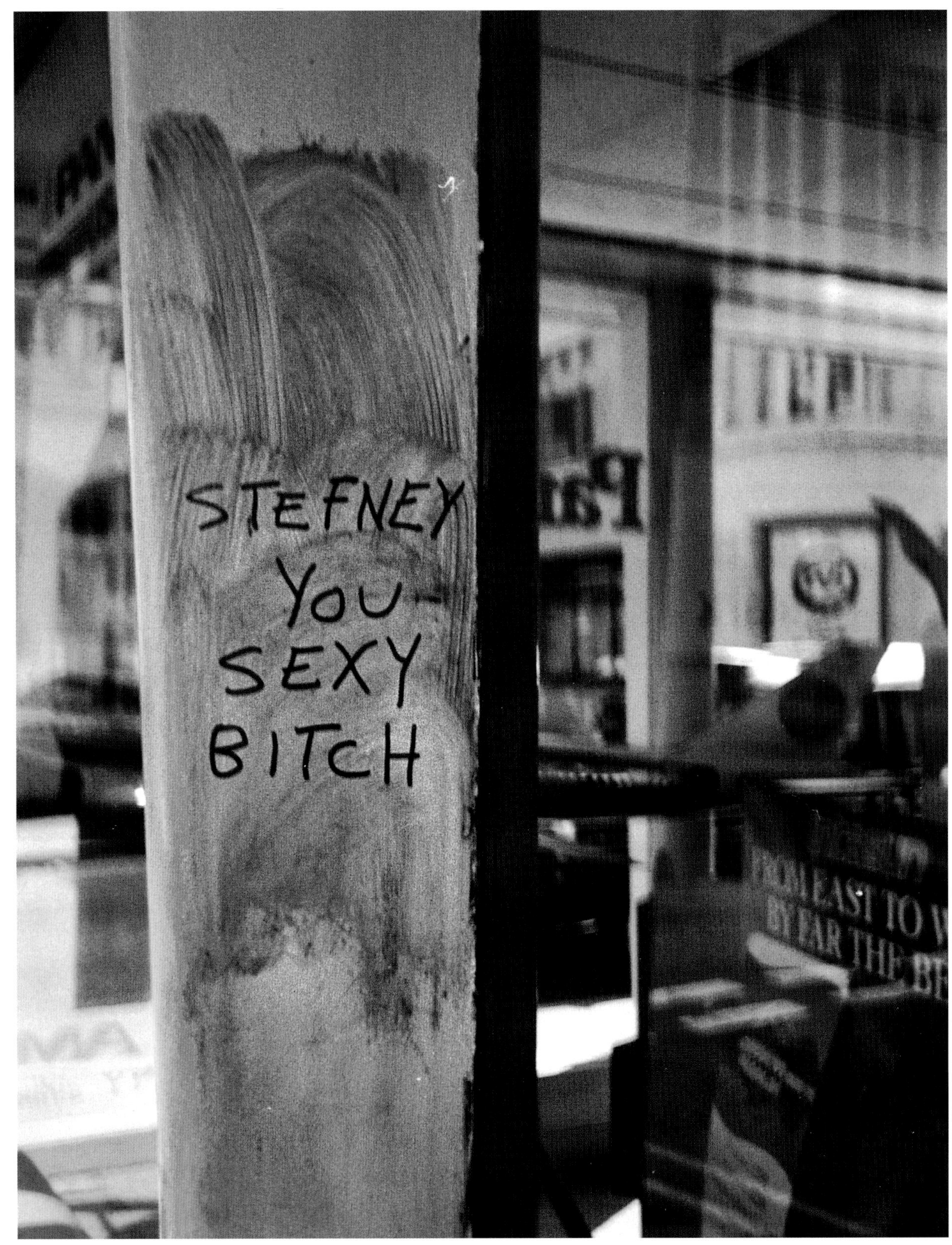

Stefney, You Sexy Bitch, c. 1985, photograph, 10 x 8 inches.

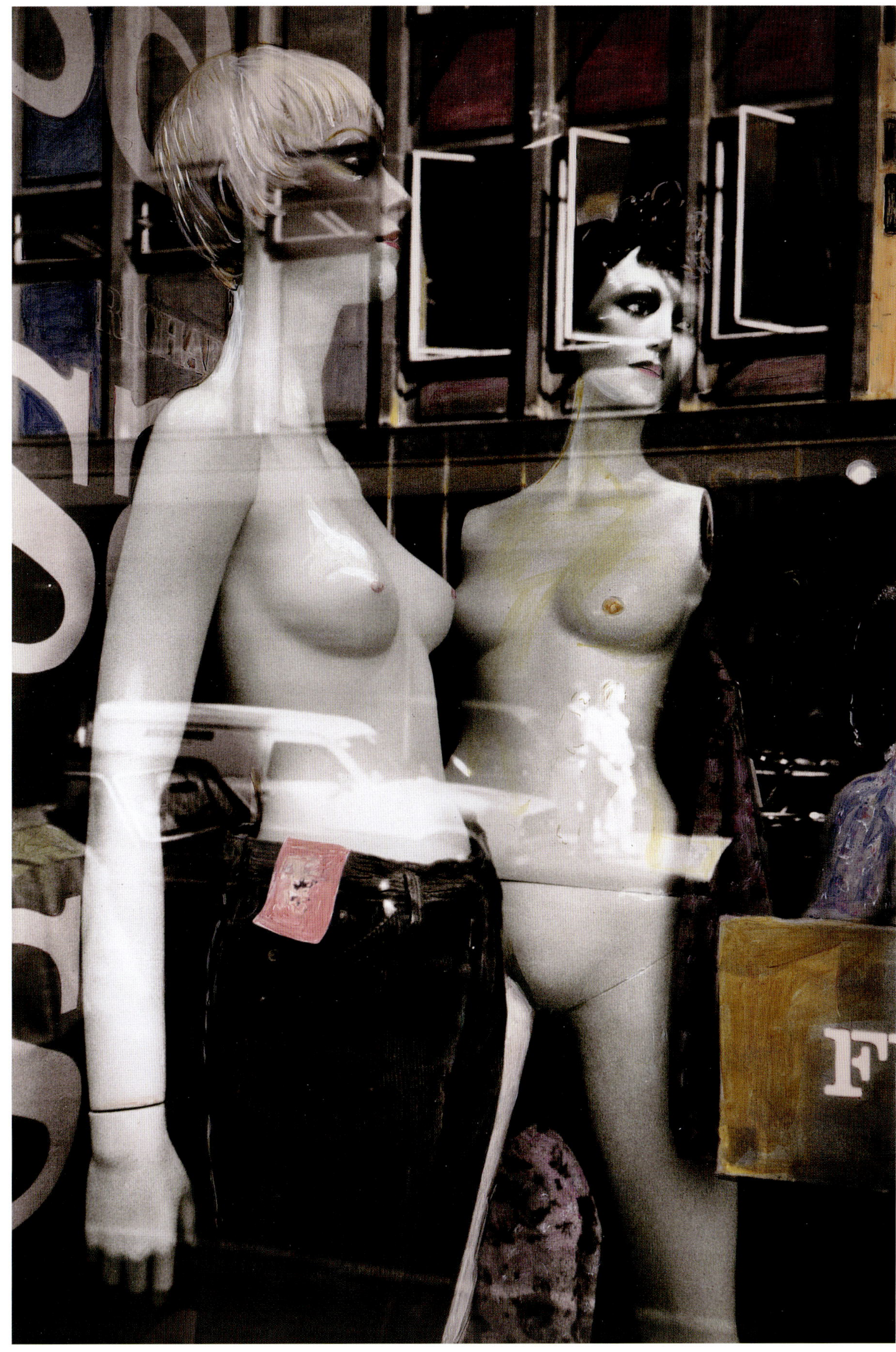

Models,
c. 1985,
photograph, color added,
42 x 29 3/4 inches.

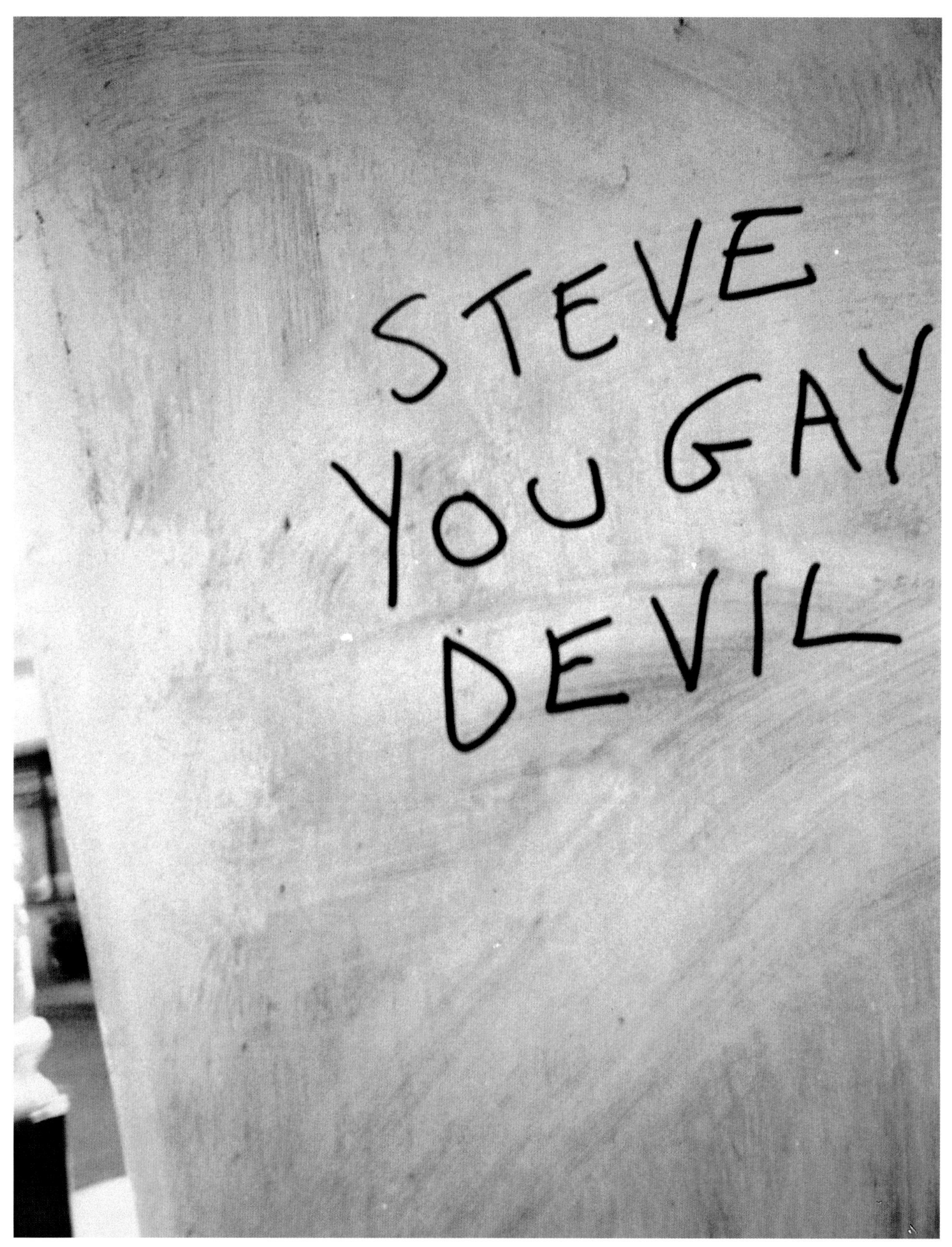

Steve, You Gay Devil, c. 1985, photograph, 10 x 8 inches.

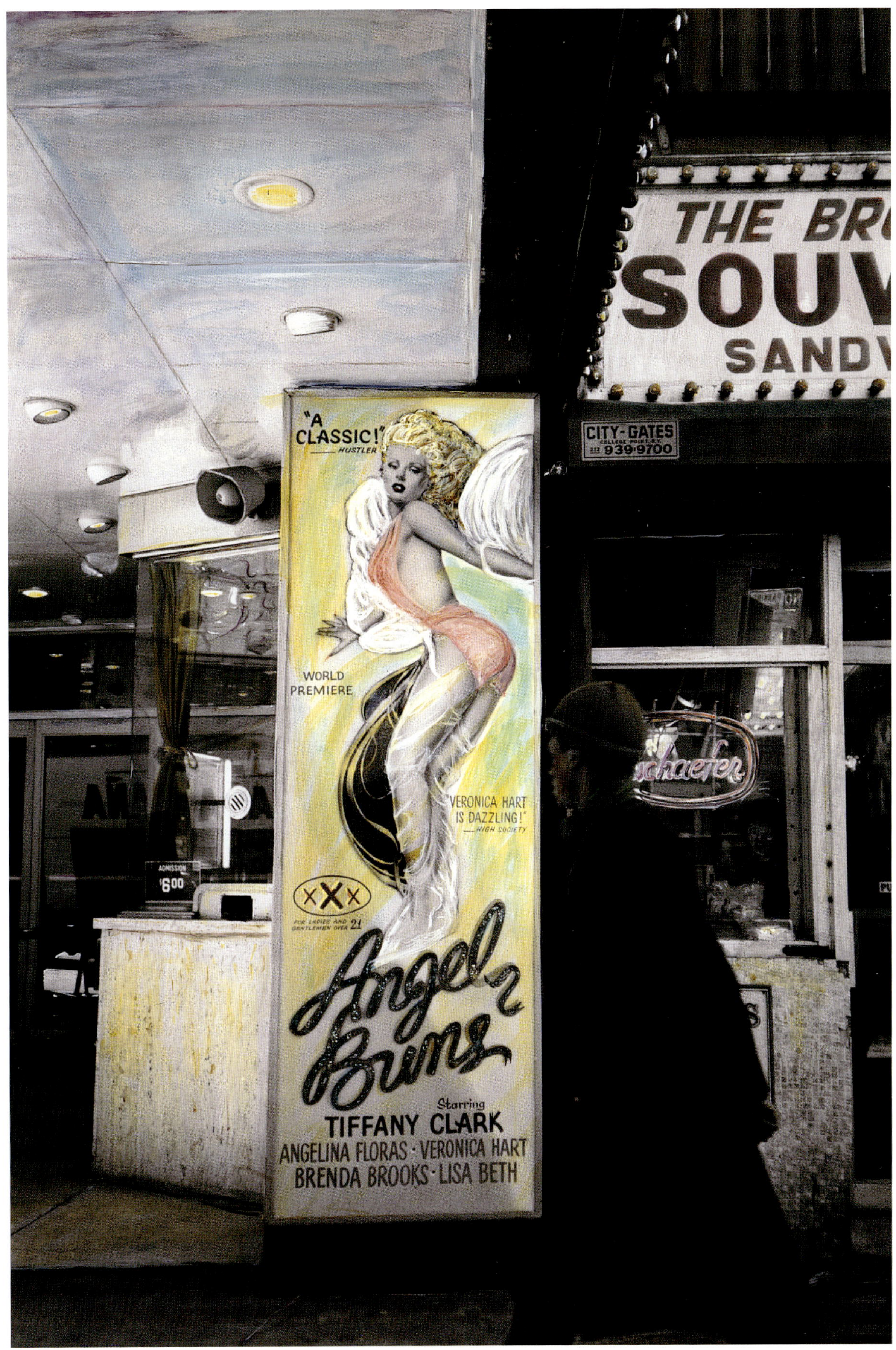

A Classic,
c. 1986,
photograph, color added,
41 1/2 x 28 1/2 inches.

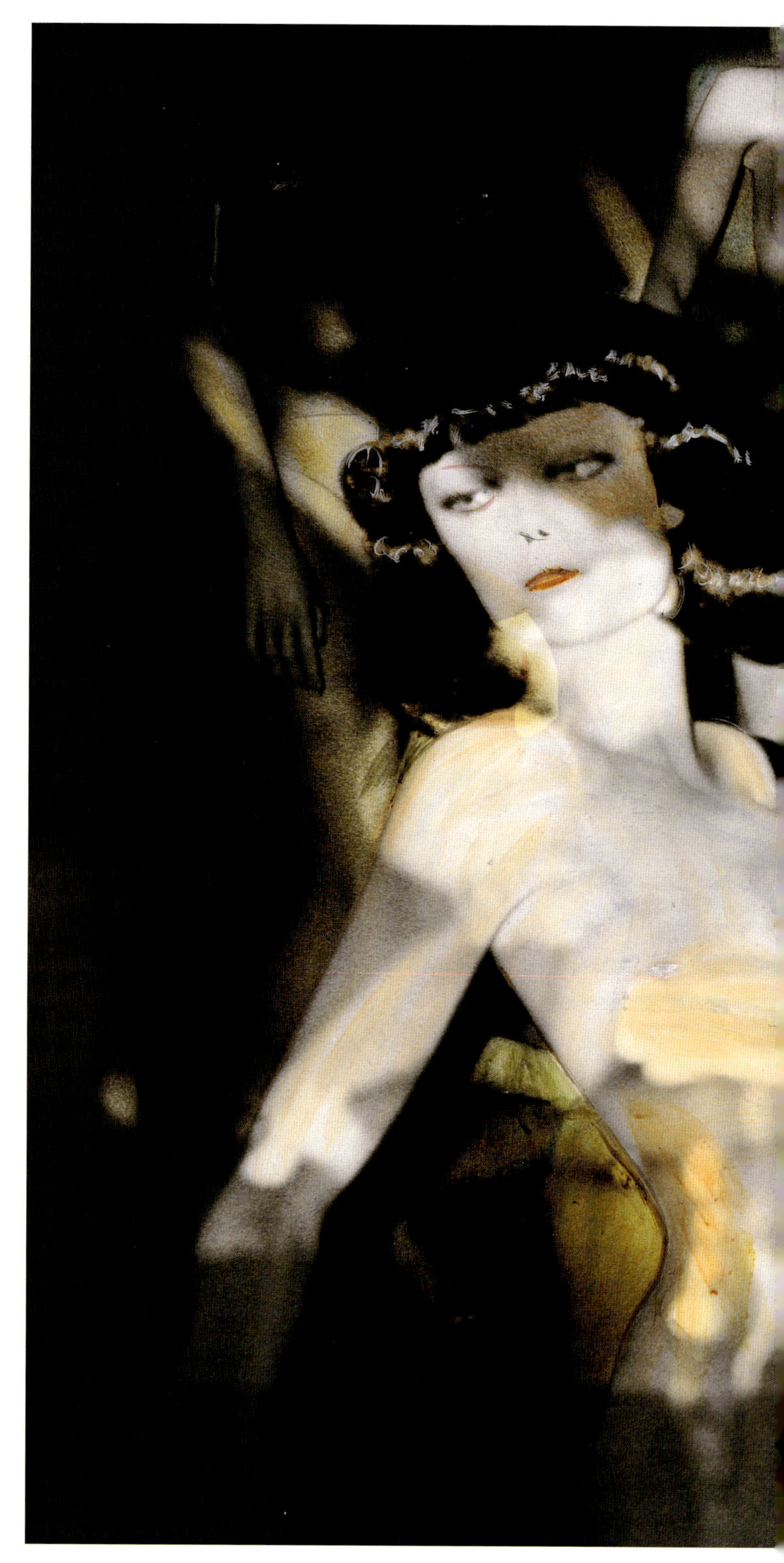

Nude Models, c. 1987, photograph, color added, 28 x 40 3/4 inches.

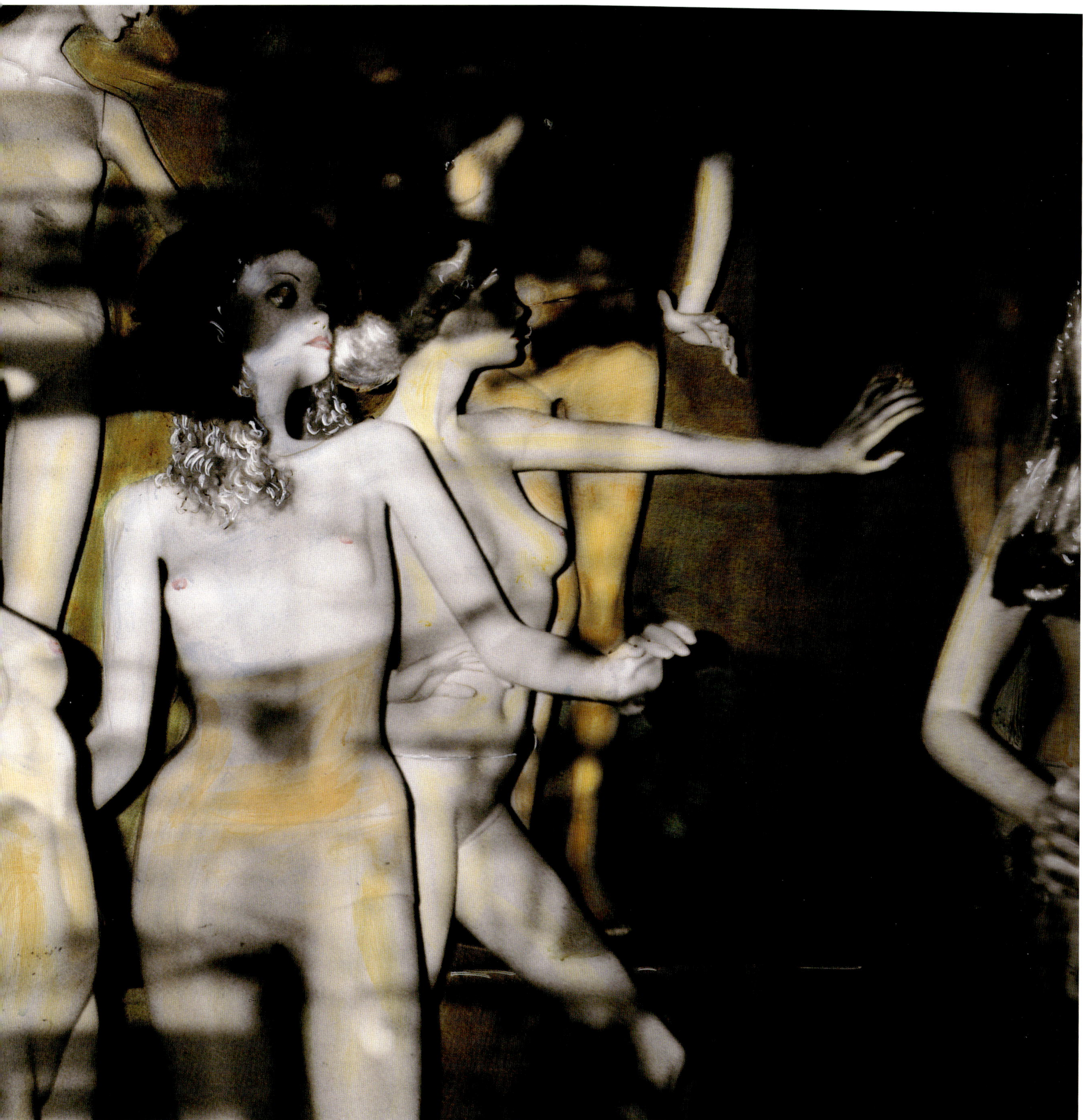

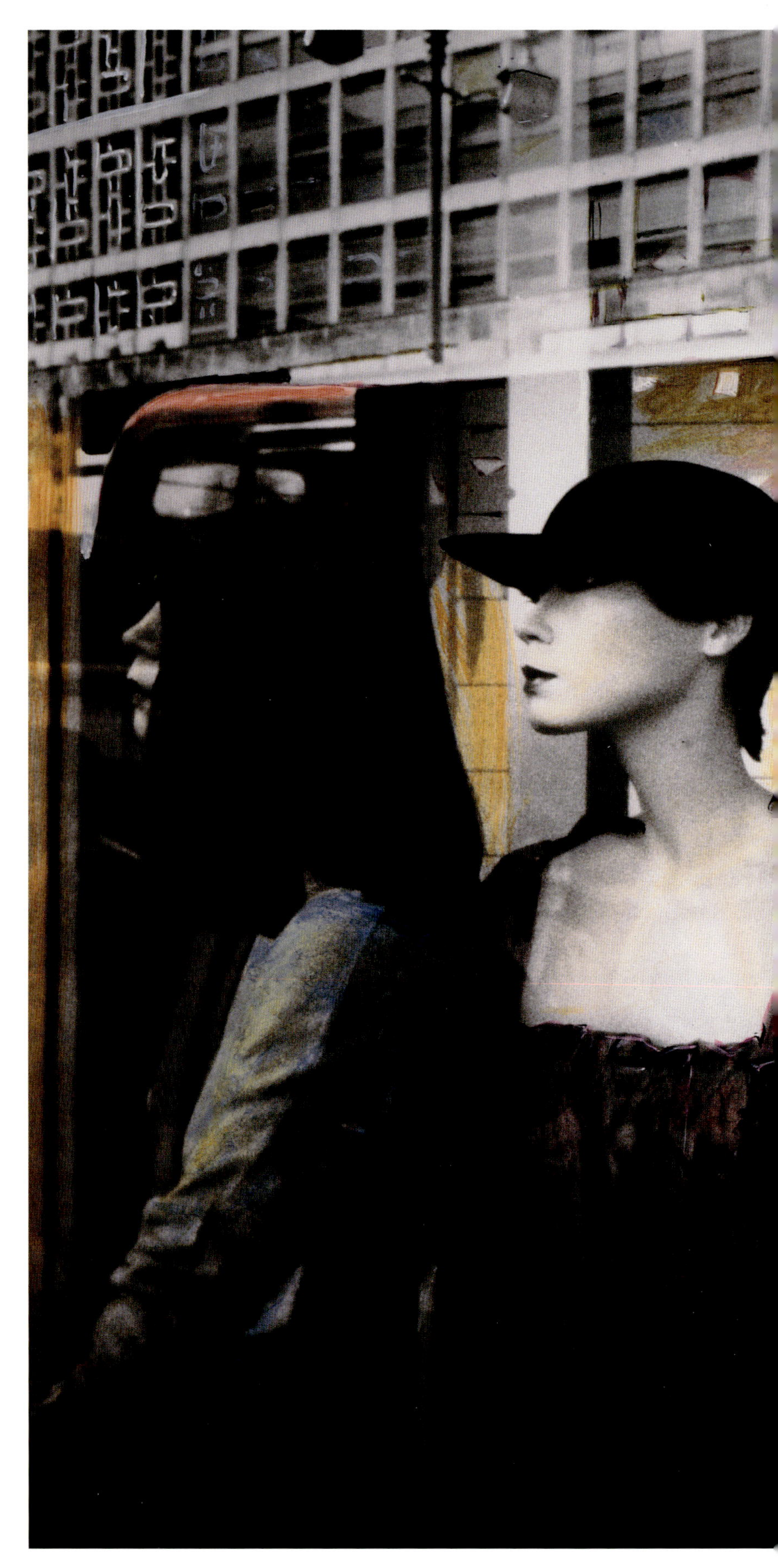

Three Models, c. 1989, photograph, color added, 27 x 40 inches.

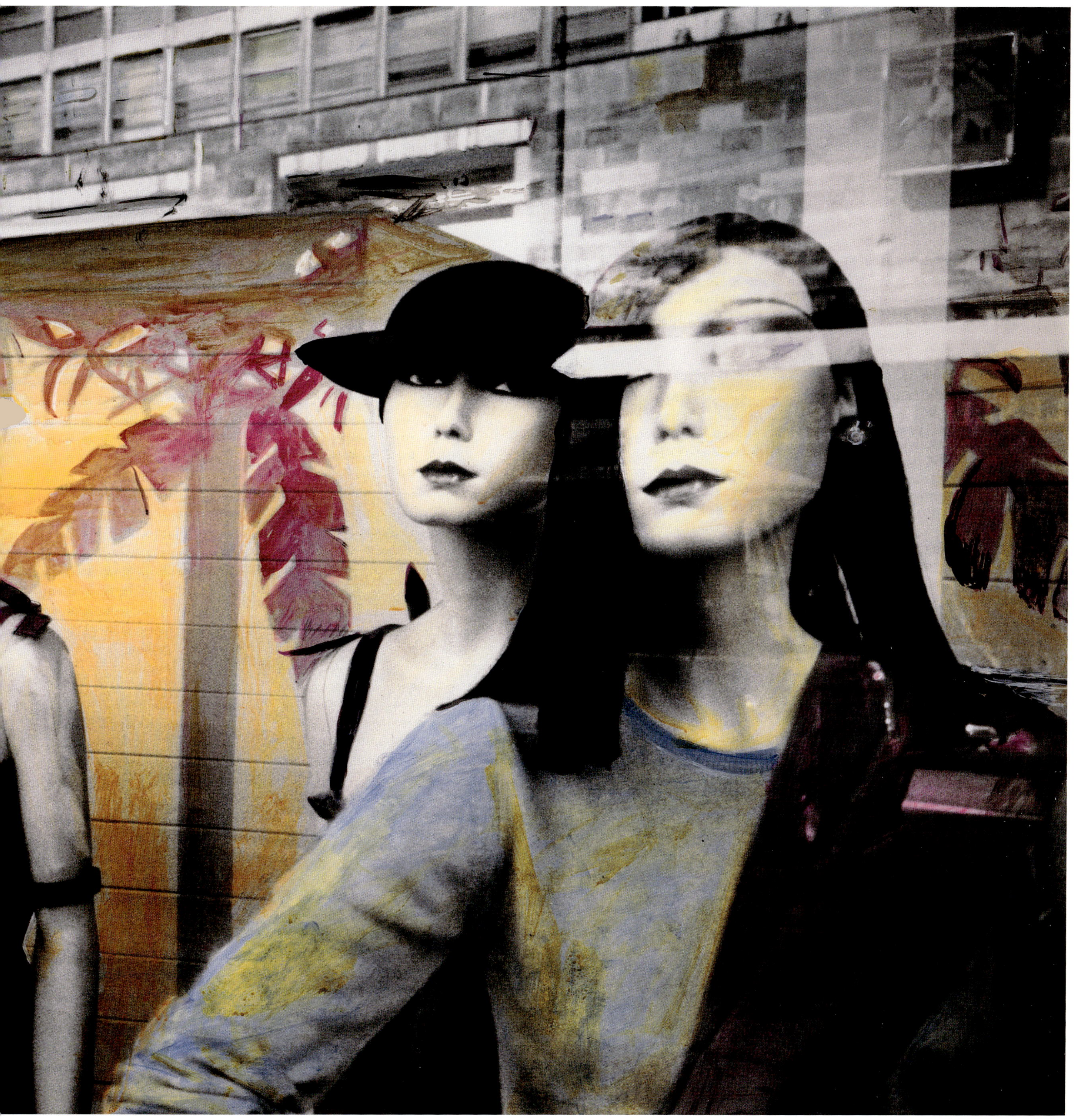

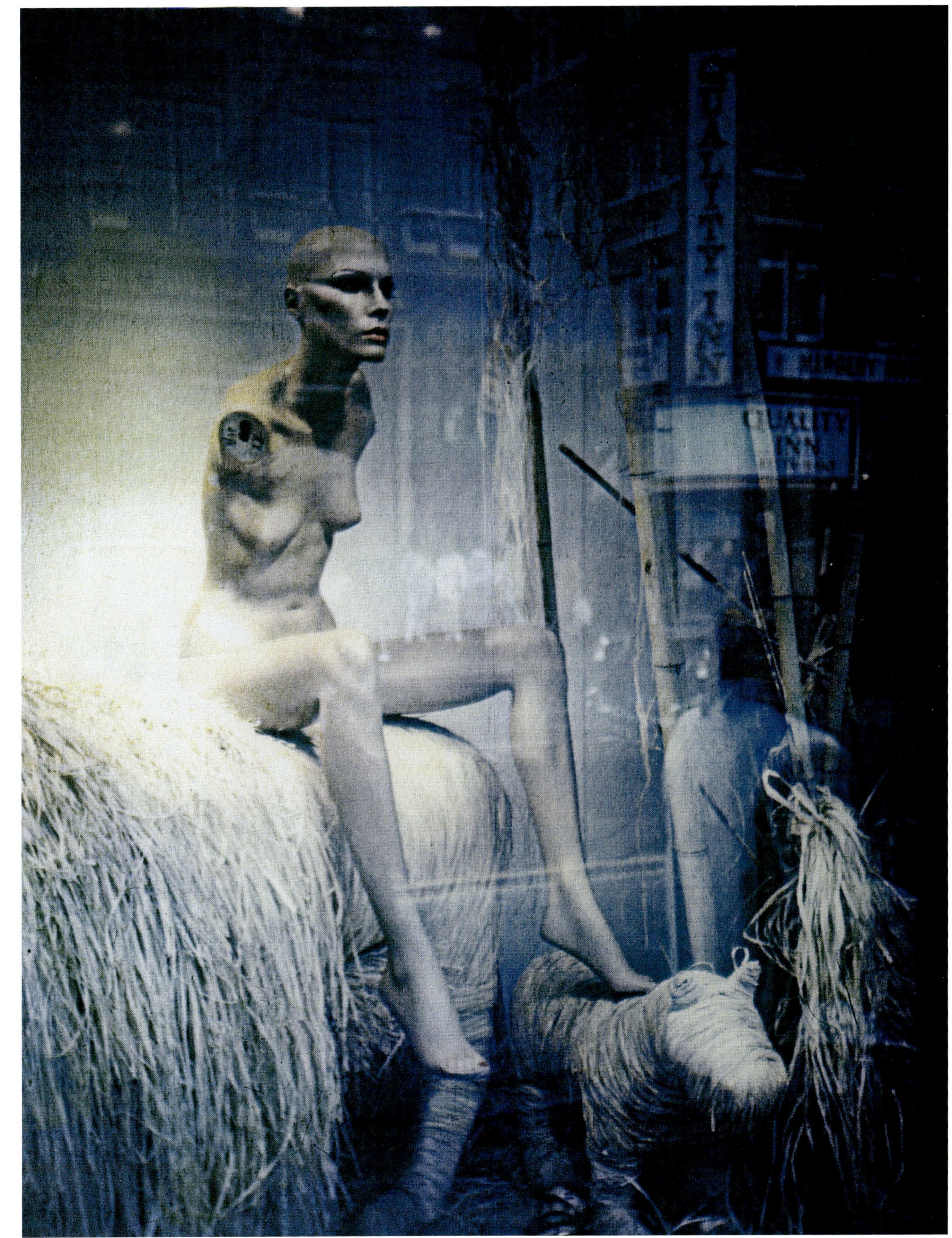

Dismembered Mannequin,
1996,
color photograph,
11 1/2 x 7 1/2 inches.

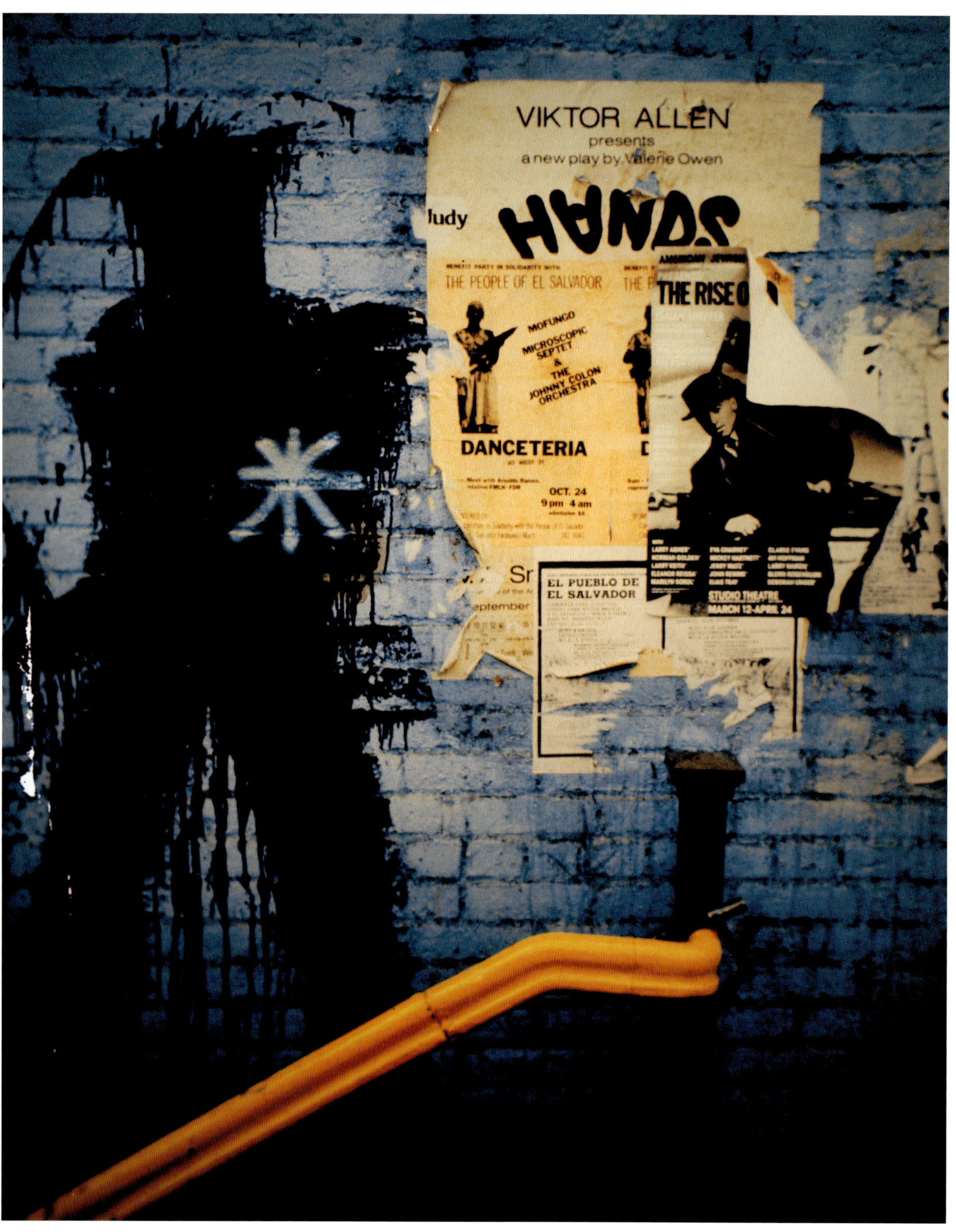

Viktor Allen,
c. 1990,
color photograph,
10 x 8 inches.

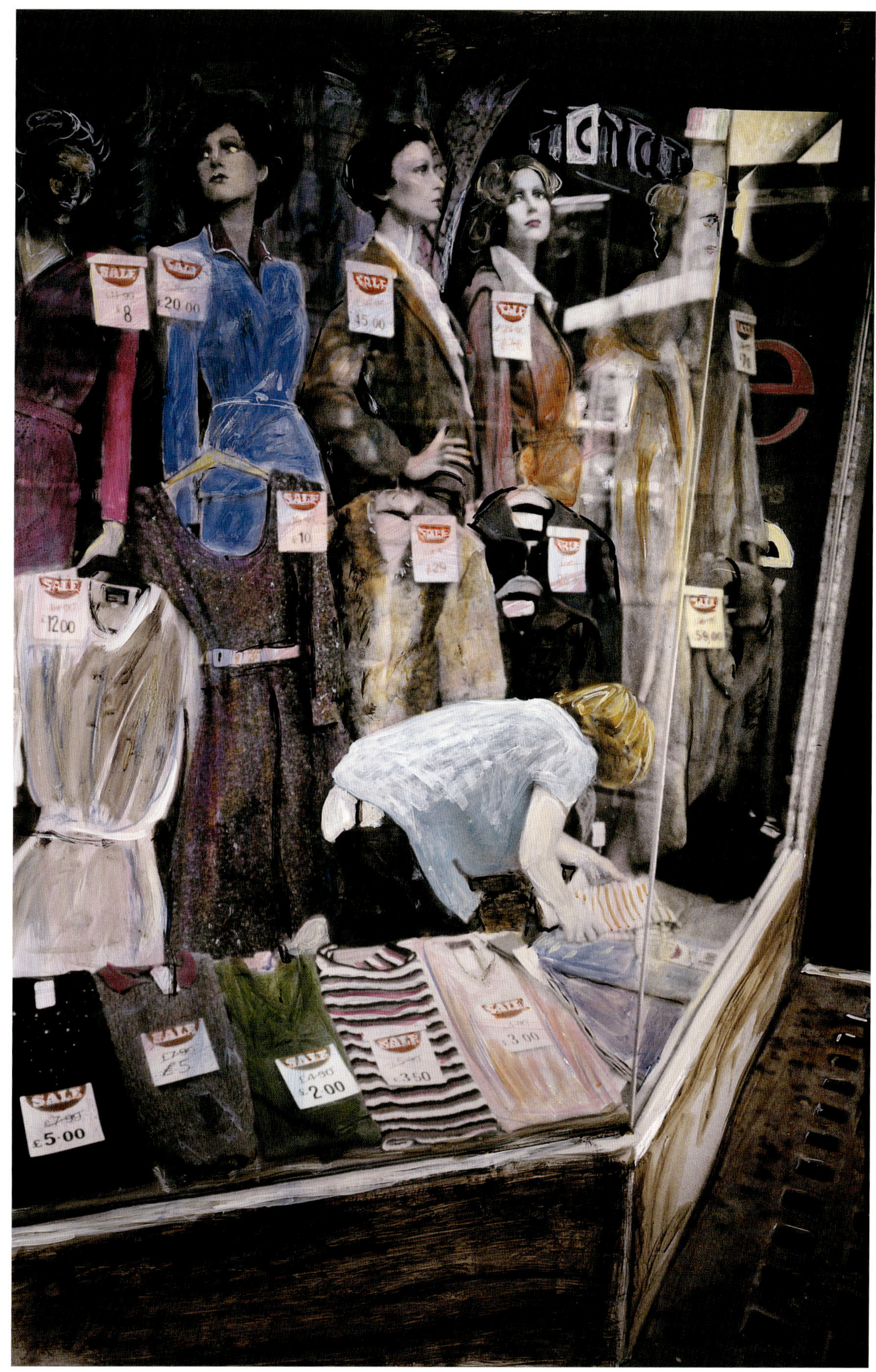

Sale,
c. 1988,
photograph, color added,
44 x 29 inches.

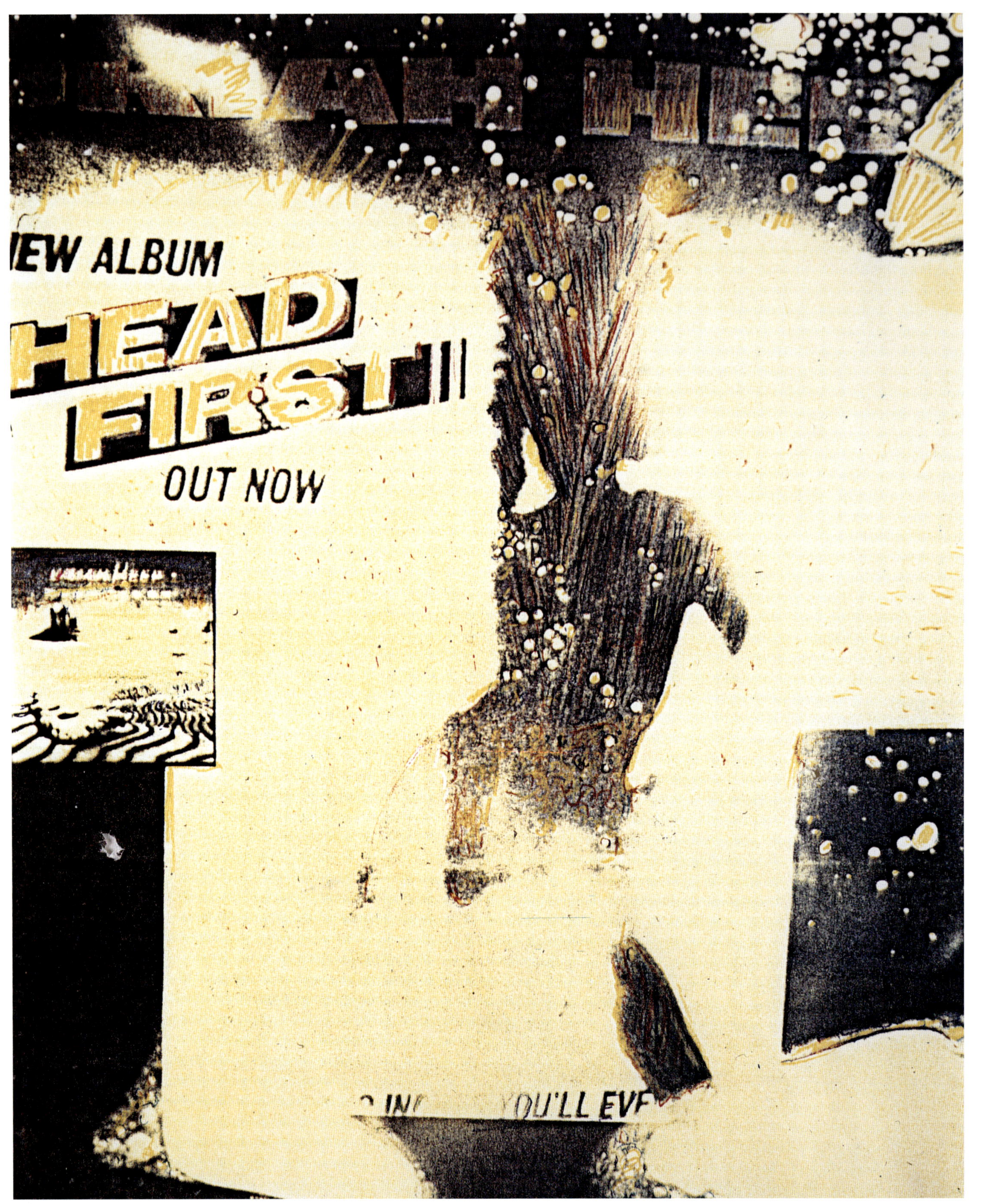

Head First,
c. 1990,
color copier print,
10 1/2 x 8 1/2 inches.

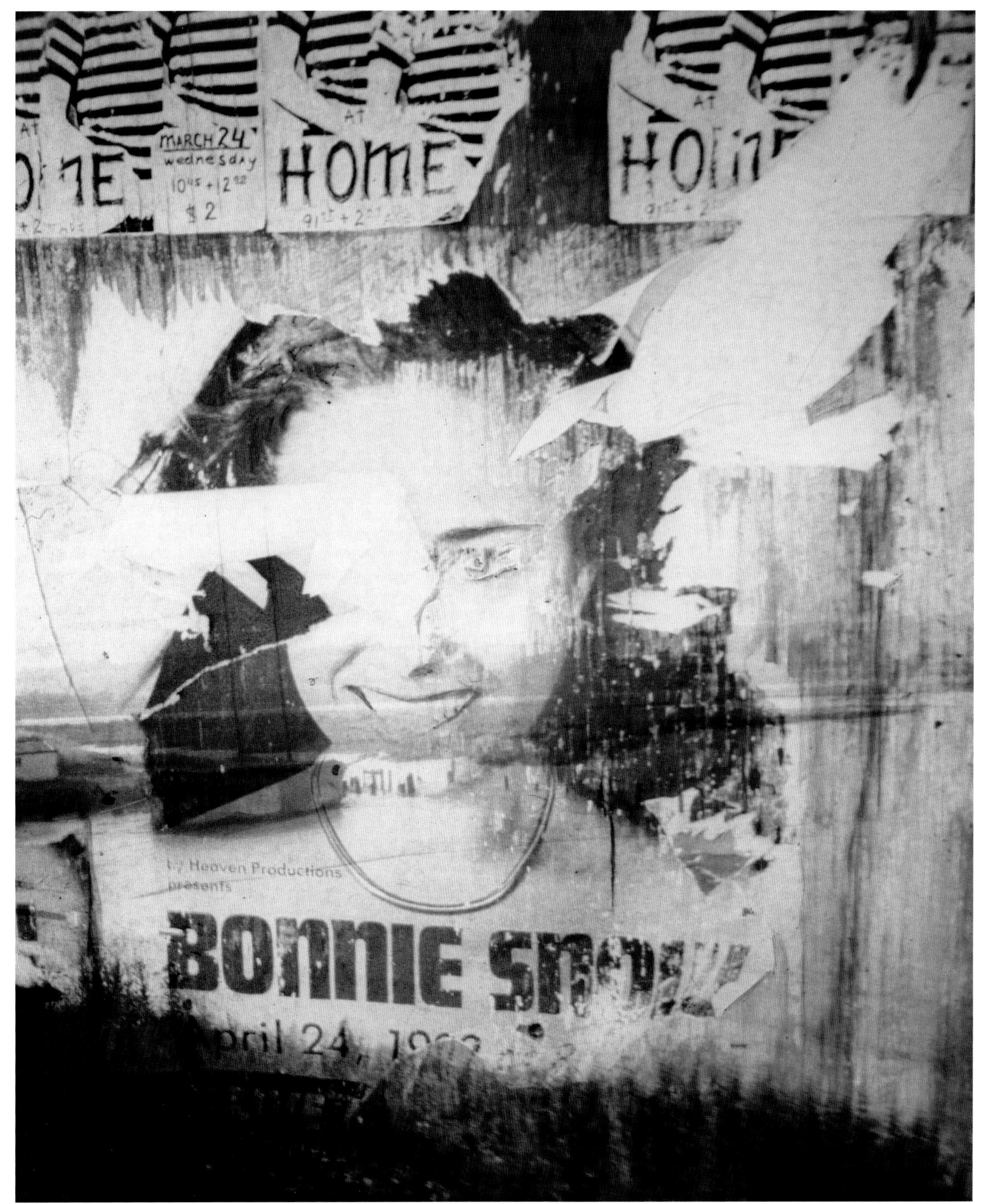

Bonnie,
1992,
color photograph,
10 x 8 inches.

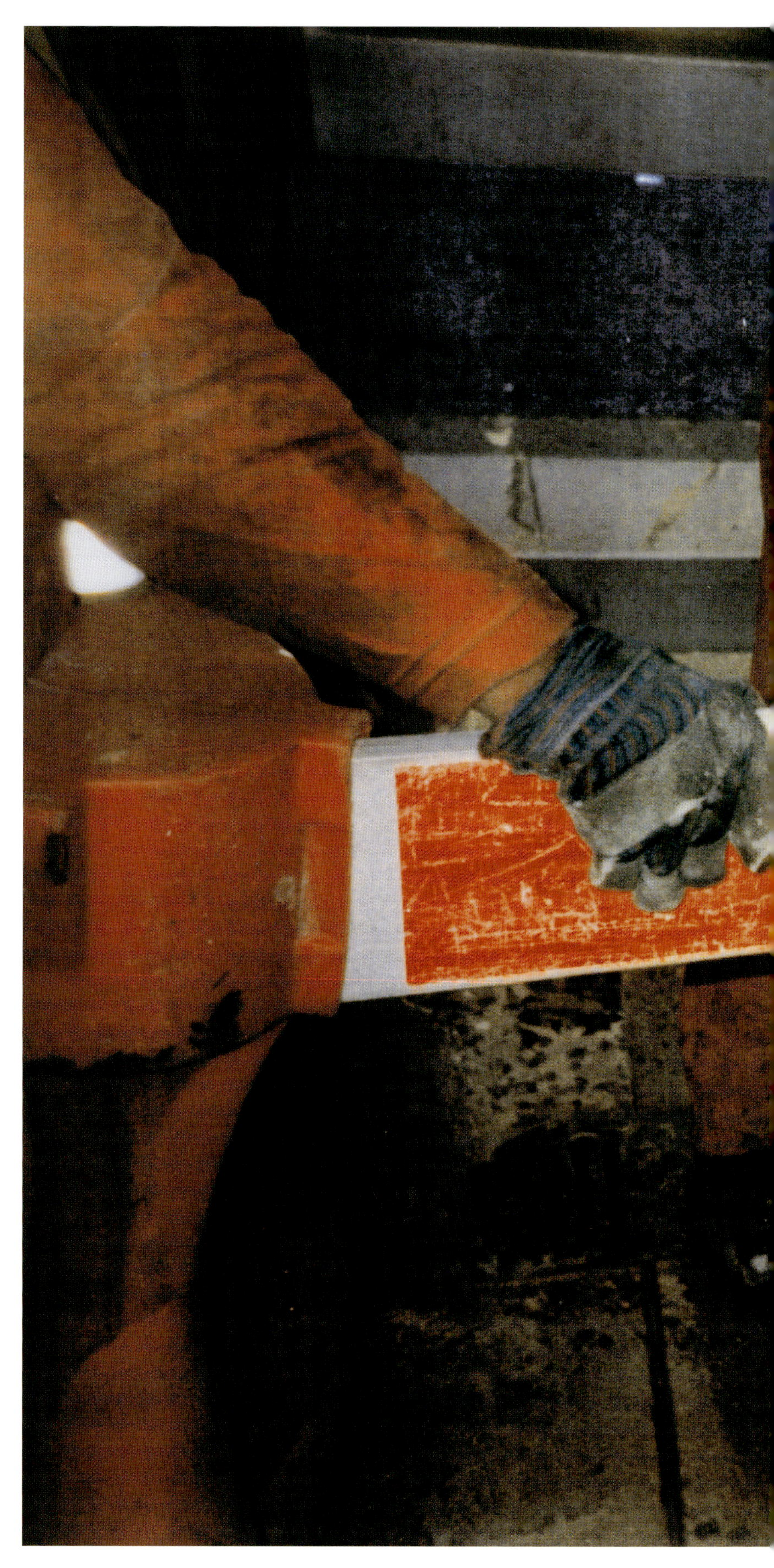

Repairs at the Ritz, 1994, color copier print, 11 x 16 inches.

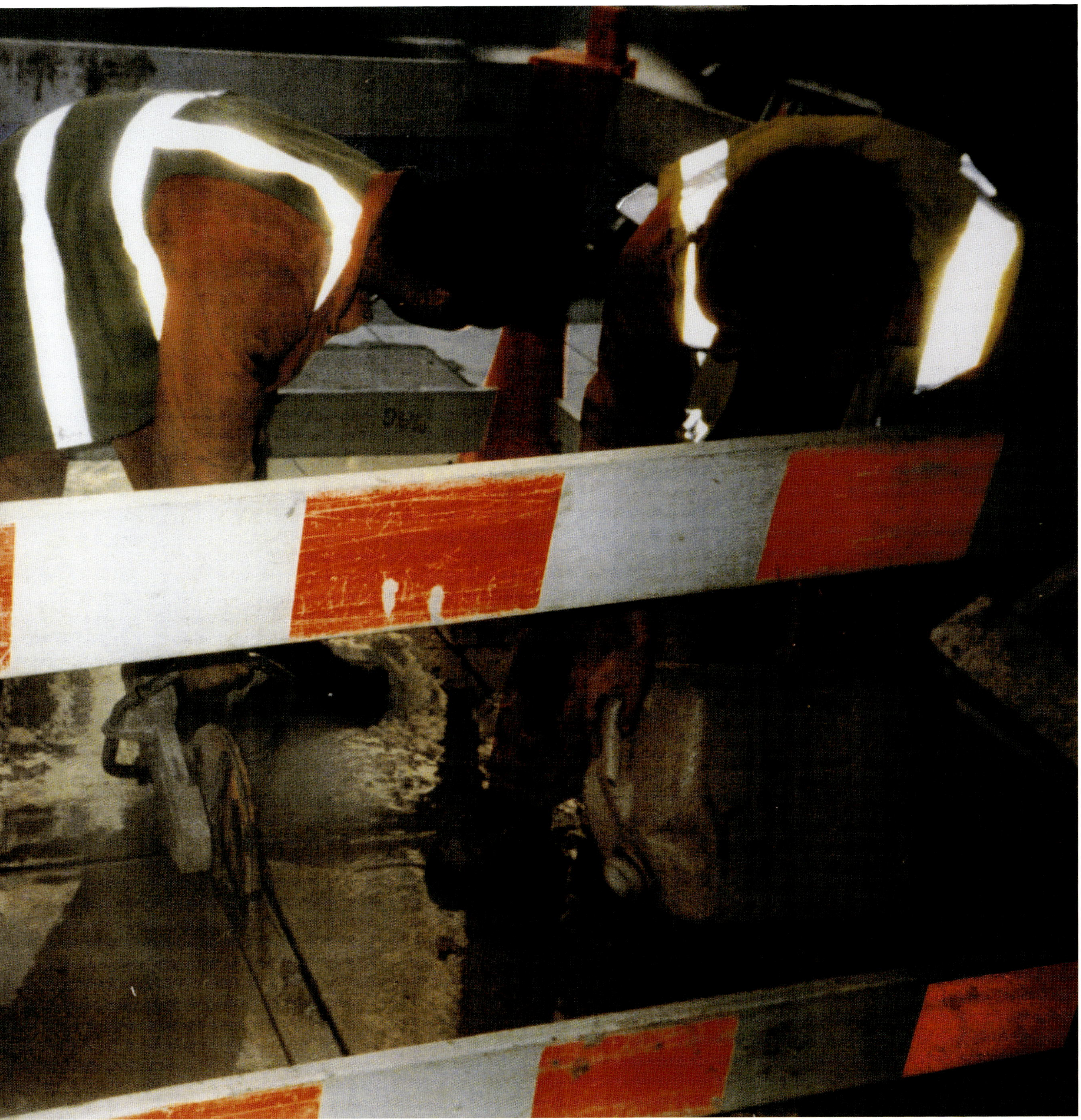

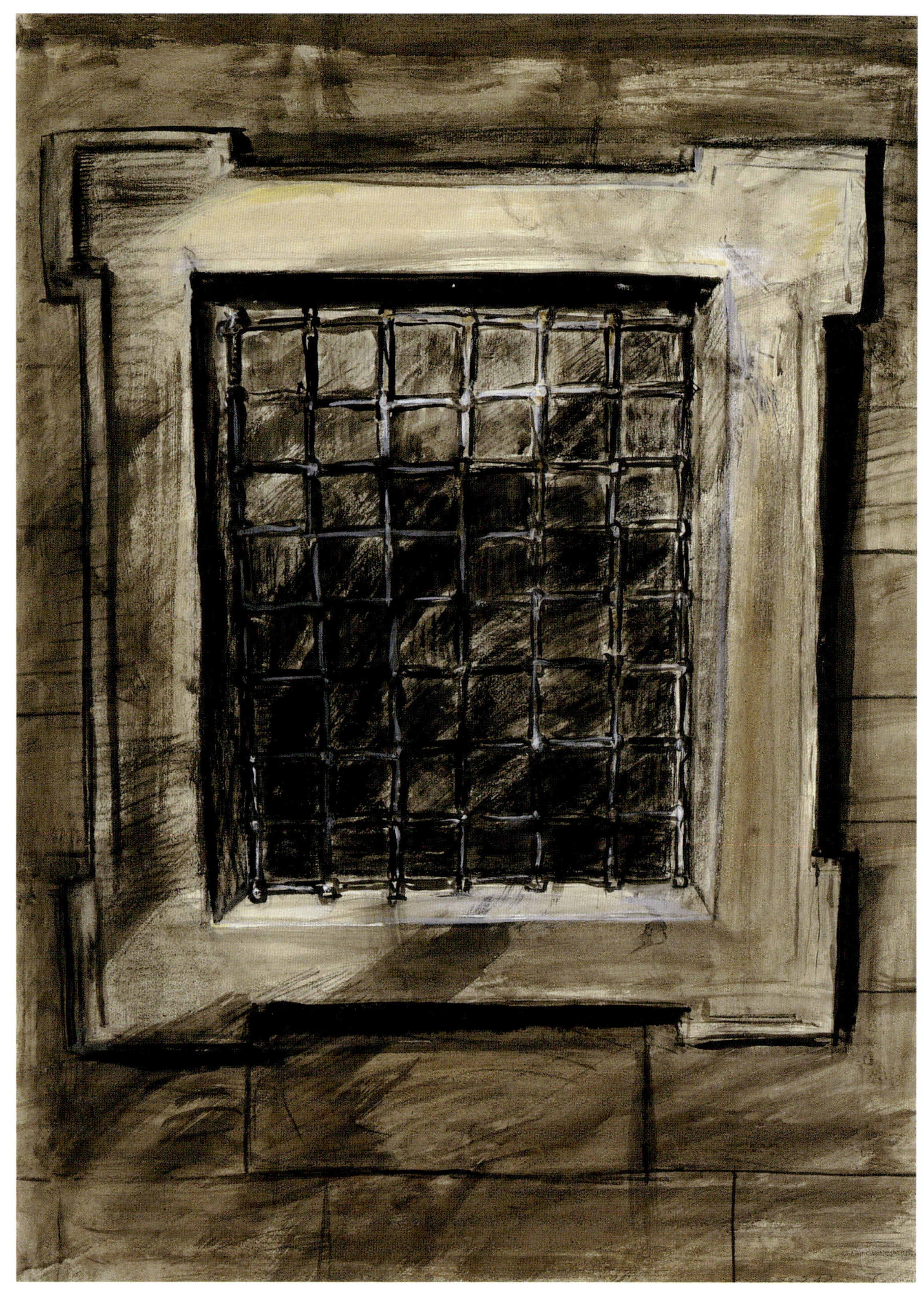

Basement Window, c. 1988, watercolor, 28 x 20 1/2 inches.

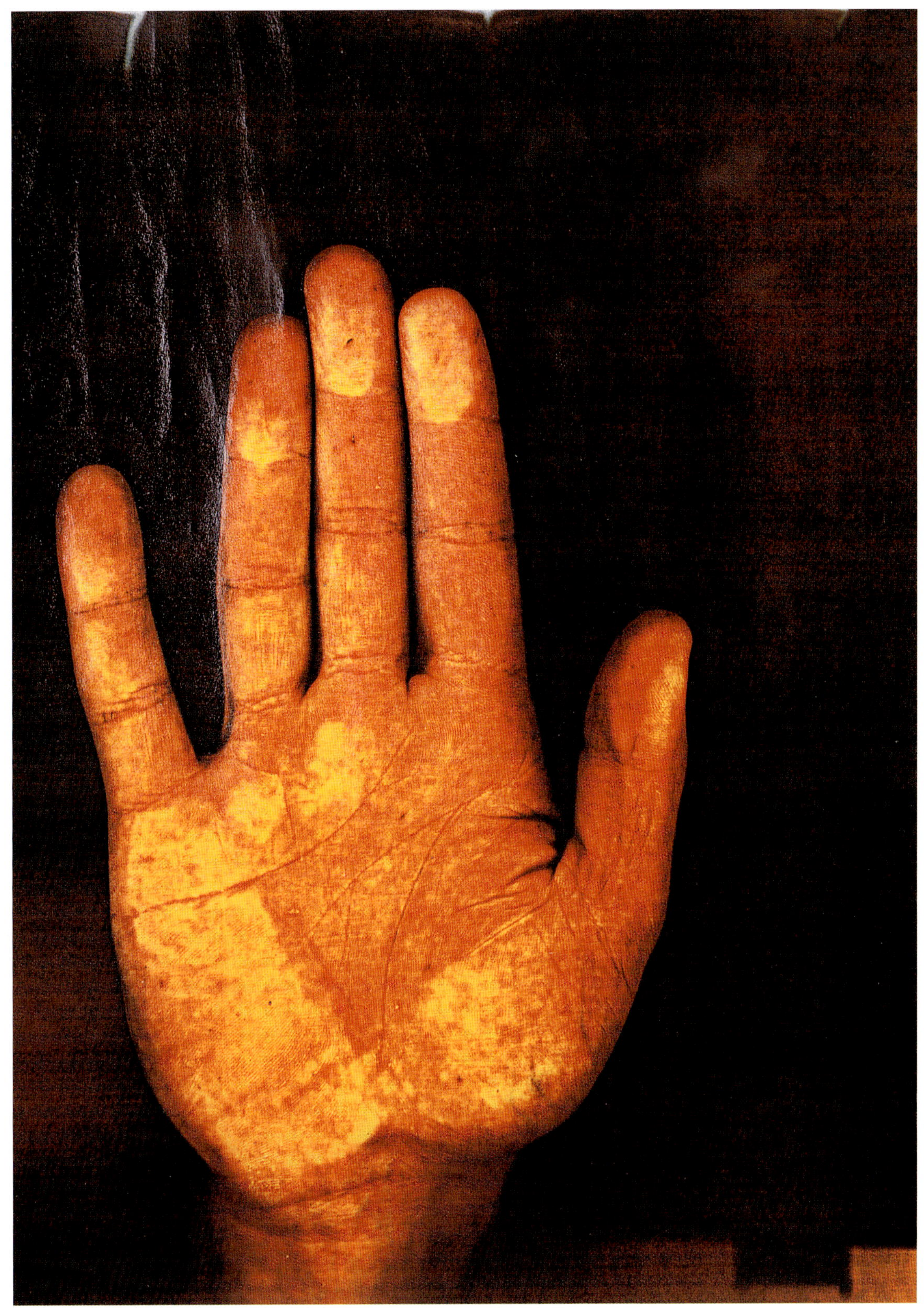

Hand, c. 1990, color copier print, 11 1/2 x 8 inches.

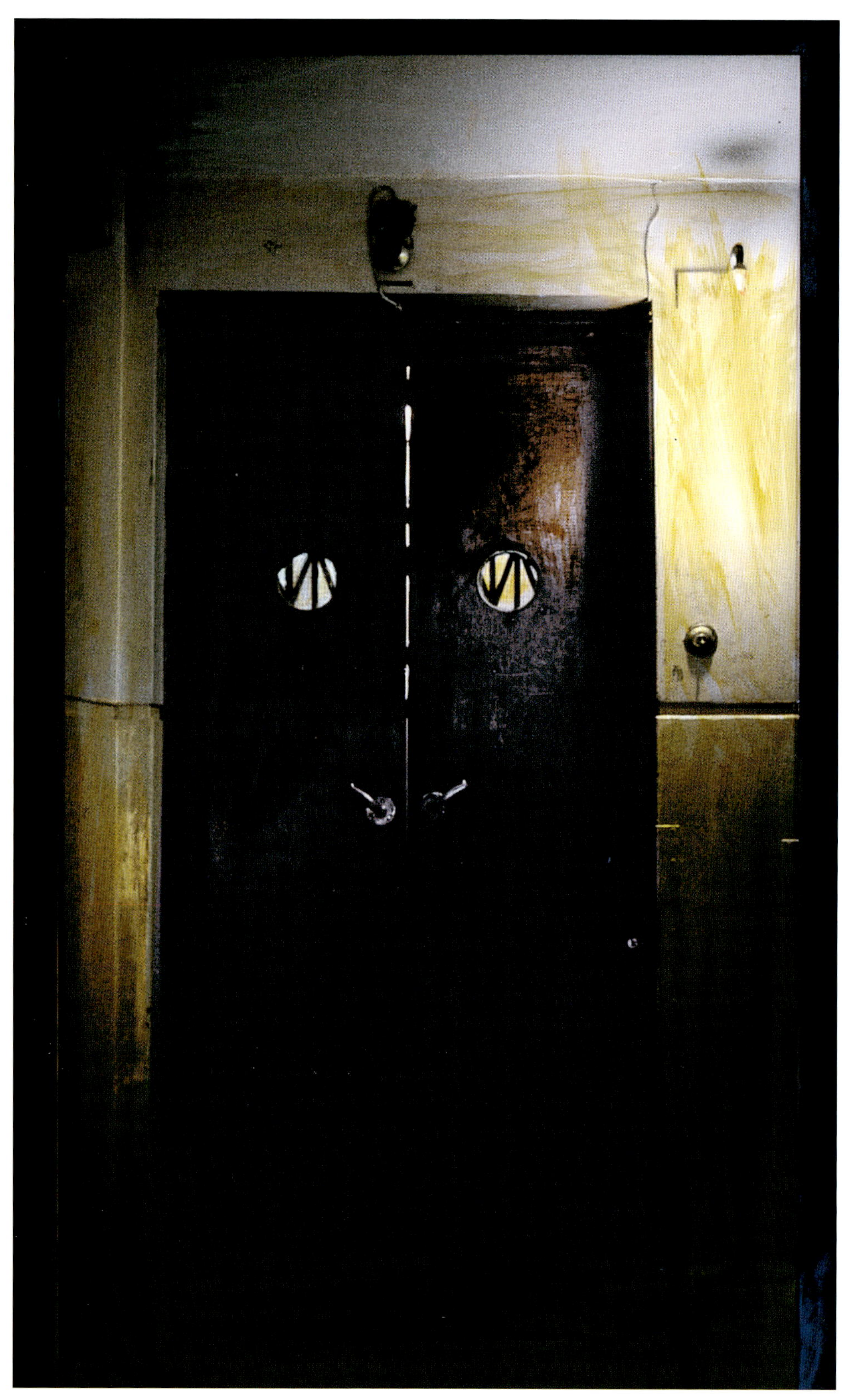

Elevator, Steinway Building, 1997, photograph, color added, 29 3/4 x 15 3/4 inches.

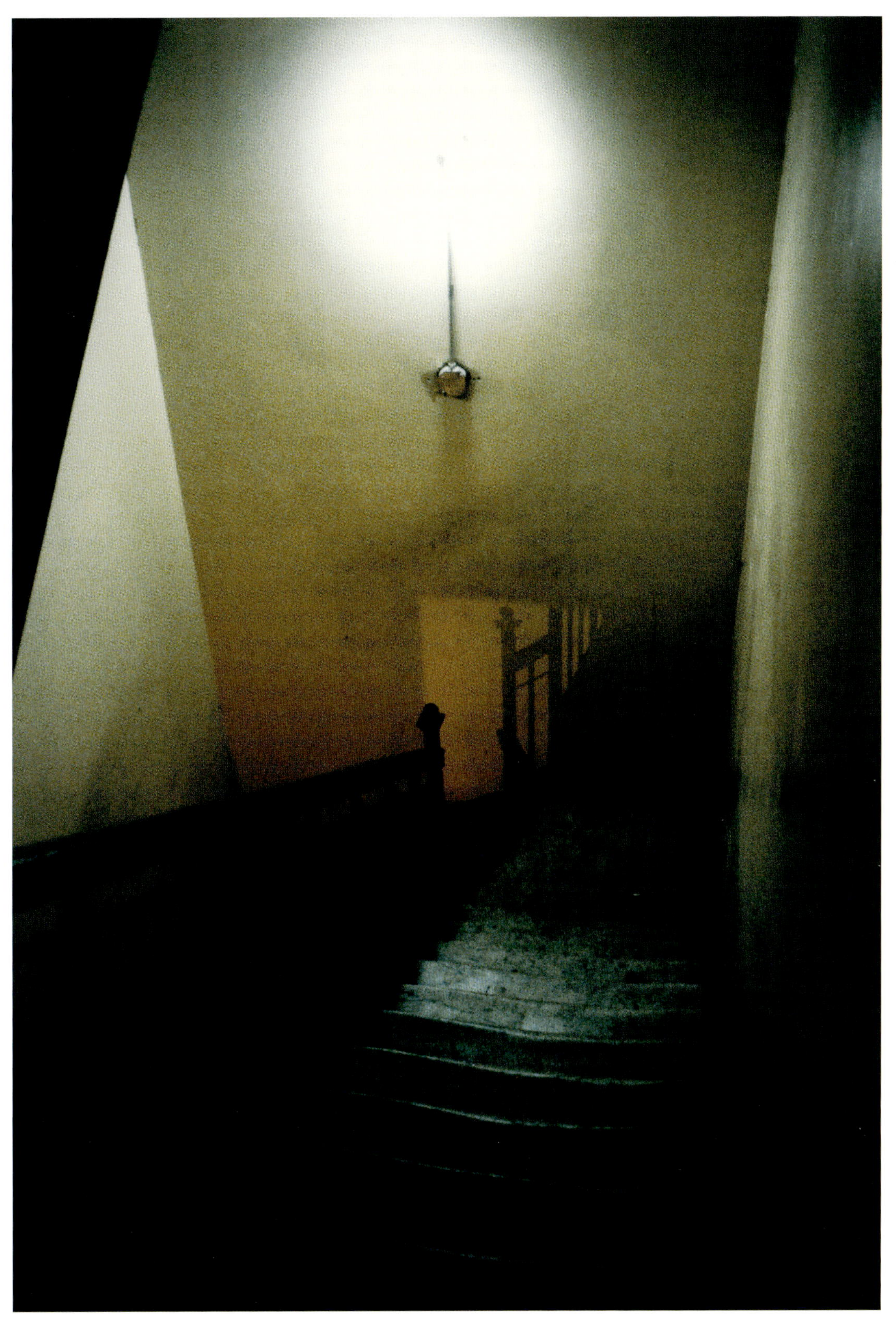

Stairs, Steinway Building, 1997, color photograph, 20 x 15 1/4 inches.

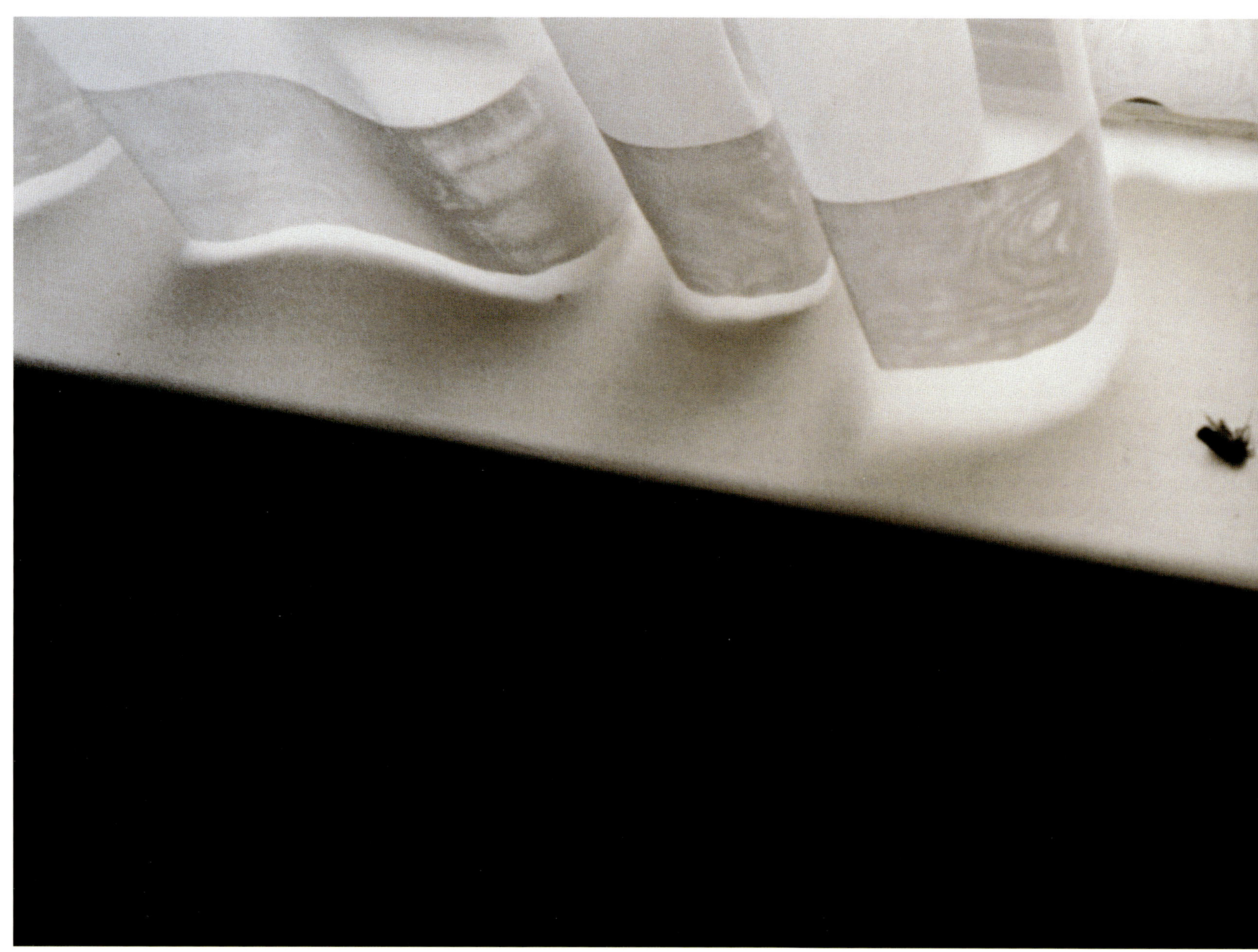

Bug, 1995, color photograph, 3 1/2 x 9 3/4 inches.

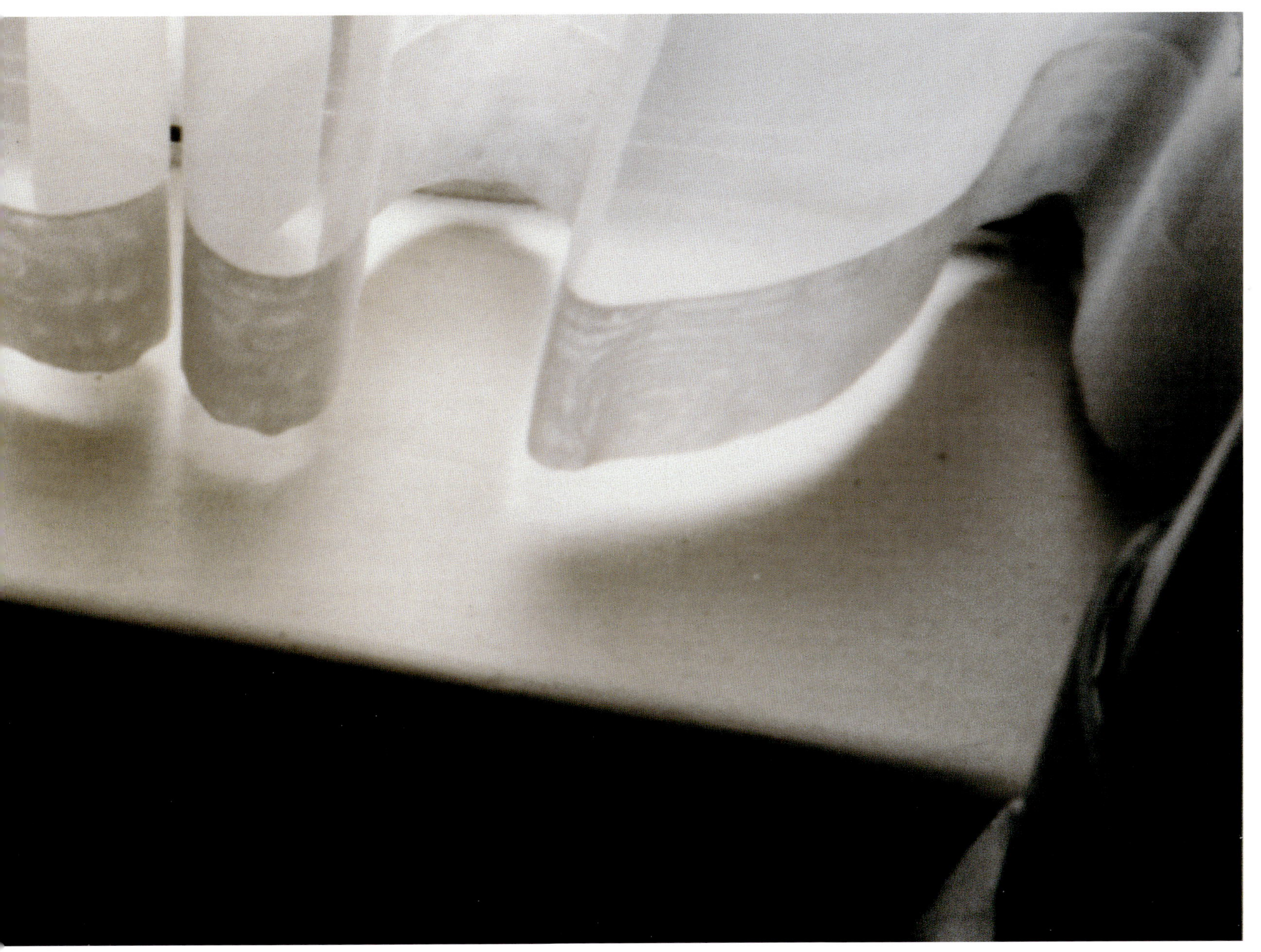

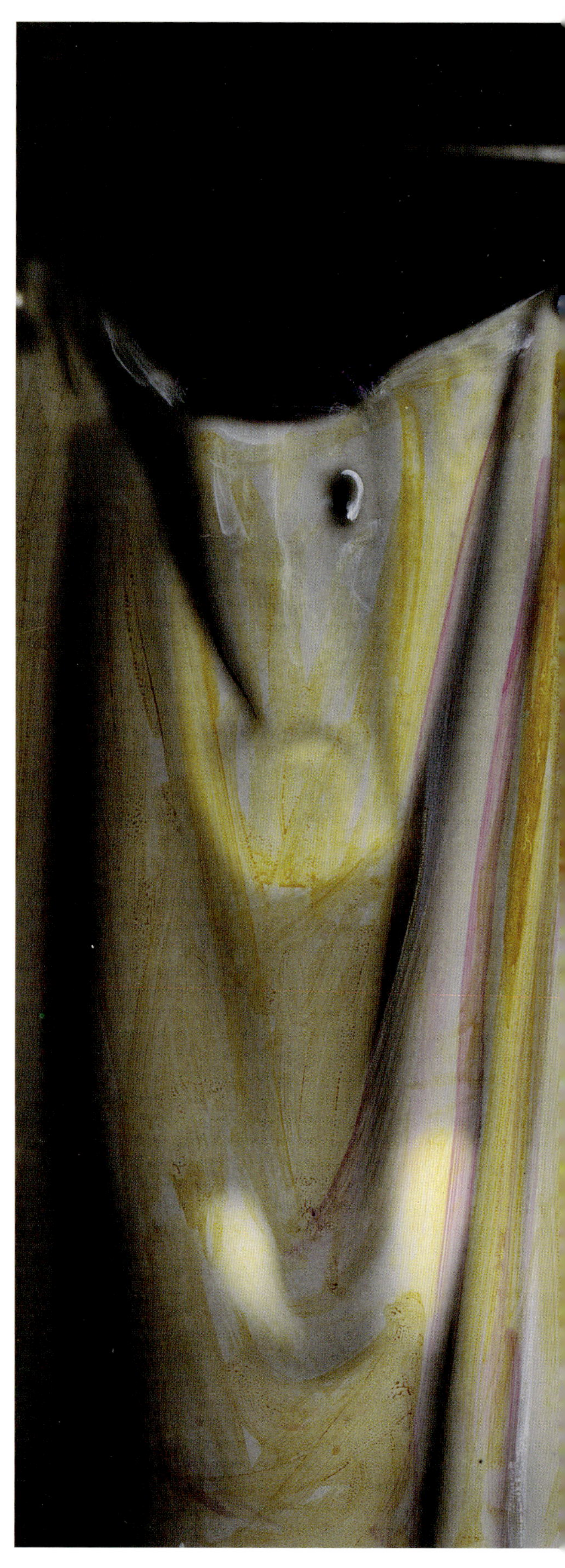

Hospital Curtain, 1981, photograph, color added, 40 1/2 x 30 inches.

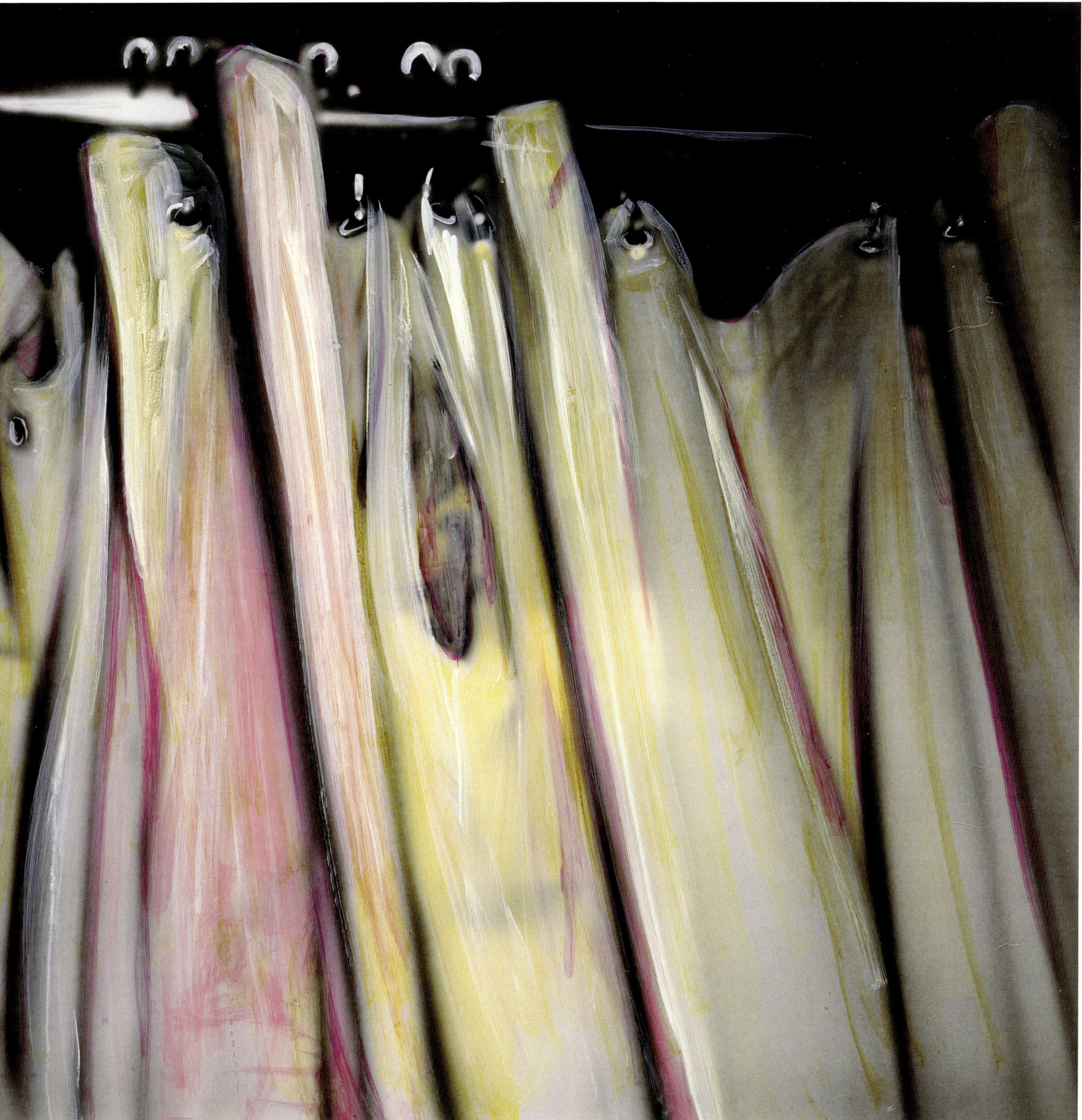

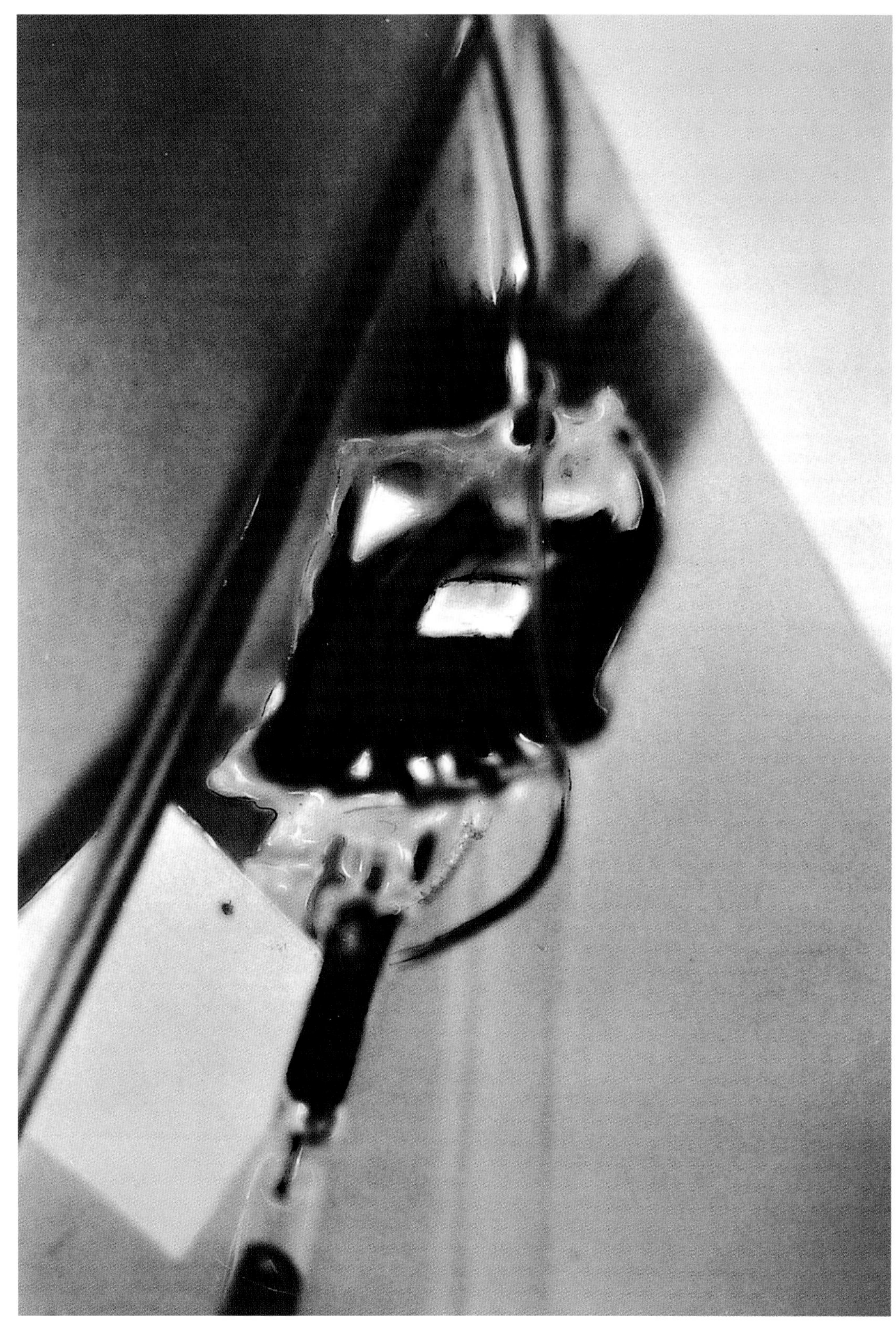

Blood Transfusion, 1981, photograph, color added, 40 x 27 inches.

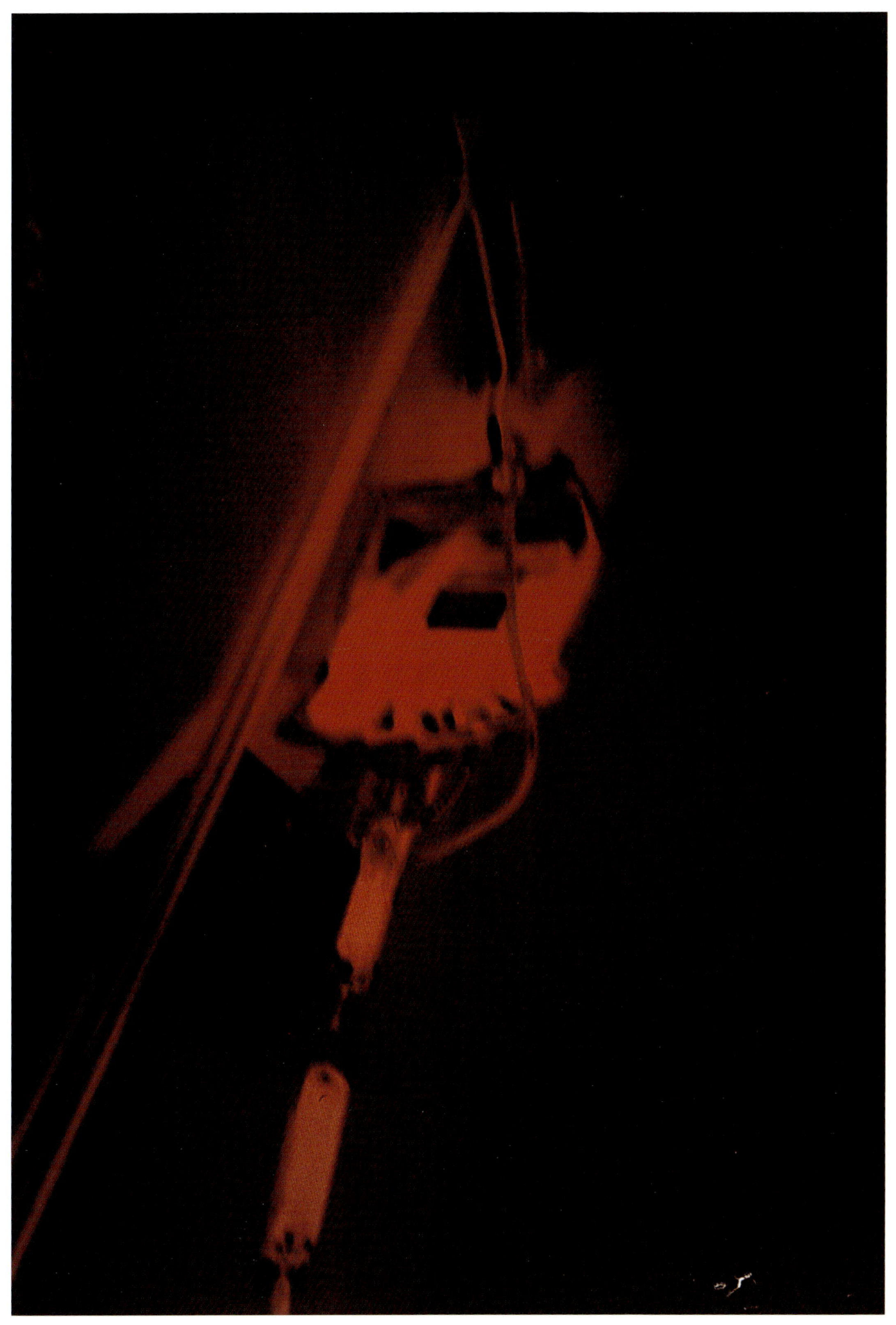

Blood Transfusion, 1981, photograph, 40 x 27 inches.

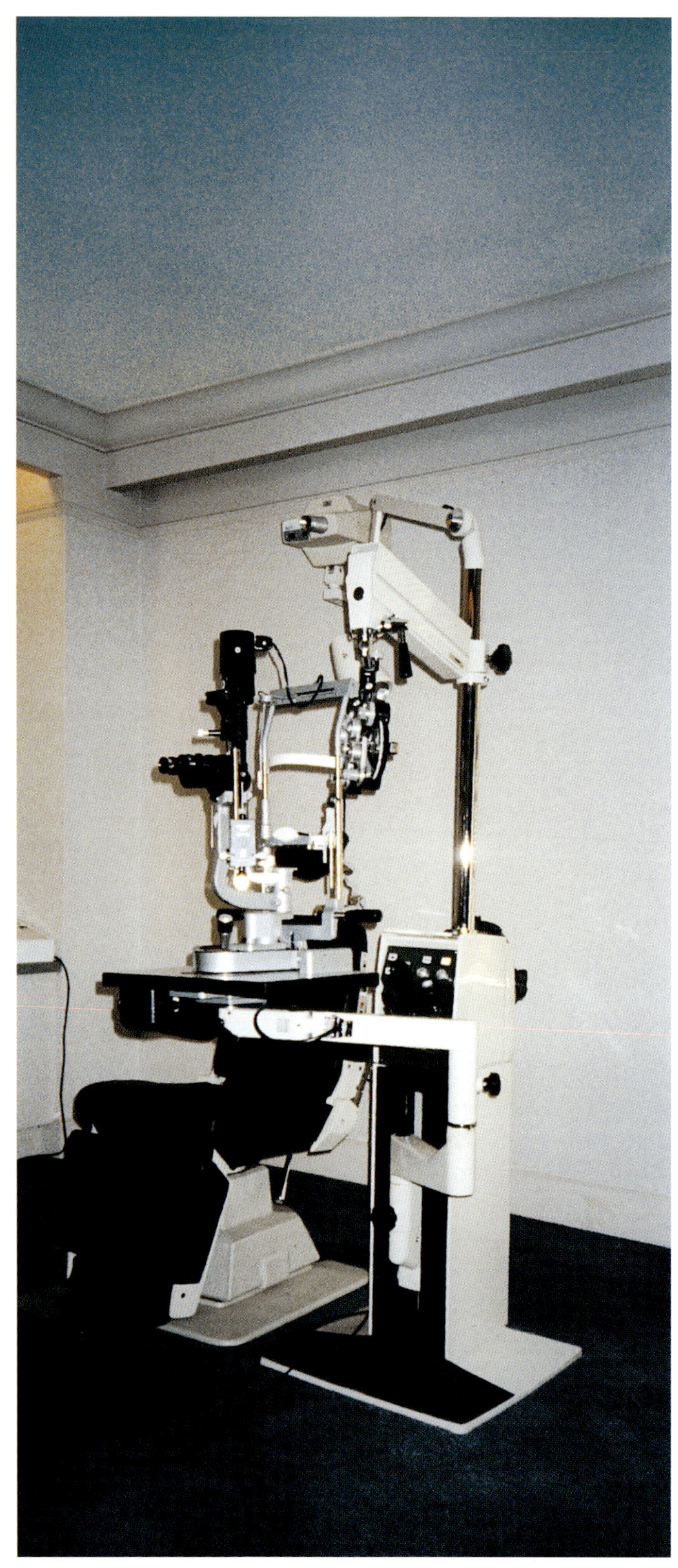

Eye Exam, c. 1992, color photograph, 30 x 11 inches.

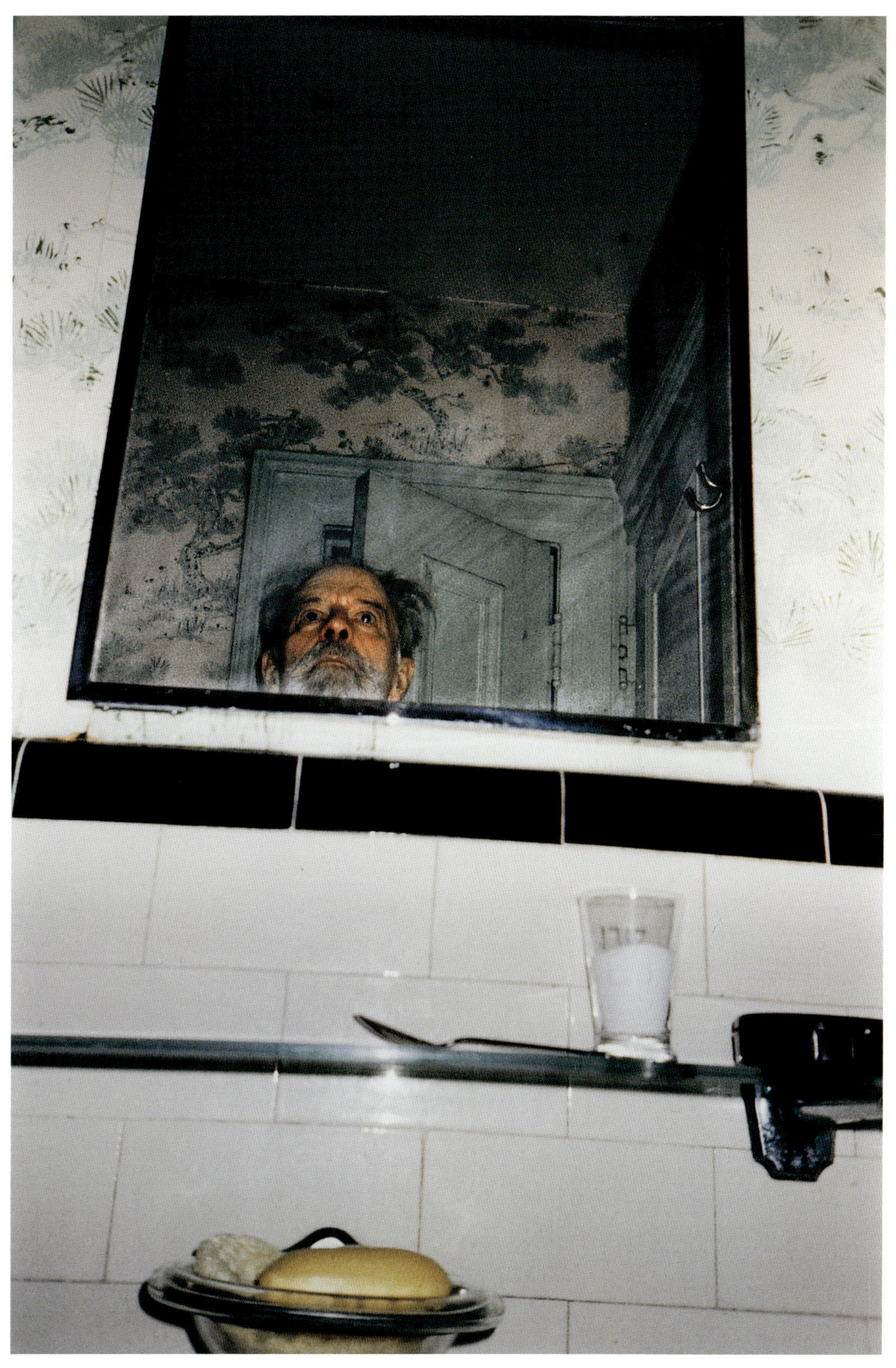

Self Portrait, 1996, color photograph, 19 1/2 x 12 3/4 inches.

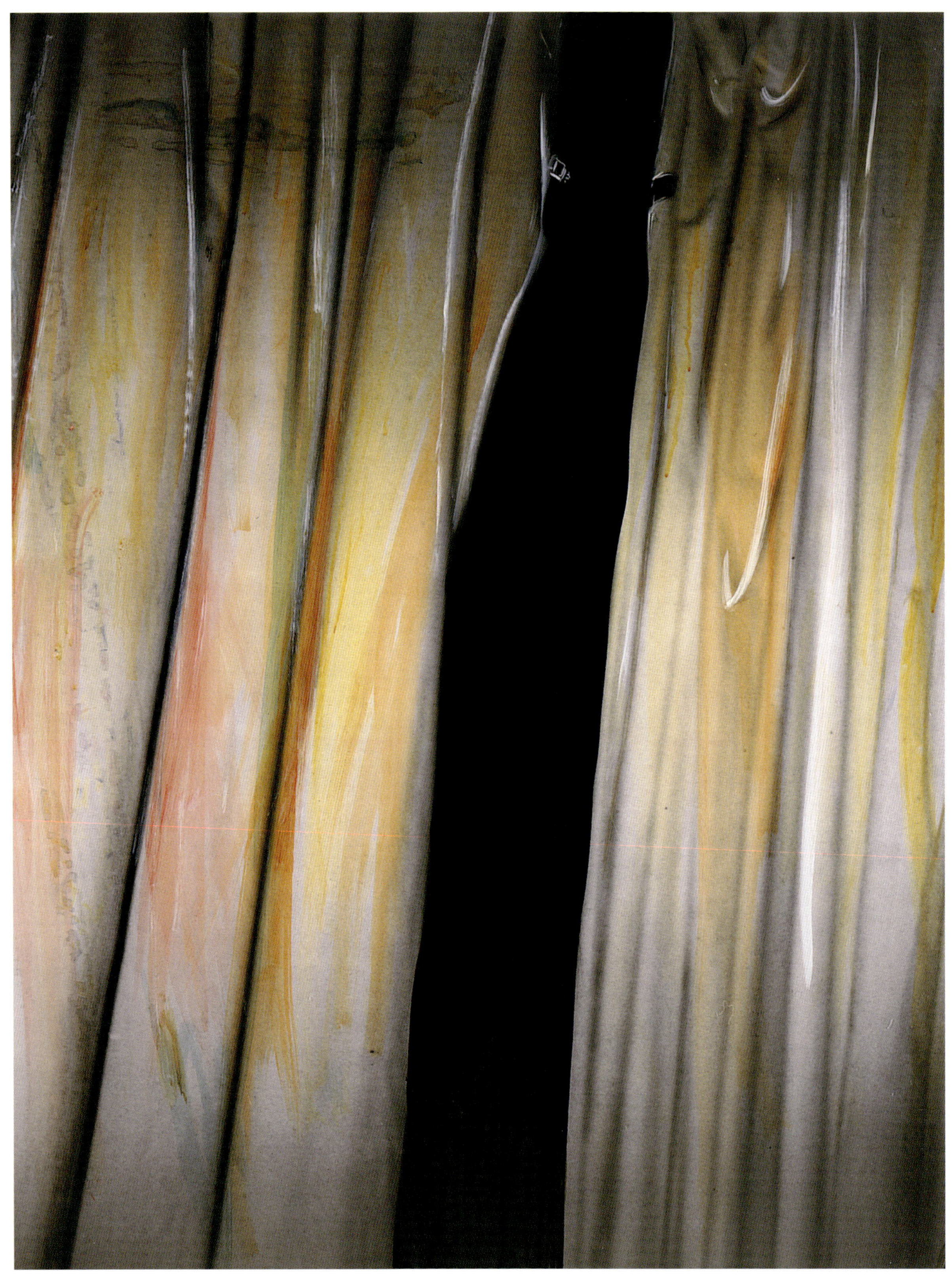

Hospital Curtain, 1981, photograph, color added, 40 1/2 x 30 inches.

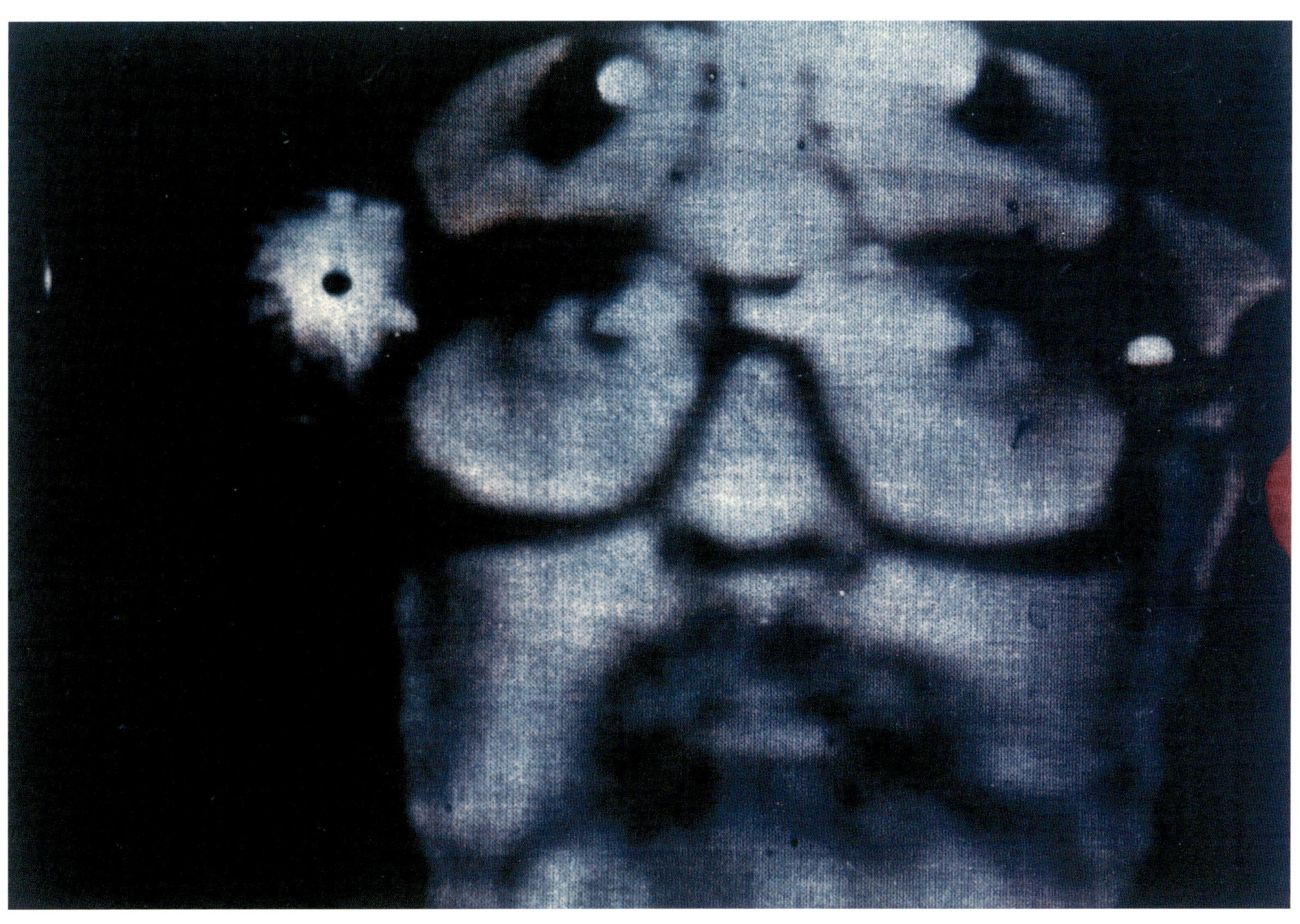

Self Portrait, 1996, color copier print, 5 x 7 inches.

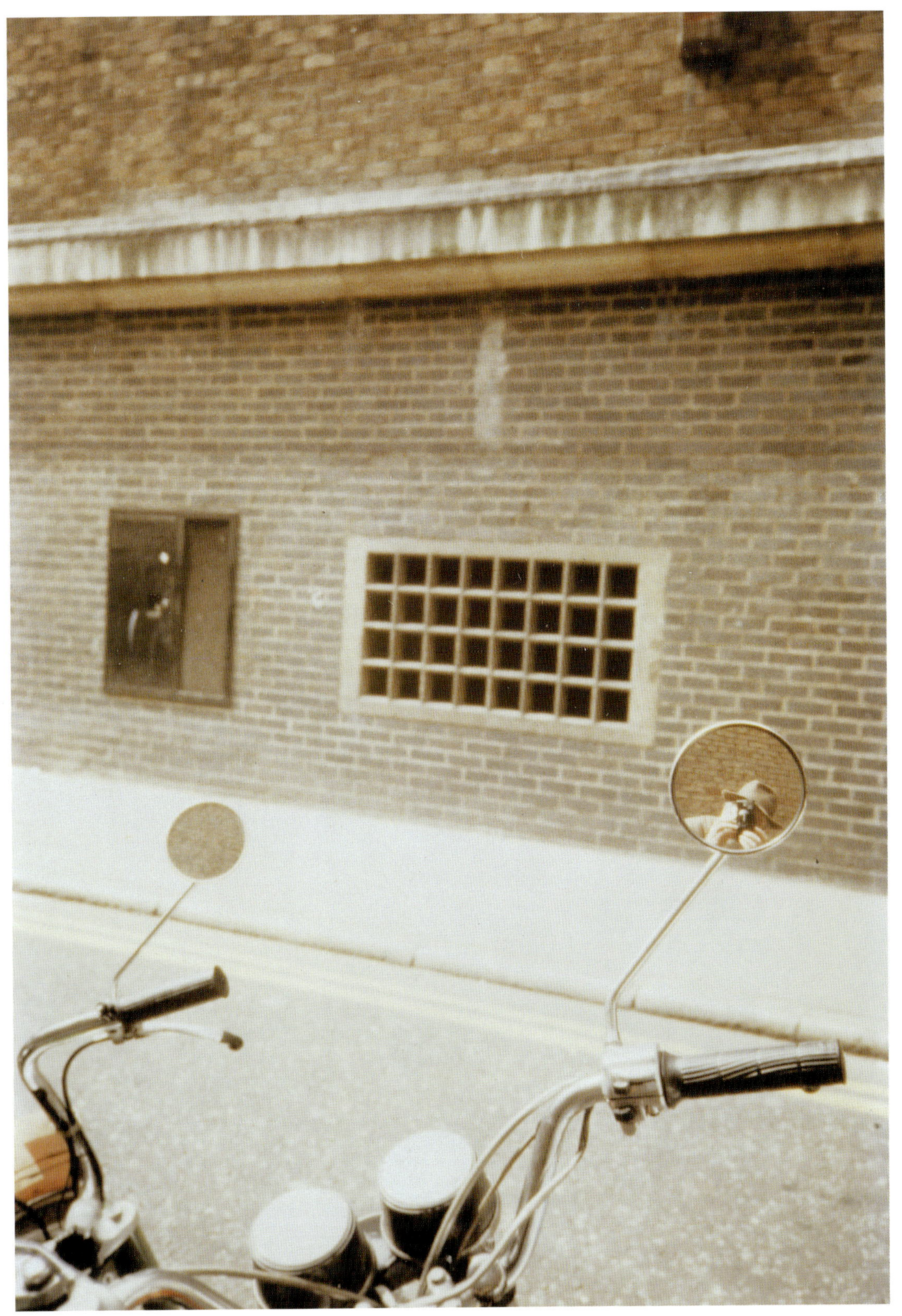

Motorcycle with Self-portrait, 1992, color photograph, 5 1/8 x 3 1/2 inches.

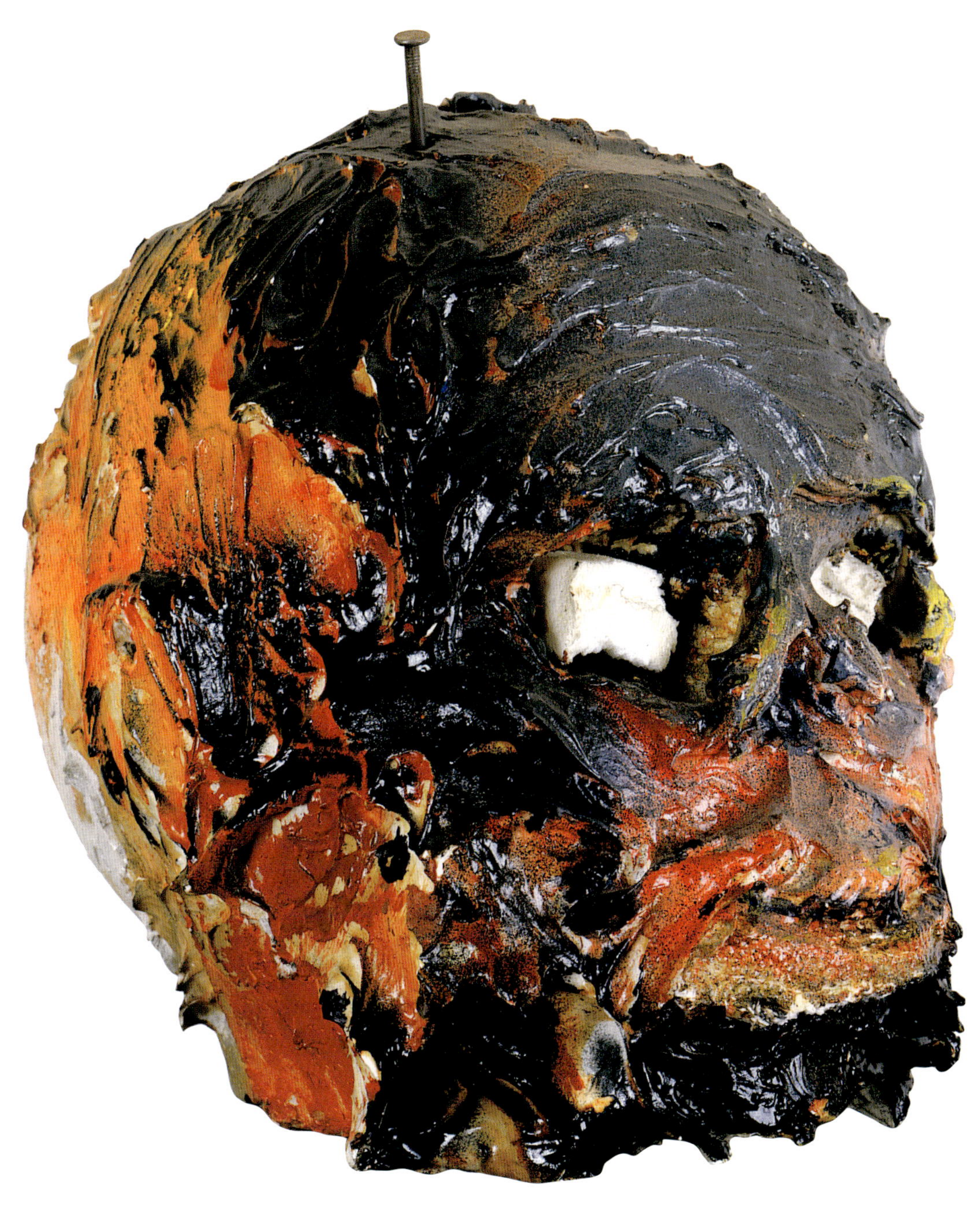

Skull with Nail, c. 1978, painted plaster over styrofoam, 7 1/2 inches high.

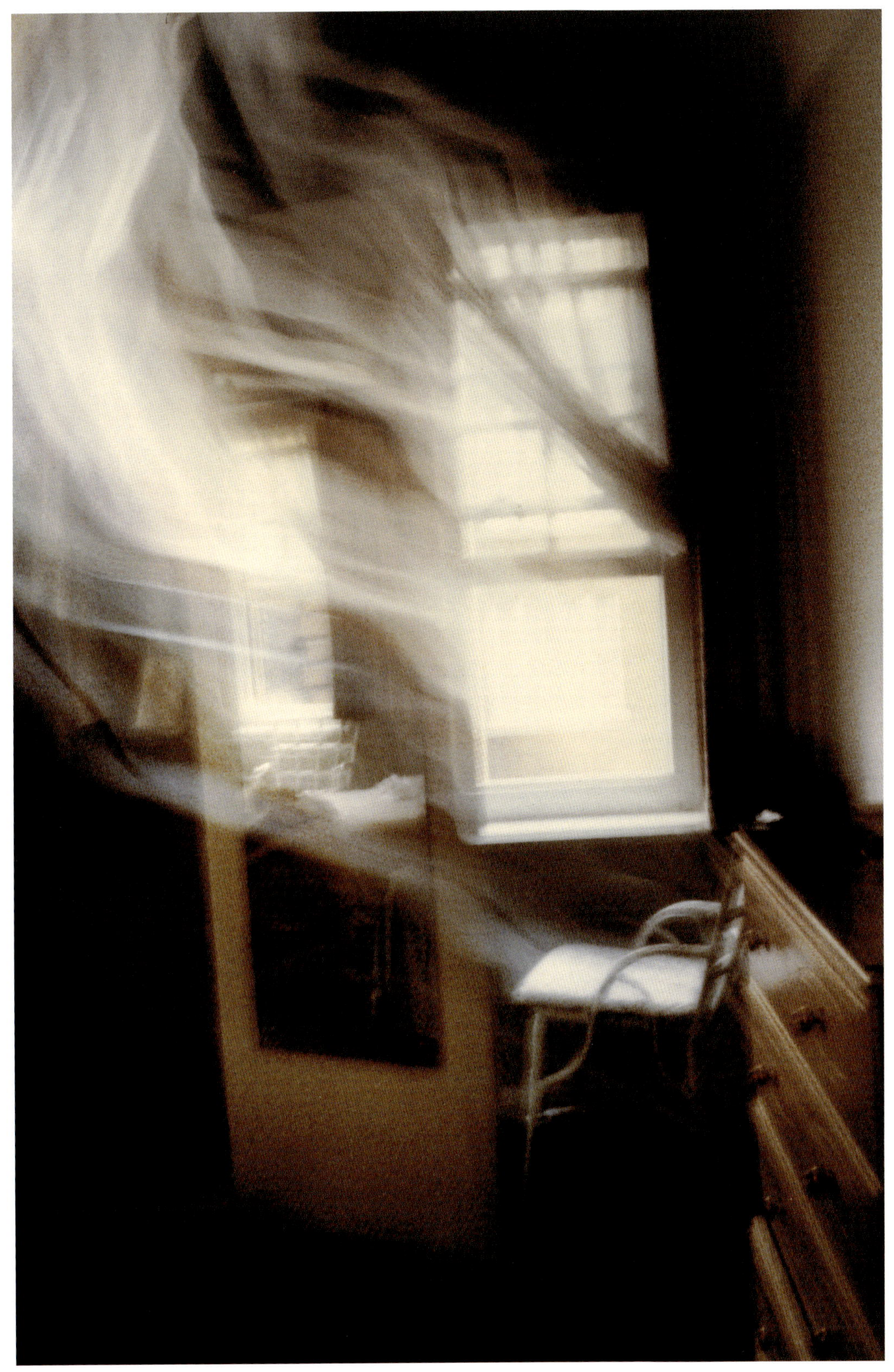

Curtain 2, c. 1990, color photograph, 10 x 8 inches.

Published in the United States by powerHouse Books,
a division of powerHouse Cultural Entertainment, Inc.
68 Charlton Street, New York, NY 10014-4601
telephone 212 604 9074, fax 212 366 5247
e-mail: info@ powerHouseBooks.com
website: www.powerHouseBooks.com

First edition, 2004

Library of Congress Cataloging-in-Publication Data:

Jones, Edward Powis, 1919-1998.
Faith, Hope and Love / artwork by Edward Powis Jones; essay by Mark Holborn. — 1st ed.
p. cm.
ISBN 1-57687-220-3 (clothbound)
1. Jones, Edward Powis, 1919-1998 — Themes, motives — Catalogs. I. Title: Faith, Hope,
and Love. II. Holborn, Mark, 1949-III. Title.

N6537.J667A4 2004
709'.2 — dc22
2003068930

Hardcover ISBN 1-57687-220-3

Separations, printing, and binding by Conti Tipocolor, Florence

Book design by Design Holborn, London
Production Consultant: Peter C. Jones
Reproduction transparencies by Zindman /Freemont, New York
Presentation dummies by Hayley Petrook

A complete catalog of powerHouse Books and
Limited Editions is available upon request;
please call, write, or visit our website.

10 9 8 7 6 5 4 3 2 1
Printed and bound in Italy